The jurisdiction and practice of the Marshalsea & Palace Courts : with tables of costs and charges, and an appendix containing statutes, letters patents, rules of court, &c..

W. Buckley

The jurisdiction and practice of the Marshalsea & Palace Courts : with tables of costs and charges, and an appendix containing statutes, letters patents, rules of court, &c..
Buckley, W. (William)
collection ID ocm30136176
Reproduction from Harvard Law School Library
Includes index.
London : S. Sweet, 1827.
iv, 238, [6] p. : forms ; 23 cm.

The Making of Modern Law collection of legal archives constitutes a genuine revolution in historical legal research because it opens up a wealth of rare and previously inaccessible sources in legal, constitutional, administrative, political, cultural, intellectual, and social history. This unique collection consists of three extensive archives that provide insight into more than 300 years of American and British history. These collections include:

Legal Treatises, 1800-1926: over 20,000 legal treatises provide a comprehensive collection in legal history, business and economics, politics and government.

Trials, 1600-1926: nearly 10,000 titles reveal the drama of famous, infamous, and obscure courtroom cases in America and the British Empire across three centuries.

Primary Sources, 1620-1926: includes reports, statutes and regulations in American history, including early state codes, municipal ordinances, constitutional conventions and compilations, and law dictionaries.

These archives provide a unique research tool for tracking the development of our modern legal system and how it has affected our culture, government, business – nearly every aspect of our everyday life. For the first time, these high-quality digital scans of original works are available via print-on-demand, making them readily accessible to libraries, students, independent scholars, and readers of all ages.

The BiblioLife Network

This project was made possible in part by the BiblioLife Network (BLN), a project aimed at addressing some of the huge challenges facing book preservationists around the world. The BLN includes libraries, library networks, archives, subject matter experts, online communities and library service providers. We believe every book ever published should be available as a high-quality print reproduction; printed on-demand anywhere in the world. This insures the ongoing accessibility of the content and helps generate sustainable revenue for the libraries and organizations that work to preserve these important materials.

The following book is in the "public domain" and represents an authentic reproduction of the text as printed by the original publisher. While we have attempted to accurately maintain the integrity of the original work, there are sometimes problems with the original work or the micro-film from which the books were digitized. This can result in minor errors in reproduction. Possible imperfections include missing and blurred pages, poor pictures, markings and other reproduction issues beyond our control. Because this work is culturally important, we have made it available as part of our commitment to protecting, preserving, and promoting the world's literature.

GUIDE TO FOLD-OUTS MAPS and OVERSIZED IMAGES

The book you are reading was digitized from microfilm captured over the past thirty to forty years. Years after the creation of the original microfilm, the book was converted to digital files and made available in an online database.

In an online database, page images do not need to conform to the size restrictions found in a printed book. When converting these images back into a printed bound book, the page sizes are standardized in ways that maintain the detail of the original. For large images, such as fold-out maps, the original page image is split into two or more pages

Guidelines used to determine how to split the page image follows:

• Some images are split vertically; large images require vertical and horizontal splits.
• For horizontal splits, the content is split left to right.
• For vertical splits, the content is split from top to bottom.
• For both vertical and horizontal splits, the image is processed from top left to bottom right.

THE

JURISDICTION AND PRACTICE

OF

The Marshalsea & Palace Courts,

WITH

TABLES OF COSTS AND CHARGES;

AND

AN APPENDIX,

CONTAINING

Statutes, Letters Patents, Rules of Court, &c.

———

By W. BUCKLEY,

TWENTY-THREE YEARS CHIEF CLERK IN THE PROTHONOTARY'S
OFFICE.

LONDON

S. SWEET, 3, CHANCERY LANE; R. PHENEY, INNER TEMPLE LANE;
A. MAXWELL, 21, AND STEVENS & SONS, 39, BELL YARD;
Law Booksellers and Publishers

1827.

UK
997
BUC

Rec Dec 22, 1898,

LONDON
W. M'DOWALL, PRINTER, PEMBERTON-ROW, GOUGH-SQUARE

CONTENTS.

———

PART III.

STATUTES.

LETTERS PATENTS.

FORMS.

INTRODUCTION.

———

THE design of the writer of the present work is, to trace the origin and jurisdiction of the Palace (or, as it is commonly called, the Marshalsea) Court, to describe its course of proceeding, and to exhibit tables of the legal costs and charges to which its suitors are liable. How competent the writer is for this task, may appear from the circumstance of his having been for the period of seven years clerk to the late Mr. Kelsall, an eminent attorney of the Palace Court, and twenty-three years chief clerk and manager in the prothonotary's office. To those acquainted with the practice of the Palace Court, it must be evident that no one can be capable of conveying this information, who has not been officially and experimentally acquainted with its proceedings.

In his examination of the practice of the Court, he regrets that he has had occasion to notice many instances of what appear to him extravagance and illegality in the items of the bills of costs, and some abuses in the process of the Court; but however unlikely a recurrence of similar practices may be, while the business and proceedings of the Court are conducted by its present highly respectable practitioners, he feels that it would not be doing justice to his subject, to omit a notice of them in this Introduction; thereby awakening the suitor's attention, and enabling him to guard against such improper proceedings, should they hereafter be attempted. And further to effect this object, the writer has, in the third part of the present publication, inserted tables of the original, and, as he conceives, the legal, costs and charges of the attornies of this Court, as founded in the schedule annexed to the letters patent, dated 8th June, in the ninth year of James the First, which costs and charges were re-appointed by the subsequent letters patent of the twenty-second year of the same reign, and of the sixth of Charles the First, (but are not incorporated in the grant of 16 Car. 2), and remained unaltered until the late Deputy Prothonotary, William Cruchley, increased the same to their present amount

The following facts will prove that abuses have existed in the process of the Court.—

An attorney has been known to include *two, three,* or even *four* defendants in one and the same writ and warrant, and to make a charge for a separate writ and warrant against each defendant. And instances have occurred of demands having been made for proceedings never instituted; which the following memorandums will substantiate:

In the year 1812, in a cause intituled Accumor and Garden *v.* Richards, writ and warrant were charged for, but none used. In Thorogood *v.* Ovenden and Others, on assignment of bail-bond, 2*l.* 12*s* 6*d* was charged, but no proceedings were had thereon. In Thorogood *v.* Lutman, Izart, and Forrest, proceedings on a bail-bond were charged to the parties, which were neither signed by counsel, nor carried into the office, whereby the Knight Marshal and Steward of the Court were deprived of fees, amounting to 11*s.* and the counsel of their fees for signing, 15*s*.* In a cause of Carter *v.* Kent, an attorney of the Court erased the name of Joseph Carter from a writ of Habeas Corpus, and inserted the name

---

* See, *post,* upon what pleadings they are entitled to fees for signing.

of Jane Dixon. This Habeas Corpus was paid for in the former cause, and charged again in the latter. In Try v. Flinn, warrant and writ charged, writ only used. In Lill v. Clarke, Same v. Chapman, Same v. Dawson, Same v. Shearing, the charges were: Chapman 1*l.* 11*s.* 6*d.*, Clarke 1*l.* 11*s.* 6*d.*, Dawson 2*l.* 10*s.*, and Shearing 1*l.* 11*s.* 6*d.*; all which sums were paid; making a total of 7*l.* 4*s.* 6*d.* for one writ and one warrant. In 1812, one attorney sued forty-two individuals between the 6th of March and the 2d of December, for which purpose he used only *sixteen* writs and *sixteen* warrants. His charge to the defendants was 67*l.* 1*s.* 6*d.* whereas he was not entitled to more than 25*l.* 4*s.* These charges are, however, not to be wondered at, as the attorney in question had been but newly admitted, and had paid to the Knight Marshal 1000*l.* for his place. In 1824, a defendant was served with a copy of writ of capias, for a debt of 7*l.* 10*s.* and on execution being levied, goods estimated at 25*l.* were sold to satisfy the debt and costs.

The augmentation of the fees and charges of the Court has been not only injurious to the suitors, but destructive of the interests of the Court and its officers; which is evident by the business of the Court being less, by three-

fourths*, than when it had the power to arrest for 40s†.

In the year 1759, it was ordered that all declarations,* as well as all other pleas, be signed by counsel on the following terms:—

In actions for words, trespass, special contract, rent, on promissory notes, and on any statute whatever, counsel should be entitled to five shillings for their signatures to each. But of late, the counsel of the Court have advanced their fees for pleading to five shillings on every *incipitur* of declaration, and the fees on their briefs to ten shillings and sixpence, and one guinea, instead of five shillings‡.

---

* This appears from the number of writs issued in three weeks in the year 1759, for, from the 6th of July to the 27th of the same month in that year, the number of writs issued was six hundred and two, and five hundred and seventeen affidavits were sworn to during the same period.

† Prior to the year 1773, the Palace Court had power to arrest for the sum of 40s., but in consequence of the malpractices of the officers of the Court, who were accustomed to take the notes of hand of persons whom they had arrested, in order that they might obtain the chance of arresting them again, Lord Beauchamp brought in a bill to render such arrests illegal.

‡ In consequence of the declension of the inferior business of the Court, by the institution of the Courts of Conscience in

The origin of this great increase of the fees taken by the counsel and attornies may possibly be attributed to the large premiums* paid by those gentlemen for the exclusive privilege of exercising their offices in the Palace Court.

At the time Sir Sydney Meadows was Knight Marshal of this Court, the premium required for the admission of an attorney was in general from 600*l*. to 700*l*.; but on the late Sir James Bland Lamb's appointment to that office, 1000*l*, 1200*l*., and in one instance 2000*l*., were the premiums paid for such admission. The like premiums have been demanded for the office of counsel to the Court. The consequence of this impolitic sale of office has been a desire on the part of the purchasers, by an increase of their fees and charges, to remunerate themselves for the large sums they had thus paid for their admission.

It is above stated, that the attornies of this Court some time ago greatly augmented their charges for fees, costs, &c. yet it is but justice to those gentlemen to observe, that they alone

and near London, the four counsel belonging to the Court were indemnified by salaries during their lives Stat. 23 Geo. 2, c. 27.

* These premiums are divided between the Knight Marshal and the Lord Steward of the Household.

were not liable to accusation on this account.
It will be seen by a comparison of the original
costs with the present, that the charges of the
Prothonotary to the attorney now exceed the
joint charge of the Prothonotary and attorney
prior to the late Deputy Prothonotary's alteration; who not only increased the costs to be paid
by the suitors of the Court, but also augmented
the fees from the officers on their admission.

The officers of the Court, at the time Sir
Sydney Meadows was Knight Marshal, usually
paid for their security-bonds 2*l*. 7*s*. 6*d*. But
when the late Sir James Bland Lamb was appointed to that office, the late Deputy Prothonotary and clerk of the securities, William Cruchley, demanded 8*l*. 8*s*.* for such bond; which the
following letter to the author will prove:

" Mr. Buckley,
"The bearer, Mr. Atfield, wishes to become an officer. Give him a petition, and request him to give the names of four persons
for his securities; and if he gives you any de-
posit, put his name up for admission. And if
the residence of his securities are near me at

* By the general rule of the Court, the clerk of the securities is not entitled to more than 1*l*. for the whole of his fees.
See post, Rule 94, p 217

Finchley, I can attest the execution there. Give
him any other information he may require. And
if the bonds are executed from the office, the
fees to be 8*l.* 8*s*   *W. C.*
        Nov. 3, 1797."

Again, when housekeepers were summoned
by the late Deputy Prothonotary on the jury,
and neglected to attend, a letter was usually written to them, stating, that if they did
not come forward and make affidavit as to
the cause of their absence, to be excused
the fine (40*s.*), their names would be returned
into the Exchequer. These affidavits were
drawn up by his dictation, and, when in Court,
he swore the parties to the affidavits himself;
and for this trouble he usually charged them *two
guineas.* This mode was irregular: his duty
was, to make a return of all defaulters into the
Exchequer, without further interference. The
regular way of proceeding is, when a person is
summoned to attend on the jury, and wishes to
be excused, he applies to the Court through the
medium of one of its attornies, who draws up
an affidavit, setting forth such excuse: which
affidavit is sworn in Court before the Judge,
and if sufficient, the party is excused. For his
trouble, the attorney is entitled to a fee. But

the affidavit in the Appendix will shew that the late Deputy Prothonotary (who was not even an attorney of the Palace Court), took all this business on himself.

We shall close our remarks on what may be considered the abuses of the Palace Court, by adducing instances of irregularity in some of its subordinate officers

The jurisdiction of the Palace Court by the statute 13 Ric. 2, st. 1, c. 3, as well as by the charter of Charles the Second, is limited to *twelve* miles round London, taking the distance from Whitehall. But some of the officers of the Court seem to have disregarded its limits, and carried its authority beyond the prescribed jurisdiction. The following statement will support the assertion:—

In the year 1824, one of the officers of the Palace Court served three defendants, residing fourteen miles from Whitehall, with copies of writs; he, however, swore that he served the defendants within the jurisdiction of the Court. It has also been the practice, when an officer makes a caption, and a bail-bond is given thereon by the party, generally to demand from 10*s*. 6*d* to 1*l* 1*s*., although the officer is entitled to 4*s*. 6*d*. only, for such bail-bond.

In thus touching upon the abuses of the
Palace Court, we are not singular. The late Sir
James Bland Lamb, prior to his becoming
Knight Marshal, wrote a work on the practices
and proceedings of this Court; which, it is to
be lamented, was suppressed on his coming into
office. It was probably from the exposure of
the practices of the Court, detailed in that publication, that Government, during the Attorney-
generalship of the late Mr. Wallace, contem-
plated the abolition of the Palace Court.

PART I.

—

THE JURISDICTION OF THE MARSHALSEA OF THE KING'S HOUSE, AND OF THE COURT OF THE PALACE OF THE KING AT WESTMINSTER

AS a preliminary step to the following information, it seems necessary to advertise the reader, that the Court of Marshalsea and the Palace Court are frequently confounded together as one and the same Court; whereas, in fact, they are two distinct Courts: the one being constituted for the administration of justice between persons belonging to the king's household, and entitled *The Marshalsea of the King's House;* the other belonging to the King's Bench, and styled, *The Court of the King's Palace at Westminster.* The former subsists by prescription, and its judges are the Lord Steward, the Steward of the Marshalsea, and the Marshal of the Household; the latter owes its institution to letters patent granted in the sixth year of Charles

the First, which were confirmed by a similar
authority in the sixteenth year of Charles the
Second; and its judges are the Lord Steward,
the Marshal of the Household* and the Steward of the Court, or his deputy, who must be a
practising lawyer.

The institution of the Marshalsea of the
king's house seems to be coeval with the common law of the land, (4 *Inst.* 130, 10 *Rep*
79 *b.*) as appears (according to the *dictum* of
Crook, J., in *Cox* and *Gray*, 1 Buls. 207,) by
L. 5 Ed. 4. fol. 129, where it is said to be one
of the most ancient courts of the realm; and
this *dictum* is supported by the authority of the
anonymous author of *Diversite des Courtes, Tit.*
Marshalsie, f. 102, by whom the Marshalsea
is placed the first in rank among the national
courts. Were any other authority wanting in
favor of its high dignity, it might be derived
from the circumstance that, until the stat. 5
Ed. 3, st. 2, c. 3, gave a writ of error to the
King's Bench, to reverse a judgment given in
the Court of Marshalsea, there was no appeal
from its decisions, but in parliament. (*Per* Fleming, Ch. J., Buls. 211; Case of the *Marshal-*
sea, 10 Rep. 79 *b. in arg.*) In its constitu-

---

* This officer, in the technical phraseology of the Court,
has received the appellation of " Knight Marshal."

tion this Court was of an ambulatory nature, and obliged to follow the king in all his progresses: *Fleta, lib.* 2, *cap.* 3. So inseparable is it from the person of the monarch, that during his residence in a foreign state it is obliged to attend him. *Ibid.* c. 3.

The jurisdiction of this Court was, by the common law, general and extensive, as it comprehended all actions real, personal, and mixed, and all pleas of the crown within the verge; *Fleta,* l. 2, c. 2; but the statute of *articuli super chartas,* 28 *Edw.* 1, c. 3, defined and abridged its jurisdiction, and ordained that the stewards and marshals of the king's house should not hold plea of freehold, debt, covenant, or contract, but only of trespass done within the king's house or verge*, of covenants and contracts where both parties are of the house. See 10 *Rep.* 71; 2 *Inst.* 549. In the construction of which statute, it hath been held, that the Marshalsea has jurisdiction over only three species of action, viz. debt, covenant, and trespass; over debt and covenant, only where both the contracting parties belong

---

* The verge, *virgata regia,* as *Fleta* terms it, lib. 2, c. 2, is defined by the stat. 13 *Ric.* 2, st. 1, c. 3, to extend twelve miles from the king's palace, or place of ordinary residence. If the Marshalsea holds plea done out of the verge, the proceedings are void, and *coram non judice. Plowd Com.* 37 *b.*

to the royal household, or are within the precincts or jurisdiction of the Court; also the contract and consideration must be laid to have arisen within the jurisdiction; but in the case of trespass it is said to be sufficient if one of the parties is in the king's domestic service, or within the precincts or jurisdiction of the Court*. *Buls.* 207; 10 *Rep.* 68; 6 *Ibid.* 20; 1 *Sid.* 105. And though the statute speaks of trespasses generally, yet it has been decided, that it is intendable of trespass *simpliciter, vi et armis,* as of battery, or taking away goods; but not of *quare clausum fregit,* nor of trespasses and ejectment, nor of trespasses on the case, nor of detinue. 10 *Rep.* 76 *a. Buls.* 205; 2 *Inst.* 508.

By what means the criminal jurisdiction of the Marshalsea became curtailed, is not precisely agreed on by writers on the subject. Lord Coke (2 *Inst.* 549,) and Staunford (*Pl. Cor.* 57,) incline to think, that it was taken away by the statute 33 Hen. 8, c. 12; an act

---

* Why, as Mr. Morice properly observes in his Essay on the Ancient Jurisdiction of the Marshalsea, it should have been decided as necessary, that in trespass one of the parties should be of the king's household, or within the precincts of the verge, is not easily seen; as the only qualification required by the statute is, that the trespass be committed *within the king's house, or within the verge*   the qualification as to being of the household is expressly confined to debt and covenant.

apparently passed to restrain this Court from encroaching beyond its true jurisdiction*: for

* Lord Coke's inaccuracy in apprehending, that it was this act that had put an end to the criminal jurisdiction of the Marshalsea, is pointed out by the author of the Essay on the Jurisdiction of the Antient Court of Marshalsea, who properly says, that this statute extends only to certain offences committed within the immediate residence of the king; whereas the jurisdiction of the Marshalsea extends *twelve miles round his residence*, and is not confined to the residence itself: besides, that the very statute itself shews that such is its meaning, for, by the 21st section, there is an express saving of the privileges of the Marshalsea. And the same writer adds, he is therefore of opinion, that the jurisdiction within the verge for the trial of pleas of the crown is still existing and inherent in the Court of Marshalsea, though it has not been exercised for a long series of years. And this position, he thinks, is confirmed by the circumstance, that there is still a coroner for the verge appointed, (Britton, fol. 1,) as well as a coroner of the king's house; the one according to the common law, the other by the stat. 33 Hen. 8, c. 12 whereas, had the statute put an end to the jurisdiction of the Marshalsea in criminal cases, which existed before the passing of it, the office of coroner for the verge would necessarily have become extinct.

While discoursing of the office of coroner of the verge, Mr. Morice has well observed, that it is his duty, in all cases of death happening within the verge, to sit jointly with the coroner of the county, to take the inquisitions; otherwise inquests not so taken will be void for want of conformity to the stat *artic. super chart.* 28 Edw 1, c. 8. And of this opinion was Sir Matthew Hale. (2 Pl. Cor. 65) See also *Katharine Wrote's* case, 4 Rep. 45.

C

it is worthy of notice, that every act made concerning the Marshalsea either restrains or explains its jurisdiction, and that no act adds any thing to it. 10 Rep. 76 *a*. Lord Bacon (charge at a Court verge by Sir Francis Bacon, Bac. Works,) and Sir Matthew Hale, (Pl. Cor 11), are of opinion that the criminal jurisdiction of this Court had not been expressly taken away, but that it had grown into disuse, and had given place to another mode of proceeding, namely, commissions of oyer and terminer, and of gaol delivery, called commissions for the verge, directed to the great officers of state, the Judges, the Steward of the Marshalsea, and others. And this seems to be the better opinion.

By the statutes 3 Hen. 7, c. 14, and 33 Hen. 8, c. 12, the method of trying offences committed in the precincts of the king's palace is pointed out, as also that of their punishment. And by the stat 5 Edw. 3, st. 2, c 3, error in the Marshalsea Court may be removed into the King's Bench.

In the above discourse the ancient jurisdiction of the Court of Marshalsea, both civil and criminal, has been described, its progress traced, its precise nature defined, and its exact limits, which are still existing, as inherent in its constitution, explained. it remains to state the

origin of the new court, entitled the *Palace Court*, which has superseded the Court of Marshalsea in its jurisdiction within the precincts of the verge; to detail its process; point out its abuses *; and furnish the reader with tables of the just and legal charges of the Court and its officers, to which the suitors of the Palace Court are subject.

It has been already said, that the Judges of the Marshalsea Court having encroached beyond their true jurisdiction, the statute of *artic. super chartas* was passed, to abridge the usurped jurisdiction: to evade therefore the provisions of the statute, in their extensive claim of cognizance of suits, the Judges resorted to the fiction of describing the defendant as of the king's household, and in the record both plaintiff and defendant were averred to be in the king's domestic service To defeat this contrivance, the stat. 15 Hen. 6, c 1, was therefore passed, by which it is enacted, that the defendant shall not be estopped by any such averment from saying that neither he nor the plaintiff was of the household of the king at the time the plea or suit at issue was commenced

* This ungracious part of our duty will be found in the Introduction to this Work

(2

Still, however, the Court of Marshalsea, unwilling to part with its usurped authority, and to lose the fruits arising from its exercise, continued to entertain suits where neither of the parties was of the king's household, and to hold plea in actions not within the statute of *articuli super chartas*, until this usurpation of jurisdiction was questioned in the cases of *Cox* and *Gray*, Buls. 218, and of *Michelbourn*, 6 Rep. 20; in which judgment was reversed on writs of error; in which the error assigned was, that neither of the parties was of the king's household at the time of the commencement of the suit, as required by the stat. 15 Hen. 6, c. 1. And these decisions of the King's Bench, receiving confirmation from the judgment of the Common Pleas, in the case of the *Marshalsea*, 10 Rep. 72 *a.*, in which the action of trespass, brought against the defendants for executing the process of the Court of Marshalsea, neither of the parties to the action being of the king's household, was held to be maintainable; the business of the Court of Marshalsea became confined to its proper jurisdiction, namely, the cognizance of causes between parties, both of whom, or at least one of them, belonged to the household of the king.

But the judges of the Marshalsea, finding

their profitable assumption of jurisdiction nearly annihilated by these decisions, immediately
applied to the Crown to relieve their pecuniary
longings; to indulge which tender propensities,
a new court of record was erected by letters
patent in the twelfth year of the reign of James
the First, under the style of " *Curia Virgi
Palatii Domini Regis,*" with the extension
of the ancient jurisdiction of the Marshalsea.
The Court constituted under these letters patent, however, did not continue its functions
longer than the sixth year of Charles the First,
when another Court was erected under fresh
letters patent, by the style of " *Curia Palatii
Regis, Westm.*"

But the legality of these letters patent being questioned in the case of *Fish* v. *Wagstaff,*
Trin. Term, 9 Car. Cro. Car. 318, in which
case a writ of error being brought in the King's
Bench, the judgment was reversed, but for
what cause does not appear; and again, on the
Restoration*, similar doubts existing as to their
legality (see the case of *Juman* v. *Batten,* 1 Sid.
180), another Court, (the present Palace Court)

---

* No historical trace is extant, to ascertain whether this Court
exercised its functions during the interregnum which inter-
vened between the dethronement of Charles the First, and
the restoration of Charles the Second

was erected by letters patent, dated the 4th October, in the sixteenth year of Charles the Second, by the title of "The Court of the Lord the King of the Palace of the King at Westminster;" and after reciting the purpose for which the Court was erected, it gives power to the judges of the Court to hold plea of all personal actions whatever, and to whatever amount* they may be, which shall arise between any person within twelve miles of the palace of Westminster (Whitehall) with exception of the jurisdiction of the city of London, and of the Court of Marshalsea; it then appoints the judges, counsel, attornies, and prothonotary of the Court, as also the usual day on which the Court must sit for the dispatch of business; and, lastly, it prescribes the mode of empanelling the juries, as also the course of the proceedings, which it precisely limits as to their duration. *See the Letters Patent, Appendix.*

The Marshalsea being the king's own Court for his palace, persons belonging to his house-

---

* Notwithstanding the Court is thus empowered to try causes to any amount, yet if the damages are stated in the declaration to amount to 5*l.* or upwards, the defendant may, by the stat. 21 Jac. 1, c. 23, remove the cause by *habeas corpus* into a superior Court.

hold can claim no privilege from arrest under its process; but persons residing within the precincts of the palace are privileged from arrest under process issuing from the Palace Court, or any other Court; and, if taken in execution, the Court from which the process issued will, on motion, discharge them. *Bartlett* v. *Hebbes,* 5 T. R. 686. And even where process issued to arrest persons not of the household, residing within the precincts of the Palace, it was usual to obtain permission from the king for that purpose, signified by the officers of his household, and the writs, in such instances, have been backed by the clerk of the Board of Green Cloth; but for many years past civil process has been executed within the said boundaries without such leave, and it has been held, that no indictment will lie against the officer making it. *Rex* v. *Stobbs,* 3 T. R 735. The Court also refused to discharge a prisoner in execution for debt, claiming privilege from arrest, on the ground, that he was one of the gentlemen of the King's Privy Chamber, it appearing that he was not a menial servant, had no stated duties to perform, received no fees in virtue of his office, and had no writ of privilege. See the case of *Tapley* v. *Battine,* 1 Dowl. & Ryl. 79. So one of the king's yeomen of the

guard having been arrested on process issued
out of the Palace Court, without leave of the
Lord Chamberlain, and the Court having refused to discharge him out of custody on filing
common bail, he removed the cause into the
King's Bench, by a writ of *habeas corpus cum
causâ*, and put in and perfected bail on *habeas*:
held that an *exoneretur* could not be entered
on the bail-piece, even supposing the defendant privileged from arrest: See *Sard* v. *Forrest*,
2 Dowl. & Ryl. 250. But in the case of *Fos-
ter* v. *Hopkins*, reported in the second volume
of Chitty's Reports, p. 46, it was decided, that
the lighter of fires and candles to the king's yeomen of the guard was entitled to be discharged
out of custody on filing common bail, it being
proved that he had sometimes executed the duties of his office in person, though they were
generally performed by his deputy.

This Court must be held in some place within the precincts of the jurisdiction, and for a
long series of years was held in King Street,
in the borough of Southwark, (within which
borough the prison of the Court is situated);
but in consequence of the decayed state of the
Court-house, which was deemed unfit to sit in,
the Court was removed to the New Sessions
House, Newington Causeway, until the pre-

sent Court-house was erected, which is situated in Great Scotland Yard, Whitehall. The Court of King's Bench may, however, by rule of Court, appoint any place in England for the holding of this Court, and within such limits as it may think proper. Com. Dig. *tit.* Imprisonment, (C)

The fees of the Court are in certain cases limited by the stat. 2 Hen. 4, c 23, and the statute gives, in case of extortion being practised on the suitor, an action to the party aggrieved, against the Marshal; which action is to be tried before the Steward of the Court, and, if the verdict be against the said Marshal, the judgment is, that he be deprived of his office, and pay treble damages to the party aggrieved

PART II.

THE MODES OF PROCESS IN THE PALACE COURT, ON THE PART OF PLAINTIFFS AND DEFENDANTS

THE proceedings in this Court are either by *capias* * or attachment, which is to be served on the defendant by one of the Knight Marshal's men†, who takes bond with sureties for his appearance at the next Court‡; on which appearance he must give bail, to answer the condemnation of the Court; and the next Court after the bail is taken, the plaintiff is to declare,

---

* But it is to be recollected that the plaint, and not the *capias*, is the commencement of the suit in this Court. *Ward* v. *Honeywood*, Doug. 61.

† In ancient times no less a person than the Earl Marshal was the minister of the Lord Steward of the Household, to execute the process of the Court. *Britton, fol.* 1.

‡ The usual day on which this Court sits is Friday, unless that happen on a holiday appointed by letters patent, in which case the Court sits on the day preceding.

and set forth the cause of his action, and afterwards proceed to issue and trial by a jury, according to the custom of the common law Courts.
If the cause is of importance, it is usually removed into the King's Bench or Common Pleas
by a *habeas corpus cum causá;* otherwise causes
are to be brought to trial in this Court, in the
space of four or five Court-days. But varia-
tions from this exact mode of proceeding frequently take place according to the circumstances and exigency of each particular case.
These are detailed in the following pages.

I. *Mode of proceeding by a Plaintiff against
a Debtor, on arrest.*

WHEN a plaintiff is desirous to proceed against
a debtor, he ought first to apply to an attorney
of the Palace Court, and consult with him,
whether any action lies for such debt, which
if found maintainable, the attorney will advise
him to issue a writ against the defendant for
the debt.

The plaintiff's attorney then draws up an affidavit for the plaintiff (after perusal thereof)
to sign; which being done, the attorney or his
clerk attends the plaintiff to the public office of

the Court, in Chancery Lane, where he is sworn
to the truth of his affidavit.   The affidavit having been sworn, the attorney applies to such public office for a writ and warrant to sue the defendant, on the ground of the affidavit; which being
obtained, and filled up either by the attorney or
his clerk, is carried back to the office to be entered.   But it is worthy of observation, that
this mode of filling up the writs is highly improper, and not the ancient practice, (having
only of late years been introduced), as the writ
ought to be filled up by the proper officer in
the public office, and not by the attorney or
his clerk.   After the writ is so obtained, it is
given to an officer of the Court, with instructions where the defendant is to be found, at the
same time giving with such instructions one
shilling, (which is called the warrant shilling);
or else the plaintiff leaves the writ and instructions with his attorney.

The writ must be executed, and the caption
made previous to the return day, which is the
Friday following the issuing of the writ, and, if
not executed previous to that day, the officer to
whom the writ was given to execute, must apply to the plaintiff's attorney, to have the writ
renewed for the week following, and so on until the officer is enabled to arrest the defendant.

Should the arrest be made on the day the writ is returnable, the plaintiff must have the writ renewed again, as by law the defendant is, on being arrested, entitled to twenty-four hours' indulgence, to give him an opportunity of procuring friends to give a bail-bond to the officer for his appearance at the return of the writ; or, on payment of the debt and costs, he is entitled to his discharge.

If the legality of the plaintiff's claim should be disputed, the defendant's attorney will then enter an appearance in the appearance-book, either at the Court on the return-day, or at the office belonging to the said Court, on the Saturday morning after such bail-bond shall have been so given for the defendant's appearance. The plaintiff's attorney should also appear for him at the same time.

But should the defendant not appear by an attorney of the Court on the return of the bail-bond, then on the Monday morning after the return of the said writ and bail-bond, the plaintiff's attorney will be entitled to assign such bail-bond, and sue out writs against the defendant and his bail. Should the officer not be enabled to serve all the defendants before the return of the writ, such writ must be renewed against those not served.

When all parties are served, if the defendant does not appear and put in bail above, before the return of such service, the bail-bond then becomes forfeited to the use of the plaintiff, and the defendant has no redress to exonerate himself and bail from paying the plaintiff the debt and costs, as also the costs of suing upon the assignment. And should the same not be paid, the plaintiff's attorney must then proceed on such assignment against the defendant and his bail, at the suit of the officer who took the bail-bond, by causing affidavits to be made of the service of process on the defendant and bail, and then filing common bail, declaring against all the defendants, and giving notice of declaration; and if these proceedings are not attended to by the defendants, the plaintiff is entitled to his judgment and execution against all the defendants severally.

II. *The Proceedings of a Plaintiff, where the Defendant had appeared and taken the necessary steps by his Attorney.*

WHEN the defendant has put in bail above to his appearance, and justified his bail, in order to save his bond becoming forfeited, the plain-

tiff is, after such justification, bound to proceed by filing his declaration, perfecting the same, and giving the defendant a rule to plead; which rule expires on the following Court-day after given, unless the defendant's attorney obtains a week's further time, which it is customary to give, and also a Monday following.   But to entitle the defendant to this enlarged time, such plea must be an issuable plea, so as not to bar the plaintiff from proceeding to trial, on the Court-day following the Monday the defendant had obtained for the purpose of pleading· and for this day the plaintiff's attorney should set down the cause for trial

In the mean time, the attornies of both plaintiff and defendant write to their respective clients, to request their attendance on the Tuesday or Wednesday morning, (also specifying the sums of money required), to receive instructions for preparing briefs; and each attorney issues such subpœnas as may be necessary, in the one case, for witnesses in support of the plaintiff's claim, and in the other, for the defendant's defence: these preparatory steps having been adopted, the cause is set down for trial on the Friday following

Should the plaintiff not be ready, and withdraw his record, then the defendant's attorney

is at liberty to set down such cause (which must be summoned by proviso); and if the plaintiff does not proceed to trial on the Court-day following such record being withdrawn, he will be nonsuited for want of evidence, and the defendant entitled to his costs; and if such costs are not paid by the plaintiff's attorney, before execution, the defendant will be entitled to his execution on the Saturday morning following

III. *Mode of Process for a Plaintiff, where the Defendant is arrested at his suit, and goes to Prison.*

THE plaintiff, by his attorney, must declare against the defendant in custody, in the course of the week following the return of the writ. otherwise the defendant will become supersedeable for want of an *incipitur* of declaration

But should the plaintiff, in the course of the week subsequent to the return of the writ, proceed in his action against the defendant in custody, and then in the course of the week following call on the defendant to plead, the preferable course is for the defendant to plead in person, denying the debt, and putting the plaintiff to the proof thereof by witnesses, or

D

else, if term draws near, he may sign a *cognovit* to confess such debt and damages, in order to get the sooner committed in execution, so that he may be enabled to obtain his weekly allowance under the Lords' Act; of which the defendant is to give notice by petition, delivered to the keeper of the prison of the Court, and left also at the public office of such Court, for the information of the plaintiff's attorney, in order that he may enquire of his client whether such defendant is to be continued in prison at his suit; and should this be the case, the plaintiff must attend his attorney, and give his note of hand to pay the defendant three shillings and sixpence *per* week, so long as he shall continue prisoner at his suit; and with such note he must pay three shillings and sixpence of lawful money of this realm, and continue such payment weekly to the prisoner on every succeeding Monday morning, from the first payment at the gaol or prison of the said Court, before the hour of eight o'clock.

Note. It is incumbent on the plaintiff to be circumspect in seeing that the money so paid is *good;* for should any part of the money paid be *base*, the defendant will, on the next Court-day, obtain his discharge on account of such unlawful payment.

IV. *Mode of Proceeding by a Plaintiff, on a common process, where the debt is* 40s., *and not exceeding* 5l.

THE plaintiff applies to an attorney of the Court for a process to serve on the defendant for a debt of 40s. and under 5l. which process is served in general by an officer of the Court, though it may be by the plaintiff himself. When so served, the defendant must, on the Court-day of the week following the service of the process, employ one of the attornies of the Court, (not concerned for the plaintiff) to appear for him and file common bail. But should the defendant omit so to do, then the plaintiff's attorney, (if he thinks proper to proceed, which is in general the case,) will order the person who served the defendant with such process, to attend on him, to make an affidavit of such service, (and this must be made within the jurisdiction of the Court); which affidavit is drawn up by the plaintiff's attorney *(see Affidavit in Appendix)*; and when signed by the person serving the process, the plaintiff's attorney attends him to the public office, and gets such affidavit sworn to before the proper officer of the Court. Having done this, the plaintiff's attorney will file

common bail and the declaration, in the second week after the return of the writ, and give the person who served the defendant with the process, a notice of such declaration having been filed in the public office of the Court, which notice should be delivered to the defendant on the Monday, or left at his place of abode; but should it not be possible to ascertain such defendant's residence, the notice must be left at his last place of abode, and a copy thereof stuck up in the public office of the Court.

Previous to the pleadings being filed they must have the signature of counsel; for which a charge of 5s. is claimed, but which was not allowed for their signature to *incipiturs* prior to 1802; nor is there any rule or order of Court for that purpose, as the special order of Court made in the year 1759, specifies the pleadings to which the signature of counsel is requisite, and for which they are entitled to 5s. but it does not mention signatures of this nature.

Should the defendant neglect to appear by an attorney of the Court, and take the declaration filed against him out of the office of the Court, then the plaintiff may (by his attorney) sign interlocutory judgment at the next Court-day after such notice of declaration so given and stuck up in the public office; he may also,

on that day, set his cause down for trial, for an enquiry to be executed against the said defendant. The plaintiff's attorney will also give the person who served the defendant with process and notice of declaration, a notice of enquiry to be executed the following Court-day, by leaving the same at his residence or last place of abode, and, if absent, by sticking the same up in the public office. In this stage of the proceedings, it is usual for the attorney of the plaintiff to write to him, desiring him to attend on the Tuesday or Wednesday morning, prepared with the sum required for proceeding, and to give instructions for drawing out the case, and preparing briefs for counsel, and, if necessary, to issue subpœnas for plaintiff's witnesses, in support of his action. Having made these preparations, and proceeded to trial, when the damages are assessed, if the defendant does not apply to prevent execution issuing against him, the plaintiff will be entitled to his execution against him on the Saturday noon following the Friday, on which the enquiry was executed.

V.

THE proceedings are the same where the damages are laid at only 39s., with this differ-

ence only, that some of the pleadings in this latter case are not charged at so high a price as in the former.

———

VI.

WHERE the damage is laid at 9*l* 19*s*. but no defence is made to the action, the proceedings are the same as in the foregoing case.   But should the defendant, where the damage is so laid, be inclined to make a defence to such action, and want longer time than is allowed by the Palace Court for that purpose, he must employ an attorney of the Court, to take the declaration out of the office; or should he not be inclined so to do, but wishes to remove such cause, he must employ an attorney of the Palace Court, should any foreign attorney have brought the *habeas corpus** for the purpose; which must be done on the Tuesday

———

* When any attorney of the superior Courts has occasion to remove a cause from the Palace Court by *habeas corpus*, he must lodge the same in the public office of such Court, where it must remain four days for the return, and for which he must pay 5*s*   should the attorney require a return to the *habeas* immediately, he must pay for such expedition an additional 2*s*. 6*d*

preceding the writ of inquiry being executed; and special bail must also be put 'in, in the Palace Court, by an attorney of the Court, with the names of two housekeepers added to such bail piece, who will be able to justify their sufficiency in open Court; and the said attorney must give notice of bail having been put in on the Tuesday, and that such bail will justify themselves in open Court, that is, on the next Court-day following such notice, as good and sufficient bail for the said defendant, on his writ of *habeas corpus* allowed in that cause.

Note Bail justifying themselves in Court, on *habeas corpus*, undertake to pay the damages and costs in such action, should the defendant fail in his defence thereto: their responsibility does not merely extend to rendering the body of the defendant in their discharge.

The defendant must on such writ of *habeas corpus* also file common bail in the superior Court to which such cause is removed, and then the plaintiff will be entitled to proceed *de novo*.

VII. *Mode of Proceeding for the Plaintiff where he has obtained a Verdict against the Defendant; and not knowing where to find him, wishes to fix his Bail.*

BEFORE a plaintiff can fix a defendant's bail either on the bail-bond for his appearance, or those who may have justified for the defendant and themselves, such plaintiff must, through the medium of his attorney, get his debt and damages ascertained by the proper officer of the Court, by such officer's taxing the same; after which the plaintiff's attorney must sue out execution, and get the same returned by the officer who arrested the defendant, " *Non est inventus.*"

On the return of such *ca. sa.* the plaintiff's attorney must sue out *sci. fa.* against the bail of the defendant, who had justified. Should such bail render the defendant on such first notice, and before the second is issued, they will thereby exonerate themselves from the damages and costs incurred by the defendant, and they will be totally discharged from any claim which the plaintiff could have had against them on the defendant's account. But should such bail not be able to render the defendant before the

issuing of the second notice oi *sci. fa.* then the defendant and his bail are absolutely fixed for the damages and costs. Bail may appear to a second *sci. fa.* although such appearance will render them no assistance, but merely incur additional expense.

———

VIII. *Mode of proceeding for a Defendant when arrested.*

WHEN a defendant is arrested by an officer of the Palace Court, and is enabled to procure two housekeepers to sign a bail-bond for his liberation, he should be very cautious (after he and his friends have executed the bail-bond,) of being .ed away by the advice of the officer or his colleague, or of permitting such officer to put in an appearance for him to such bail-bond, at the return thereof; but the defendant should, himself, employ an attorney for that purpose. Another contrivance of office, which it seems necessary also to put the defendant on his guard against, is, that such officer frequently obtains money from defendants, to put in appearances for them, perhaps 6*s.* 8*d.* or 2*s.* according to circumstances; whereas the only money the officer can legally demand for

the bail-bond is 4s. 6d., and the sheriff of the county is not entitled to any more than this sum by law. And should any officer of the Court persist in demanding more than 4s. 6d. for such bail-bond, the defendant has his remedy, either by applying to the Court, to which such officer belongs, or by indicting him for extortion.

It is therefore recommended to defendants, strictly to attend to this advice; and previous to the return of such writ and bail-bond, (if they have any defence to make to the action), to apply to an attorney of the Palace Court, before the return of the writ on which they have been arrested, and give such attorney the name of the plaintiff, and instructions to appear for the defendant, at the return of the bail-bond and writ By attending to this advice, the defendant will save himself a great deal of trouble and anxiety, both on the part of himself and his friends who bailed the action, and will likewise prevent additional expense being incurred by the plaintiff's attorney taking any advantage of him, and he will moreover debar him from assigning the bail bond for want of an appearance

In the subsequent week after such appearance is entered, the defendant must attend on the attorney who appeared for him to his

said bail-bond, and who generally writes to require such attendance and the money necessary to proceed; yet it is most advisable for defendants not to wait the receipt of such letter, but to secure the safety of themselves and friends by attending their attorney personally, and giving him the names of two housekeepers. The attorney will then attend with the defendant and his friends, to be acknowledged as bail before the Judge, which acknowledgment must be made in the week following the appearance being entered. By adopting this course of proceeding (if the bail are good) the defendant will have no occasion to trouble his friends to go to Court to justify. But should the plaintiff's attorney take exceptions, he will give a rule for better bail on the Court-day following such bail having been put in, file his declaration, and at the same time give a rule for the defendant to plead on the day such bail justifies in Court. Should it so happen that the defendant's bail should not be enabled to justify on such rule given, the defendant's attorney may obtain further time to justify such bail, (*viz.* the week following), by taking what is termed a *sto bas.* for which the defendant's attorney must give the plaintiff's attorney 2*s.*

Should the defendant then justif͟ his bail, and plead to the plaintiff's declaration, the plaintiff will be entitled to set down his cause for trial on the day the defendant pleads, namely, the Friday following; unless the defendant plead specially, or bring a *habeas corpus,* which he is c͟ titled to do, if he pleases, on the day such cause is set down for trial; but it would be the safest way for the defendant to bring his *habeas* before the cause is set down for trial, and also, should the defendant be in any wise apprehensive (where his attorney has taken a week's further time to justify his bail) that such bail will not be able to attend, in that case it is preferable for the defendant's attorney, before the second rule for better bail under the head of *sto bas.* be taken, to bring his *habeas,* than to bring a *habeas* after such *sto bas ;* as he will thereby stay the proceedings in such Court

Having adopted this course, the defendant's attorney should wait till the plaintiff's attorney gives a rule (if in vacation a six day rule, if in term a four day rule,) to put in good bail in the Court in which the *habeas corpus* is brought. When such rule to put in bail is given, the defendant's attorney will then know how to proceed in future. The reason why it is above

suggested to bring a *habeas corpus* before the second rule for better bail given in the Palace Court, is, that in case the defendant should not be able to justify bail to his writ of *habeas corpus* in the superior Court, and such cause should revert by *procedendo* into the Palace Court for want of justification, the defendant will then have the liberty of justifying his bail in the latter Court, as at first; and should he not be able so to do, in order to prevent his friends being fixed with the bail-bond given for his appearance, the bail on the bail-piece (should the same have been acknowledged before the Judge, which is most essential to be done,) may render him in open Court, in their discharge, on the Court-day following such writ of *procedendo* being allowed in the office of such Court. Should the defendant be rendered by his bail, he can, by his attorney, or himself, force the plaintiff to trial, and should the plaintiff not proceed to trial, the defendant may, by his attorney, summons such cause for trial by proviso; and should the plaintiff not be able to establish his claim against the defendant, nor appear to such trial, the defendant will be entitled to his discharge, as in the case of *non pros.* for want of evidence. But should the plaintiff substanti-

ate his claim, then the defendant ought (as to the proper time of doing so the defendant must consult his attorney,) to give the plaintiff a rule to commit such defendant in execution, so that he may (as the law allows in such cases,) compel the plaintiff to give his note to him for the sixpences granted under the Lords' act, and to pay therewith three shillings and sixpence; which sum the plaintiff must continue to pay every Monday morning, before the hour of eight o'clock: for, in default of such payment, the defendant will be entitled to his discharge.

Where a defendant requires time, and the vacation draws near, it is advisable for him to bring a *habeas corpus* to remove the cause from the Palace Court, in an early stage of the proceedings; and he should be careful to put in bail above in the Palace Court, previous to such removal, more particularly if it be near the vacation.

The defendant will be obliged to put in bail above (special bail) to this writ of *habeas corpus* in the superior court; but he is not compelled so to do until the plaintiff's attorney gives a judge's rule to put in good bail on such writ.

When such bail is put in before one of the judges of the Court to which the cause h as

been removed, the defendant should give the plaintiff notice of such bail having been put in, and before whom, with the names and residences of such bail. And on the plaintiff's attorney giving a judge's rule for better bail, the defendant's attorney must give notice that the bail which had been put in will justify themselves in open court, on the first day of the ensuing term, that is, the term subsequent to the writ of *habeas corpus* having been allowed

Should the defendant neglect to put in special bail to such writ of *habeas corpus* (having previously neglected to put in bail above in the Court from which the cause was removed), and the same cause should revert to the Palace Court by *procedendo*, the bond given to the officer of the Palace Court on the arrest becomes forfeited, and no render can be made to relieve the bail, who are thus fixed with the debt and costs.

Note The defendant's attorney should be particularly attentive, where such defendant's bail-bond is supposed to be assigned, in searching the public office of the Court, to see whether an assignment has been made or not, and whether any writs have been issued against the defendant and his bail on such assignment; as

instances have occurred in which defendants have been charged with proceedings on a supposed assignment of the bail-bond, when no such bond had been assigned, and no proceedings instituted thereon.

IX. *Mode of proceeding for a Defendant in Custody, who employs an Attorney of the Superior Court to bring a* habeas corpus *for him.*

WHERE an attorney for a defendant in custody is to bring a *habeas corpus*, he must, after receiving instructions, apply to the keeper of the prison of the Palace Court for a copy of causes by which the defendant is detained in custody; and then, having obtained the writ of *habeas corpus* filled up, signed, and sealed, he must lodge the same, together with the copy of causes, at the public office of the Palace Court, where, on leaving the writ, he must pay 5*s*. and with the paper of causes 1*s*.; if more than one cause, 1*s*. for every additional cause. If in vacation, it is most proper to have the writ returned immediately, as the judges are then not always to be met with. When he has settled

what judge he intends taking the prisoner before, he must leave the writ of *habeas corpus* at the prison, and appoint a time for the keeper to bring the prisoner before such judge, to be by him committed: when the judge will order the gaol fees, 10*s*. 10*d*. to be paid previous to such commitment, and will at the same time sign the order for the prisoner's commitment. The keeper of the prison of the Palace Court will then surrender such prisoner to the custody of his Lordship's tipstaff.

X. *Mode of proceeding where a Defendant is arrested, and afterwards proves himself to be an Attorney.*

WHERE the defendant is an attorney, he has no occasion to give bail to the officer, or to go to the prison of the Palace Court; but, while l e is in custody at the officer's house, (where he is by law allowed to remain twenty-four hours), he should get his writ of privilege allowed, sig i ed, and sealed, and lodge the same in the pub lic office of the Palace Court, where he will have to pay 3*s*. for allowing such writ; and the clerk will thereupon issue a *supersedeas* to such

E

officer, to discharge the defendant, without giving a bail-bond; for which the defendant will have to pay 1*s.*

The officer, on the receipt of such supersedeas, must immediately discharge the prisoner; against whom, when so discharged out of the custody of the officer, the plaintiff, by his attorney, should enter a *cassetur* at the public office of the Palace Court. And should the plaintiff be then inclined to proceed against the defendant, he must proceed *de novo*, by filing a bill against such defendant in the court of which he may be an attorney.

XI. *Mode of proceeding for a Defendant who has been arrested, and for whom Bail at Peril has been put in by his Attorney previous to Bond being given, on which the Officer receives a supersedeas.*

In former years it was usual, where a defendant had been arrested, for him to apply to an attorney of the Palace Court, and lodge the debt and costs in such attorney's hands; when the attorney, being so indemnified, put in bail

at peril for such defendant, and gave the officer
a *supersedeas*, instead of a bail-bond; a mode
of proceeding which saved much trouble to
the defendant, and prevented him from requiring his friends to become bail for him.

The mode of process in the case of bail at peril is, that the plaintiff is at liberty to proceed *instanter* against the defendant, by filing and perfecting his declaration, and giving a rule to force
the defendant to plead on the Friday following.
But it is a rule, that, after such declaration is
filed and perfected, should the defendant not
be prepared to plead thereto, he may have a
week's further time for that purpose, which is
usually given; and should the defendant not then
be prepared, his attorney may on the following
Friday take what is termed *a lunar*, that is,
leave to plead on the Monday following. But the
plaintiff in that case, is not to be debarred from
summoning his cause for trial, which he may
set down for that purpose, on the Friday preceding the Monday the defendant must plead;
whose plea must be either—general issue, *non
assumpsit*, or judgment recovered. Should the
last mentioned plea be entered, then the plaintiff's summoning such cause for trial is rendered nugatory, and he must proceed in the regular way, by replying to such plea, &c. &c.

But in general, in interlocutory pleadings, the object of the defendant is, to get all the time he can; and, if he wants further time, he must, previous to the plaintiff's joining in demurrer, bring his *Habeas Corpus;* otherwise, after joining in demurrer, his writ of *Habeas Corpus* will not avail him, but the plaintiff may proceed to trial, and get final judgment against him: in which case the defendant has no other redress, than that afforded by a writ of error, which must be bespoke, and obtained before the trial, so as to be ready to be lodged at the office on the day the writ of inquiry is executed; in default thereof, the plaintiff will have his execution against the defendant, or the attorney who put in bail at peril for him

If the defendant should sue out a writ of error, he will pay for lodging the same at the public office 1*l.* 11*s.* 6*d*; and should he be obliged to transcribe such writ, he will have to pay the secondary 6*s* 8*d. per press,* every press to contain forty-two lines. Should the plaintiff in error omit transcribing the writ, the defendant in error will be entitled to his *nonpros* for want of such transcribing, and may proceed to execution.

The like proceedings may occur, where a defendant is arrested, and a bail-bond is given

XII. *Mode of proceeding for a Defendant, when arrested out of the Jurisdiction of the Court*

I𝐹 a defendant should be arrested by an officer of the Palace Court out of the jurisdiction thereof, such defendant in general gives the officer making such arrest a bail-bond for his appearance at the next Court, which will be on the return day of such writ on which the defend‑ ant was arrested, should such arrest have been made previous thereto.

The defendant having thus complied with the rules of the Court, must apply at the next Court to have such bail-bond cancelled, and to be discharged from such arrest. For which purpose he must employ an attorney of the Palace Court to draw up an affidavit, setting forth the distance from Whitehall where such defendant was arrested, and on this affidavit the Court is moved by counsel *.

Should the Court be satisfied with such affi‑ davit, an order will be made thereon for the de‑ fendant's discharge, and the cancelling of the

* Formerly, in order to save expense, the Court on this and the like occasions permitted the attornies to make mo‑ tions.

bail-bond.   When the defendant will be entitled to his remedy against the Knight Marshal of the Court, by an action for trespass and false imprisonment.   This is the usual course; but the best mode a defendant can adopt, when arrested out of the jurisdiction of the Palace Court, is, not to bail the action, but immediately to go to gaol, and employ an attorney of one of the superior Courts to bring an action in such Court against the Knight Marshal, for trespass, damages, and false imprisonment.

XIII. *Mode of proceeding where the Defendant is served with a Copy of Process, out of the Jurisdiction of the Court.*

WHEN a defendant is served with process out of the jurisdiction of the Palace Court, he should take no notice of it, but let the plaintiff proceed, make affidavit of service, file declaration, and give notice of the filing thereof; and when the defendant receives such notice of declaration, he should apply to an attorney of the Court, to take the declaration out of the office, and then plead "*the jurisdiction of the Court.*"

The plaintiff must then either reply to such plea, or enter a *cassetur;* and the defendant will thus for a time stay the proceedings.

In case the plaintiff replies to such plea, and the Court decides against such replication, the defendant will then be entitled to his costs, and can afterwards bring his action against the Knight Marshal for trespass, and also indict the party, who swore the affidavit of service, for wilful perjury. (*See form of Affidavit in Appendix*) The defendant has the same remedy should the plaintiff discontinue, provided affidavit of service has been made.

XIV. *Mode of proceeding by a Defendant when arrested, and in case of* Nonpros *for want of his Plaintiff's proceeding.*

WHEN a defendant is arrested by a writ issued from the Palace Court, and gives the officer who arrested him a bail-bond for his appearance at the return of the writ, he should immediately on giving such bail-bond employ an attorney of the Court, (who is not concerned for the plaintiff), to appear for him at the next ensuing court-day after he has been arrested Should

the defendant neglect so to do, the plaintiff's attorney will (for want of such appearance) assign the defendant's bail-bond, and sue out writs against the defendant and his bail, whereby he will be put to the additional expense of 2l. 12s. 6d. and which he must pay immediately on such assignment and writs issued against his bail.   And as soon as the assignment is paid for, his attorney must put in bail above, that is, before the following Court after the return of the writ and bail-bond. Having complied with these directions, it is advisable for the defendant not to wait for the plaintiff's attorney giving a rule for better bail, but to attend on his own attorney, with his bail, whose names are to the bail-piece; and if they should not be housekeepers, then the defendant should get the names of two housekeepers added to the bail-piece so put in, and attend with them and his attorney at the next Court subsequent to that on which the bail was put in, and justify their sufficiency in open Court, as good bail for him.

But if such additional bail should attend to justify, and not those on the bail-piece in the first instance, the defendant's attorney must give notice to the plaintiff's attorney on the Tuesday preceding, that such bail will justify

themselves in open Court for the said defendant, so that the plaintiff's attorney may have time to make inquiries as to their sufficiency, unless he should be satisfied without.

When the defendant, by his attorney, has taken the precaution of securing the safety of himself and bail, and the plaintiff's attorney has not proceeded to declare against him, his attorney must, at the next court-day, give a rule to force the plaintiff to declare; and if the plaintiff should then merely declare, and not perfect his declaration, nor obtain any time for so doing, the defendant's attorney may, at such Court, give the plaintiff a rule to perfect his declaration; which, if he neglects to do, the defendant's attorney is entitled to *nonpros* for want of the plaintiff's so perfecting his declaration. And should the plaintiff not discontinue his action, by entering such discontinuance at the office, and paying the costs incurred, the defendant will be entitled to his execution against the plaintiff for his costs.

XV. *Mode of proceeding for Defendant when served with Copy of Process, and in case of Nonpros for want of Plaintiff's proceeding.*

WHEN a defendant is served with copy of a writ issued from the Palace Court, and he has a defence to make to the action, he should, on the return of the writ, or on the following court-day, apply to an attorney of the Court to enter an appearance, and file common bail for him, at the court-day following the return. The plaintiff must then, on the next ensuing court-day, declare against the said defendant; and should he not declare on the court-day subsequent to the defendant's filing common bail, or take a rule for further time to declare, then the defendant's attorney must give the plaintiff a rule to declare on the following court-day. Should the plaintiff then declare, (which consists in carrying an *incipitur* into the office), but neglect to perfect his declaration, or to obtain a rule for further time for that purpose; then the defendant's attorney should give a rule for the plaintiff to perfect his declaration; and should he omit so to do, the defendant's at-

torney must sign a *nonpros*, which will entitle the defendant to his costs; and if these be not paid, the defendant is entitled to his execution against the plaintiff.

***

XVI. *Mode of proceeding for Defendant when arrested by a wrong Name.*

SHOULD a person be arrested by a writ issued from the Palace Court, and the party be not called and known by the name in the process, as well as by his right name, it is advisable for such person to go to prison, and then give notice to the Knight Marshal, and the officer making the arrest—" That unless they liberate him, " he will bring an action against them for tres- " pass, damages, and false imprisonment."

***

XVII. *Mode of proceeding for Defendant when served with Process in a wrong Name.*

WHEN any person is served with the copy of a process issued either from the Palace Court, or any of the superior Courts, and the party is not

called or known by the name in the process, as
well as by his right name, he is not bound to
appear to, or take any notice of such writ.—
And should the plaintiff be advised to proceed
in such action, and the supposed defendant be
taken in execution, the plaintiff in such suit will
be liable to an action for damages and false imprisonment; and the party swearing the affidavit of service, will be liable to an indictment for
perjury.

But should the party wish to get rid of the
business at the commencement, he must move
the Court in which such action is brought, to
set aside the proceedings; which motion must
be grounded on an affidavit stating the facts.

PART III.

———

A GENERAL VIEW OF ORIGINAL COSTS IN THE PALACE COURT.—CONTAINING

ORIGINAL COSTS.

———

[The following Bills of Costs having been drawn prior to the passing of the stat. 55 Geo 3, c 184, the amount of the Stamp Duty charged on the respective Proceedings, may be ascertained by referring to the fifth division of these Tables, and which appears at page 95, *post*]

———

I.—COSTS ON TAKING OUT A WRIT.

Fees paid to the Attorney on suing out a Writ to hold a Defendant to Bail.

FOR the affidavit stamp	£0	1	0
Stamp on the writ	0	2	0
Swearing the affidavit of debt	0	1	0
To the prothonotary for filling up the writ	0	1	6
Fee to the attorney	0	2	0

———

For suing out a Writ to serve Defendant with a Copy, if the Debt be 40s. or upwards.

Stamp for the writ	£0	2	0
To the prothonotary for filling up the same	0	1	6
Fee to the attorney	0	1	4

If the Debt be under 40s.

To the prothonotary for signing the writ £0 1 6
Fee to the attorney 0 1 4

Note. If there are more than one defendant, the attorney charges 4*d.* each for the copies of the writ.

If a writ is sued out after the hours appointed for the office to be kept open, the Prothonotary charges 6*d.* more than the above fees. If after ten o'clock at night, 2*s.* 6*d.*

If the Prothonotary or his Clerk attends at the Fleet prison, King's Bench prison, or any short distance, to take an affidavit, he is entitled to 6*s.* 8*d.* for his attendance and swearing the affidavit.

Note. The Officer to whom the writ is delivered to execute, is entitled to 1*s.* on giving him the writ, which is called the *Warrant Shilling*, and is allowed in costs.

The Attorney's charge for several Articles which are not in Bills of Costs.

Assigning a bail-bond £0 2 4
Writ, copies, and Officer for service 0 6 6
    If more than one bail, 4*d.* is charged for each copy; and the Officer is entitled to only 1*s* each for serving, unless six weeks have expired from the return of the writ on which the

defendant was arrested, to the time of assigning the bail-bond, &c in which case the charge is *2s. 6d.* each

For withdrawing a record	£0	2	2
For a rule against an officer	0	2	8
For withdrawing one security of an officer	0	7	0
For filing a bill against an officer	0	8	2
For a procedendo	0	19	2
For a habeas corpus in term	1	6	8
If in vacation	1	7	8

COSTS ON A DISCONTINUANCE BEING ENTERED.

For Plaintiff on the Return of the Writ.

Appearance	£0	2	0
Rule to discontinue	0	2	0
Discontinuance and entry	0	5	4
Fee and bill	0	2	4

For Defendant on the Return of Writ.

Bail-bond, duty, Knight Marshal's fee	£0	4	6
Rule for time to put in bail	0	2	0

For Defendant where the Discontinuance is entered on Wednes-
day (before 12 o'Clock) next after Return of Writ.

Bail-bond, duty, and Knight Marshal's fee £0 4 6
Rule for time to put in bail 0 2 0
Fee and Bill 0 2 4

For Defendant where Discontinuance is entered (after 12
o'Clock) on Wednesday next after Return of Writ.

Bail-bond, duty, and Knight Marshal's fee £0 4 6
Rule for time to put in bail 0 2 0
Bail-piece, duty, entry, and judge's clerk 0 6 6
Fee on rule to discontinue 0 1 8
Fee and Bill 0 2 4
Letters 0 1 0

For the Defendant where an Arrest has been made, General
Issue pleaded, Cause summoned for Trial, Retraxit, and Dis-
continuance entered by Plaintiff.

Bail-bond, duty, and Knight Marshal's fee £0 4 6
Rule for time to put in bail 0 2 0
Bail-piece, duty, entry, and judge's clerk 0 6 6
Imparlance, and copy of declaration 0 4 0
Rule for time to plead 0 2 0

F

Plea of general issue, duty, and entry   0   3   2
Fee on summons for trial   0   1   8
Drawing brief, and copies for counsel   0   2   8
Subpœna and tickets   0   8   6
Two counsel   0   10   0
Fee on plaintiff's withdrawing record   0   1   8
Fee on rule to discontinue   0   1   8
Fee and bill   0   2   4
Letters   0   1   0

COSTS ON PAYING MONEY INTO COURT.

Bill of Costs for the Plaintiff, on paying Money into Court, at Return of Writ, where a Bail-bond has been taken.

Affidavit of debt, swearing, writ, signing, and officer for arrest £0   13   6
Appearance   0   2   0
Fee and bill*   0   2   4

* Not allowed between party and party, but charged to the client

For Plaintiff on paying Money into Court after the Return of the Writ, and before 12 o'Clock on the Wednesday next ensuing.

Affidavit of debt, swearing, writ, signing, and officer for arrest £0   13   6

Appearance 0 2 0
Fee and Bill 0 2 4

———

For Plaintiff on paying Money into Court after 12 o'Clock on the Wednesday next ensuing the Return.

Affidavit and swearing, writ and signing, and offi-
    cer for arrest £0 13 6
Appearance 0 2 0
Fee on rule to pay money into court 0 1 8
Fee and bill 0 2 4

———

For Plaintiff on paying Money into Court at the Time of plead-ing the General Issue

Affidavit and swearing, writ and signing, and offi-
    cer for arrest £0 13 6
Appearance 0 2 0
Inquiring into the sufficiency of the bail, and rule
    for the defendant to justify bail 0 1 8
Opposing the justification of the bail in court ... 0 1 8
Declaration 0 5 6
Perfect special, and counsel 0 12 6
Fee on rule to plead 0 1 8
Opposing motion for further time till Monday . . 0 1 8

F 2

Fee on rule to pay money into court £0   1   8
Fee and bill 0   2   4

———

For the Plaintiff on paying Money into Court on a Process Cause where the Debt is 40s or upwards, at the Return of the Writ.

Writ, copy, and service £0   8   4
Appearance 0   2   0
Fee and bill 0   2   4

———

For Plaintiff on paying Money into Court at the Return of the Writ, where the Debt is under 40s

Writ, copy, and service £0   4   10
Appearance 0   2   0
Fee and bill 0   2   4

———

For Defendant on paying Money into Court at the Return of the Writ

Rule to pay money into court £0   2   0

For Defendant on paying Money into Court after the Return of the Writ, and before 12 o'Clock on the Wednesday next ensuing.

Rule to pay money into court	£0	2	0
Fee and bill	0	2	4

For Defendant on paying Money into Court after 12 o'Clock on the Wednesday next ensuing the Return of the Writ.

Rule for time to put in bail	£0	2	0
Rule to pay money into court	0	2	0
Fee and bill	0	2	4

For the Defendant on paying Money into Court at the Time of pleading the General Issue.

Rule for time to put in bail	£0	2	0
Bail-piece, duty, entry, and judge's clerk	0	6	6
Rule for time to justify bail	0	2	0
Rule for former bail to be absolute	0	2	0
Imparlance, and copy of declaration	0	4	0
Rule for time to plead	0	2	0
Plea of general issue, duty, and entry	0	3	2
Rule to pay money into court	0	2	0
Fee and bill	0	2	4

Note. It is usual with the attornies, when orders are given to pay money into court, at the return of the writ, to take 4*s.* viz. 2*s.* for the appearance, and 2*s.* for the rule to pay money into court: sometimes they take 6*s.* 4*d.*

Bill of Costs for the Plaintiff on an Arrest, where the General Issue is pleaded, with an Allowance of Witnesses, if paid before Execution is sued out.

Affidavit of debt, writ, signing, and officer for arrest	£0	13	6
Entering appearance	0	2	0
Declaration	0	5	6
Perfect	0	5	6
Rule to plead	0	1	8
Venire facias, duty, record, and summoning the jury	0	6	8
Drawing brief, and copies thereof for counsel ...	0	2	8
Subpœna and tickets	0	6	6
Two counsel	0	10	0
Court fees, (which include the jury, verdict, and judgment thereon), officers in waiting, attorney's fee, attending the trial, and bill of costs	0	17	2
Note. If any exhibits, charge 1*s.* each.			
Rule to allow witnesses	0	2	0
Paid four witnesses from Deptford	0	6	6
Fee	0	2	4
Letters	0	1	0

For Defendant on an Arrest where General Issue pleaded, and Verdict for the Defendant, if paid before Execution made out

Bail-bond, duty, and Knight Marshal's fee	£0	4	6
Rule for time to put in bail	0	2	0
Bail above, duty, entry, and judge's clerk	0	6	6
Rule for time to justify bail	0	2	0
Rule for former bail to be absolute	0	2	0
Imparlance, and copy of declaration	0	4	0
Fee on rule for time to perfect	0	1	8
Rule for time to plead	0	2	0
Plea of general issue, duty, and entry	0	3	2
Fee on plaintiff's summons	0	1	8
Subpœna	0	8	6
Brief, and copies for counsel	0	2	8
Two counsel	0	10	0
Court fees	0	17	2
Fee	0	2	4
Letters	0	1	0

For Plaintiff on an Arrest, where General Issue pleaded, Verdict for Plaintiff, and Execution sued out

Affidavit, writ, and arrest	£0	13	6
Appearance	0	2	0
Rule for better bail*	0	1	8

* If same bail justified that were put in above, this charge is omitted, and not allowed in any case for the plaintiff

Opposing justification of bail *	0	1	8
Declaration	0	5	6
Special perfect and counsel	0	12	6
Rule to plead	0	1	8
Opposing motion for further time	0	1	8
Venire, and summoning the jury	0	8	8
Brief and copies	0	2	0
Subpœna and tickets	0	8	6
Two counsel	0	10	0
Court fees	0	17	2
Reading, if any exhibits, 1s. each			
Execution and service	0	9	0

* If same bail justified that were put in above, this charge is also omitted, and not allowed in any case for the plaintiff

---

For Plaintiff on an Arrest, where Defendant pleads a special Plea, with Subpœna for Witnesses, and Execution

Affidavit, writ, and arrest	£0	13	6
Appearance	0	2	0
Declaration	0	5	6
Perfect	0	5	6
Rule to plead	0	1	8
Copy of special plea	0	2	8
Rule for time to reply	0	1	8
Replication and counsel	0	8	8
Summoning the cause	0	8	8
Brief, and copies for counsel	0	2	0
Subpœna and tickets	0	8	6

Two counsel	0	10	0
Court fees	0	17	2
Rule to allow witnesses	0	2	0
Paid four from Greenwich	0	8	0
Execution and service	0	9	0

For Defendant, where Bail at the Peril of Defendant's Attorney, Supersedeas issued, and Special Plea pleaded.

Searching for plaint, and paid	£0	2	2
Bail	0	6	6
Paid Knight Marshal's fee thereon	0	2	4
Paid for supersedeas	0	1	0
Rule for bail to be absolute at peril of defendant's attorney	0	2	0
Fee on rule for time to declare	0	1	8
Imparlance, and copy of declaration	0	4	0
Fee on rule for time to perfect	0	1	8
Rule for time to plead	0	2	0
Special plea, and paid signing	0	11	6
Rule to reply	0	2	0
Copy of replication	0	2	8
Fee on plaintiff's summons	0	1	0
Briefs	0	2	0
Two counsel	0	10	0
Subpœna	0	8	6
Court fees	0	17	2
Execution and service	0	9	0

*For Defendant, where there is a Bail-bond, General Issue plead-
ed, with Notice of Set off—Verdict for Defendant.*

Bail-bond	£0	4	6
Bail above, duty, and entry	0	6	6
Rule for time to justify bail	0	2	0
Rule for former bail to stand	0	2	0
Imparlance, and copy of declaration	0	4	0
Rule to plead	0	2	0
Plea of general issue	0	3	2
Notice of set-off, copy, and service *	0	2	0
Fee on plaintiff's default	0	1	8
Fee on plaintiff's summoning the cause	0	1	8
Subpœna and tickets	0	8	6
Drawing brief and copies	0	2	0
Two counsel	0	10	0
Court fees	0	17	2
Execution	0	9	0

* Not allowed on taxation

*For Defendant, where served with Process, the General Issue
pleaded, Summons and Retraxit by the Plaintiff, Summons by
Proviso, and Verdict for Defendant.*

Appearance *	£0	2	0
Common bail, and paid Knight Marshal's fee	0	7	4

* Not allowed on taxation

Imparlance, and copy of declaration	0	4	0
Rule to plead	0	2	0
Plea of general issue	0	3	2
Fee on plaintiff's summons	0	1	8
Brief and copies	0	2	0
Subpœna and tickets	0	8	6
Two counsel	0	10	0
Fee on plaintiff's withdrawing the record	0	1	8
Summons by proviso	0	8	8
Two counsel	0	10	0
Court fees	0	17	2
Execution	0	9	0

For Defendant, where Motion is made in Arrest of Judgment, and Judgment arrested.

Bail-bond	£0	4	6
Bail above, duty, and entry	0	6	6
Rule for time to justify bail	0	2	0
Rule for former bail to stand	0	2	0
Imparlance, and copy of declaration	0	4	0
Rule to plead .. ..,	0	2	0
Plea of general issue	0	3	2
Fee on plaintiff's default	0	1	8
Fee on plaintiff's summons	0	1	8
Brief and copies	0	2	0
Subpœna and tickets	0	8	6
Two counsel	0	10	0
Motion and rule to stay judgment and execution, unless cause	0	2	0

Copies of the proceedings for the steward and counsel in arrest of judgment	0	7	6
To counsel therewith	0	10	0
Rule continued	0	2	0
Rule to hear judgment	0	2	0
Attending the court, when judgment given for the defendant	0	2	0
Rule for judgment accordingly	0	2	0
Signing judgment	0	5	4
Execution	0	9	0

For Plaintiff on an Arrest, where Special Plea pleaded, Verdict for Plaintiff, Motion in Arrest of Judgment, and Judgment affirmed.

Affidavit, writ, and arrest	£0	13	6
Appearance	0	2	0
Rule for better bail	0	1	8
Opposing justification of bail	0	1	8
Declaration	0	5	6
Special perfect and counsel	0	15	6
Rule to plead	0	1	8
Opposing motion for further time	0	1	8
Venire, and summoning the jury	0	8	
Brief and copies	0		
Subpœna and tickets	0		
Counsel		10	
		1	

Copies of the proceedings for the steward and coun sel on arrest of judgment	0	7	6
To counsel therewith	0	10	0
Rule continued	0	2	0
Rule to hear judgment	0	2	0
Attending the court when judgment was affirmed .	0	2	0
Rule accordingly	0	2	0
Signing judgment	0	5	4
Execution	0	9	0

For I ounty where the Defen'n t is served wih Process, Debt 40s or upnards, Special Plea, and Verdict for Plaintiff.

Writ, copy and service	£0	8	4
Appearance	0	2	0
Declaration	0	5	6
Perfect	0	5	6
Rule to plead	0	1	8
Copy of special plea	0	2	8
Rule for time to reply	0	1	8
Publication .. tn cl	0	8	8
d caus	0	8	8
Briefs and copies for counsel	0	2	0
Subpoena nd tickets	0	8	6
Two counsel	0	10	0
Witnesses ....,...	0	17	2
Execution	0	9	0

For Plaintiff where Defendant is served with Process, Debt 39s. General Issue pleaded, and Verdict for Plaintiff.

Writ, copy, and service	£0	4	10
Appearance	0	2	0
Declaration	0	5	6
Perfect	0	5	6
Rule to plead	0	1	8
Summoning the cause	0	8	8
Brief and copies	0	2	0
Subpœna and tickets	0	8	6
Two counsel	0	10	0
Court fees	0	17	2
Execution	0	9	0

For Plaintiff on Process, Debt 40s. or upwards where Defendant does not appear, and Plaintiff files Bail according to the Statute, and Inquiry executed.

Writ, copy, and service	£0	8	4
Appearance	0	2	0
Affidavit of service, and officer*	0	5	0
Filing common bail, and paid Knight Marshal's fee	0	7	4
Declaration	0	5	6
Imparlance, and copy of declaration	0	4	0

* If served by plaintiff, 3s. will be taken off

Perfect special, and counsel	0	9	10
Rule to plead	0	2	0
Notice of declaration being filed, copy, and service*	0	2	0
Judgment	0	5	4
Summoning the jury	0	8	8
Notice of inquiry, copy, and service*	0	2	0
Subpœna and tickets	0	8	6
Brief and copies	0	2	0
Two counsel	0	10	0
Court fees	0	17	2
Execution	0	9	0

* Only 1s is allowed on taxation

For Plaintiff on Process, Debt 39s where he serves the Writ himself. Defendant does not appear, and Plaintiff files Bail, Common, Perfect, and Inquiry executed.

Writ, copy, and service	£0	4	10
Appearance	0	2	0
Affidavit of service, plaintiff	0	2	0
Filing common bail and paid Knight Marshal's fee	0	7	4
Declaration	0	5	6
Imparlance, and copy of declaration	0	4	0
Perfect	0	2	10
Rule to plead	0	2	0
Notice of declaration being filed, copy, and service	0	1	0
Judgment	0	5	4

Summoning the jury	0	8	8
Notice of inquiry, copy, and service	0	1	0
Subpœna and tickets	0	8	6
Brief and copies	0	2	0
Two counsel	0	10	0
Court fees	0	17	2
Execution	0	0	0

For Plaintiff, where a Demurrer to a Declaration, and Judgment for Plaintiff.

Affidavit, writ, and arrest	£0	13	6
Appearance	0	2	0
Rule for better bail	0	1	8
Opposing rule for bail to be absolute	0	1	8
Declaration	0	5	6
Perfect*	0	5	6
Rule to plead	0	1	8
Copy of demurrer	0	2	8
Fee on rule to join in demurrer	0	1	8
Joinder in demurrer, and counsel	0	8	8
Rule to read record	0	2	0
Rule for concilium	0	2	0
Three copies of paper book for the judge and counsel	0	7	6
To counsel therewith	0	10	0

* In this case charge 12s 6d for a special perfect, and 5s 6d for a common perfect, instead of 9s 10d or 2s 10d or else add the difference to the joinder in demurrer, but the first way is most eligible.

Rule for judgment 0 2 0
Judgment 0 5 4
Venire facias, and summoning the jury 0 8 8
Brief and copies 0 2 0
Two counsel with briefs 0 10 0
Court fees 0 17 2
Execution 0 9 0

For Plaintiff on Copy of Process, where the Verdict is subject to the Opinion of the Court.

Writ, copy, and service £0 8 4
Appearance 0 2 0
Declaration 0 5 6
Perfect 0 5 6
Rule to plead 0 1 8
Plea of general issue 0 2 2
Venire facias, and summoning the jury 0 8 8
Brief and copies 0 2 0
Subpoena and tickets 0 6 6
Two counsel 0 10 0
Court fees 0 17 2
Rule for plaintiff's verdict to be subject to the opinion of the court 0 2 0
Rule to hear counsel for the plaintiff in support of the verdict 0 2 0
Brief, and copies for that purpose 0 2 0
Two counsel 0 10 0
Rule to hear counsel 0 2 0
The like 0 2 0
Attending the argument* 0 1 8

* Not allowed on taxation

G

Rule for judgment   0   2   0
Signing judgment 0   5   4
Paid entering, continuance, and judgment.   _____

N B The prothonotary takes 4d for each continuance, and
    the attorney charges 2s. for each continuance, and a fee
    of 2s. 4d
Where judgment is given for the same party as the verdict,
    signing judgment (5s 4d.) should not be allowed, it being
    charged in the court fees.

—

For Plaintiff, where a Special Plea pleaded, Replication, Re-
joinder, &c. and Demurrer to Replication argued by Con-
cilium.

Affidavit, writ, and arrest £0 13 6
Appearance . . ..-----.. ...   0   2   0
Rule for better bail   0   1   8
Opposing justification of bail   0   1   8
Declaration   0   5   6
Perfect   0   5   6
Rule to plead   0   1   8
Opposing rule for further time   0   1   8
Copy of special plea   0   2   8
Rule to reply   0   1   8
Rule for time till Monday*   0   2   0
Replication and counsel   0   8   8
Rule to rejoin   0   2   0
Opposing rule till Monday .... ○   0   1   8
Copy rejoinder   0   2   8
Rule to join in demurrer   0   1   8
Joinder and counsel   0   8   8

* Not allowed on taxation

Rule to read record	0	2	0
Rule for concilium	0	2	0
Three copies of paper book	0	7	6
To counsel to move	0	10	0
Rule for judgment	0	2	0
Judgment	0	5	4
Venire and summons	0	8	8
Brief and copies	0	2	0
Two counsel	0	10	0
Subpœna and tickets	0	8	6
Court fees	0	17	2
Execution and service	0	9	0

For Defendant where General Issue is pleaded, and Verdict for the Defendant.

Common bail, and paid Knight Marshal's fee	£0	7	4
Imparlance, and copy of declaration	0	4	0
Rule for time to plead	0	2	0
Plea of general issue	0	3	2
Fee on plaintiff's summons	0	1	8
Brief and two copies	0	2	0
Subpœnas and tickets	0	8	6
Two counsel	0	10	0
Court fees	0	17	2
Execution and service	0	9	0

For Plaintiff where a copy of Process is served, General Issue pleaded, and Verdict for Plaintiff, if paid before Execution is sued out

Writ, copy, and service*	£0	3	4
Appearance	0	2	0

* If damages are only laid at 39s this charge is only 4s 10d.

Declaration	0	5	6
Perfect	0	5	6
Rule to plead	0	1	8
Venire facias and summoning the jury	0	8	8
Brief and copies	0	2	8
Subpœna and tickets	0	8	6
Two counsel	0	10	0
Court fees	0	17	2
Fee	0	2	4
Letters	0	1	0

For the Defendant, where copy of Process is served, General Issue pleaded, Verdict for Defendant, if paid before Execution sued out.

Appearance £0	2	0
Common bail, and paid Knight Marshal's fee ...	0	7	4
Imparlance, and copy of declaration	0	4	0
Rule to plead	0	2	0
Plea of general issue	0	3	2
Fee on plaintiff's summons	0	1	8
Brief and copies	0	2	8
Subpœna and tickets	0	8	6
Two counsel	0	10	0
Court fees	0	17	2
Fee	0	2	4
Letters	0	1	0

For Defendant, if in Custody of the Keeper of the Prison, where General Issue is pleaded, and Verdict for Defendant, if the Rule to try is given by an Attorney.

Rule to try, and copy £0	2	0
Advising defendant what to plead	0	1	8

Fee on plaintiff's summons	0	1	8
Briefs and copies	0	2	0
Subpœna and tickets	0	8	6
Two counsel	0	10	0
Court fees	0	17	2
Paid gaol fees	0	10	10
Execution and service	0	9	0

For the Defendant in custody, where General Issue pleaded, and Verdict for Defendant, if Rule to try is given by Petition.

Rule to try	£0	0	6
Fee on plaintiff's summons	0	1	8
Brief and copies	0	2	0
Subpœna and tickets	0	8	6
Two counsel	0	10	0
Court fees	0	17	2
Paid gaol fees	0	10	10
Execution and service*	0	9	0

* If paid before execution is sued out, this charge is omitted, and a fee of 2s 4d, and Letters, 1s added in its stead

For Plaintiff where the Defendant is in Custody, General Issue pleaded, and he is committed in Execution

Affidavit, writ, and arrest	£0	13	6
Appearance	0	2	0
Declaration in custody	0	6	0
Rule to try, and copy	0	1	0
Perfect special, counsel, and paid entry*	0	12	6

* If common perfect, only 5 6d

Calling defendant in court to plead, and paid ...	0	1	6
Notice of trial, copy, and service	0	1	0
Summoning the cause for trial	0	8	8
Brief and copies	0	2	0
Two counsel	0	10	0
Subpœna and tickets	0	8	6
Paid court fees	0	17	2
Rule to charge the defendant in execution	0	2	0
Charging defendant in execution	0	6	6

For Plaintiff where Defendant is in Custody, and gives a Cognovit.

Affidavit, writ, and arrest	£0	13	6
Appearance	0	2	0
Declaration in custody	0	6	0
Rule to try, and copy	0	1	0
Perfect special, and counsel*	0	9	10
Calling defendant to plead, and paid	0	1	6
Notice of trial, copy, and service	0	1	0
Rule to confess the damages	0	2	0
Confession and entry	0	6	6
Rule to charge defendant in execution	0	2	0
Charging defendant in execution	0	6	6

* If common perfect, only 2s 10d

For Plaintiff where Defendant is in Custody, General Issue pleaded, and the Debt is paid without being committed in Execution.

Affidavit, writ, and arrest	£0	13	6
Carrying the defendant to gaol	0	2	6
Appearance	0	2	0
Declaration in custody	0	6	6

Rule to try, and copy	0	2	2
Notice of trial, copy, and service	0	2	0
Summoning the cause for trial	0	8	8
Briefs	0	2	8
Two counsel	0	10	0
Subpœna and tickets	0	8	6
Rule to allow witnesses	0	2	0
Paid four from Woolwich	0	10	0
Court fees	0	17	2
Fee	0	2	1
Letters	0	1	0

COSTS ON NONPROSS.

*For Defendant when served with a Copy of a Process, and
Nonpross is signed for want of Declaration.*

Common bail, and paid Knight Marshal's fee .. £0		7	4
Fee on rule to declare	0	1	8
Signing nonpross	0	5	4
Searching plaint	0	0	6
Execution and service	0	9	0

*For Defendant where served with a Process, and Nonpross
signed for want of Perfect.*

Common bail, and paid Knight Marshal's fee £0		7	4
Fee on rule to declare	0	1	8
Imparlance, and copy of declaration	0	4	0
Fee on rule to perfect	0	1	8
Signing nonpross	0	5	4
Searching plaint	0	0	6
Execution	0	9	0

Note. If the plaintiff refuse to take a rule to declare, give a rule to declare, sitting the court, (for which rule *4d.* is charged), and in that case charge *2s.* instead of the fee of *1s. 8d.* on plaintiff's rule.

In all cases where issue is joined, charge your perfect; if special and signed by counsel, 12*s. 6d.*; if common, 5*s. 6d.* the plaintiff being charged 2*s. 8d.* more in the prothonotary's office when issue is joined. If judgment by *nil dicit*, then only 9*s. 10d.* for a special perfect, and 2*s. 10d.* for a common perfect.

Where there is a plea in abatement, instead of "Imparlance and copy of declaration 4*s.*" charge specially—"Imparlance special, and copy of declaration, 5*s.*"

For Defendant on an Arrest, where Special Plea pleaded, and Nonpross signed for want of Replication.

	£		
Bail-bond, and paid Knight Marshal's fee	£0	4	6
Bail above, duty, and entry	0	6	6
Rule for better bail	0	2	0
Rule that former bail be absolute	0	2	0
Imparlance, and copy of declaration	0	4	0
Rule to plead	0	2	0
Special plea and counsel	0	11	6
Rule to reply	0	2	0
Signing nonpross	0	5	4
Searching plaint	0	0	6
Execution and service *	0	9	0

* If paid without an execution, this charge is omitted, and instead of it, appearance 2*s.* and fee and letters 3*s. 4d.* are to be added.

II.—COSTS RESPECTING OFFICERS OF THE COURT.

For Plaintiff against an Officer of the Court on a Bill filed.

Bill and rule to appear	£0	8	2
Rule that Mr. ——— file common bail for the defendant	0	2	0
Perfecting the bill, and counsel	0	12	6
Rule to plead	0	1	8
Venire facias, and summoning the jury	0	8	8
Brief and copies	0	2	0
Two counsel	0	10	0
Court fees	0	17	2
Execution	0	9	0

N. B. When an officer is sued by bill, a writ should be issued in order to ground the bill, and charge it in the bill of costs.

Bill of Costs against an Officer and his Sureties.

[Thompson *agt.* Brooks.]

Rule against Jones, the officer, on behalf of the plaintiff	£0	2	8
Motion and rule to pay the plaintiff the debt and costs, and the costs of the complaint, within a month	0	2	0
Motion and rule to suspend the officer for non-payment of the debt and costs	0	2	0
Rule to assign his security bond	0	2	4
Rule to indemnify the Knight Marshal	0	2	0
Paid indemnifying the Knight Marshal	0	3	8

Paid for the names of securities	0	1	0
Attending for that purpose*	0	1	8
Fee*	0	2	4

[Meadows *agt* Jones, officer]

Writ, and copies	£0	6	10
Paid serving the defendant*	0	2	6
Appearance	0	2	0
Affidavit of service, and officer	0	5	0
Filing common bail, and paid Knight Marshal's fee .	0	7	4
Declaration	0	5	6
Imparlance, and copy of declaration	0	4	0
Paid for copy of security bond	0	2	6
Attending to bespeak and examine same*	0	1	8
Fee and bill*	0	2	4

[Meadows *agt* the Security]

Paid serving the defendant	£0	2	6
Appearance	0	2	0
Affidavit of service	0	5	0
Filing common bail	0	7	4
Declaration	0	5	6
Imparlance	0	4	0
Perfecting the declaration	0	2	10
Rule to plead	0	2	0
Signing judgment	0	5	4
Execution	0	9	0
Fee and bill*	0	2	4
Letters*	0	1	0
If writ renewed against the defendant, charge			
Writ renewed against one of the security	0	2	4

* Not allowed on taxation

Fees allowed to be taken by the Officers for an Arrest, or serving the Defendant with a Copy of Process.

The officer has a right to take of the plaintiff, for
arresting a defendant, besides the warrant
shilling £0   5   0

For serving a defendant with a copy of process* .   0   2   6

For a bail-bond of the defendant   0   4   6

        * See Act 2 Hen. 4, in Appendix

Note. If the defendant is desirous of remaining at the officer's house, after the time given by the act of parliament, the plaintiff must give his consent in writing; and on the officer's delivering that consent (signed by both parties) to the prothonotary's office, he has an order made out accordingly; for which he pays 2s. 6d. And also 10s. 10d. for the gaol fees to the prothonotary, who receives it for the use of the keeper of the prison.

If any officer in waiting is absent on calling over his name, but comes soon after the court sits, he pays to the prothonotary 1s. 6d.; but if absent during the whole sitting of the court, he is fined 5s. and suspended to take off which, he must pay in the whole, 7s. 6d.

FEES TO BE PAID BY COUNSEL, ATTORNIES, AND OFFICERS, ON THEIR ADMISSION.

Fees paid on the Admission of a Counsellor.

The Knight Marshal's secretary £10   10   0

Steward of the Court   10   10   0

Lord Steward's secretary   10   10   0

Deed of appointment (stamp 9d.)   6   0   6

Deputy prothonotary   2   2   0

Steward's clerk   0   10   6

Crier of the court	0	10	6
Officers in waiting	0	10	6
Steward's servant	0	2	6
	41	6	6

◄──►

Fees paid on the Admission of an Attorney.

Lord Steward	£50	0	0
Knight Marshal	50	0	0
Lord Steward's secretary	10	10	0
Knight Marshal's secretary	10	10	0
Steward of the court	10	10	0
Deed of appointment, and stamp	6	0	6
Deputy prothonotary	2	2	0
Steward's clerk	0	10	6
Crier of the court	0	10	6
Officers in waiting	0	10	6
Steward's servant	0	2	6
	141	6	6

◄──►

Fees paid on being admitted an Officer of the Court.

To the prothonotary for a certificate	£0	2	6
For an order thereon for admission	0	2	6
To the clerk of the securities on signing the security bond, and for the whole of his fees except the stamp*	1	0	0
To the Judge's clerk	0	10	0
To the prothonotary for swearing in	0	2	6
To his clerks, 2s. 6d. each	0	5	0
To the crier	0	5	0
	2	7	6

* This is ordered by the General Rule of the court, No. 94
See Appendix.

Fees paid by an Officer on an Order to have a new Writ, or to return his Writ, and for a Bill of Sale.

For an order to have a new writ	£0	2	6
For an order to return his writ	0	2	6
For a bill of sale	0	15	6
For the Knight Marshal's fee on returning a writ, if delivered into the office on the day the writ is returnable	0	2	4
If on the next day after the return .:..........	0	2	6

III.—PROTHONOTARY'S CLERKS.

Fees belonging to the Clerks in the Prothonotary's Office.

For every habeas corpus allowed by a foreign attorney	£0	0	4
For every execution on a nonsuit	0	0	6
For copy of a writ or plaint	0	1	4
For carrying every writ or affidavit to court	0	1	0
For every return of a writ, if made on the day following the return of such writ	0	0	2
For searching for a rule of court	0	0	4
For searching for a bail-bond	0	0	4
For searching for a return of a writ	0	0	4
For copy of a bail-bond	0	1	0
For every officer sworn in	0	5	0
For the copy of a record, 4d. per sheet.			
For copy of a rule of court	0	0	4
For entering a declaration of the last week	0	0	6
For copy of an affidavit	0	1	4
If more than four sheets, 4d. per sheet.			
For every writ after the office hours	0	0	6
If late at night	0	2	6

For every affidavit taken out of the office	0	5	8
For searching for a plaint or writ	0	0	6
For every writ made out at the suit of an officer .	0	0	6
Christmas box from the Knight Marshal, every year*	1	0	0
From the Steward of the Court, every year*	2	2	0
From the Clerk of the Securities, every year* ...	1	1	0
From the Attornies of the Court, for entering the places of abode of the attornies who allow habeas corpuses, 2s. 6d. each, yearly			
For every discharge on special bail	0	1	0
For every discharge on the lord's act.	0	1	0
For every discharge on common bail	0	0	6
For expedition in returning an habeas corpus ...	0	2	6
For taking off an officer's suspension	0	0	6

* These items were formerly charged by the deputy prothonotary in his accounts, but were never paid to the clerks, either by the late Mr Cruchley, or his predecessor, Mr. Evan Jones.

IV.—JUDGE'S CLERK.

Fees belonging to the Judge's Clerk.

For every affidavit sworn at court	£0	1	0
For every officer sworn in	0	10	0
For every bail acknowledged before the Judge ...	0	0	6
For every certificate for the admission of an officer	0	2	6
For every order made thereon	0	2	6
For every copy of process at the suit of an officer .	0	1	6
For every writ at the suit of an officer, if bailable .	0	2	0
For every order to take off an officer's suspension for not waiting	0	2	0

For every order excusing an officer from attending the court 0 2 0

For every order for an officer to bring an habeas corpus, or return a writ 0 2 0

For carrying the patent of the court to Westminster on a subpœna 0 10 6

For an order to alter an officer's seal 0 2 6

For every order to take off an officer's suspension in a cause 0 1 0

V.—PROTHONOTARY.

Fees to be taken by the Prothonotary for all Business done, and Entries made by the Attornies of the Court, in his Office, likewise an Account of such Fees as are allowed to be charged to Foreign Attornies, (that is, the Attornies of other Courts), for Writs, Copies of Records, allowing Habeas Corpuses, Writs of Error, and transcribing the same.

For every special bail entered by an attorney of the court £0 2 2

For every common bail (unless out of custody) .. 0 4 6

For every declaration 0 3 8

For every imparlance 0 1 4

For every issue and imparlance (stamp 2d.) if rule before 0 2 6

For every issue and imparlance (stamp 2d.) if no rule before 0 2 10

For every issue (stamp 2d) 0 1 6

Issue special 0 3 4

Imparlance special 0 1 0

Issue special and imparlance 0 4 4

Patria	0	2	8
Patria special	0	3	8
Replication pro patria	0	3	8
Rejoinder, and every subsequent pleading	0	1	0
Every pleading after scire facias	0	1	0
Venire facias (stamp 2s.)	0	7	0
Subpœna (stamp 2s.)	0	4	6
Verdict, judgment, and nonsuit on evidence	0	5	4
Verdict without judgment	0	3	4
Judgment thereon	0	2	0
Judgment on demurrer or nul tiel record	0	2	0
Satisfaction acknowledged	0	2	0
New entry	0	2	0
Nil dicit and nonsuit	0	3	0
Nolle prosequi, discontinuance, or non informatus	0	3	0
Assets, quando, cognovit, and relicta verif.	0	4	0
Remittitur of damages	0	1	0
Ca. sa. post sci. fa. (stamp 2s.)	0	3	0
Execution (stamp 2s.)	0	4	0
Execution renewed (stamp 2s.)	0	2	6
Subpœna renewed (stamp 2s.)	0	2	6
Execution against bail (stamp 2s.)	0	3	0
Execution against bail renewed (stamp 2s.)	0	3	0
Venire execution or subpœna (if poor)	0	0	6
Committitur	0	2	0
Habeas corpus or certiorari	0	4	8
Procedendo	0	2	4
Returning an habeas corpus for every cause after the first	0	1	0
For returning the statute under £5, one cause	0	2	0
The like, two causes	0	4	0
The like, three causes	0	6	0
For returning the statute six weeks between return of writ and issue joined	0	6	0
The like habeas corpus, and procedendo before	0	6	0

The like upon a render by bail, after a writ of error transcribed	0	5	0
Supersedeas on a writ of error (stamp 2s.)	0	4	6
For allowing a writ of error	1	2	0
Executio judicii	0	2	4
Forejudging an officer	0	2	8
Scire facias (stamp 2s.)	0	4	6
Entering every discontinuance	0	0	4
Withdrawing a record	0	0	6
For allowing a writ of privilege	0	2	8
Supersedeas thereon	0	1	0
Returning habeas corpus, one cause, in execution	0	2	0
For the return of every writ, if returned on the day the writ is returnable	0	2	4
For the return of every writ, if not returned till the Saturday	0	2	6
For allowing an habeas corpus by a foreign attorney	0	5	0
For swearing every affidavit	0	1	0
For signing every writ	0	1	6
For every trial	0	1	6
For every exhibit on a trial	0	1	0
For every execution on a nonpros	0	0	6
For copy of a writ or plaint	0	1	4
For carrying a writ or affidavit to court	0	1	0
For searching for a bail-bond	0	0	4
For searching for a rule of court	0	0	4
For searching for a return to a writ	0	0	4
For copy of a bail-bond	0	1	0
For every officer sworn in	0	17	6
For copy of a record, 4d. per sheet.			
For copy of a rule of court	0	0	4
For entering an incipitur as of the last week	0	0	6
For copy of an affidavit	0	1	4
If special, and more than four sheets, 4d. per sheet.			

H

For every writ made out after office hours, extra .	0	0	6
If after ten at night, extra	0	2	6
For swearing every affidavit out of the office	0	6	8
For searching for a writ or plaint	0	0	6
For every writ made out at the suit of an officer of the court (stamp 2s.)	0	5	6
If a copy of process (stamp 2s.)	0	3	6
For every discharge on special bail	0	1	0
For every discharge on common bail	0	0	6
For every discharge on the lords' act	0	1	0
For expedition in returning an habeas corpus	0	2	6
For taking off an officer's suspension in a cause ..	0	1	6
If for not waiting	0	2	6
If for want of security	0	1	6
For transcribing a writ of error, 6s. 8d. per press, every press to contain 42 lines			
On the discharge of a complaint against an officer .	0	0	6
For every rule of court	0	0	4
For every rule against an officer of the court, either on a complaint, bill filed, or to withdraw security	0	0	8
For every rule to assign an officer's security bond	0	0	8
For every rule to indemnify the Knight Marshal .	0	3	4
For every rule for the bond to stand assigned until bail justify	0	1	0
For every rule to shew cause	0	0	8
For every bail acknowledged before the judge ...	0	0	6
For a bill of sale on an execution	0	15	6
For attending on a subpœna, and carrying the patent to Westminster	1	1	0
Allowed by the Sub-Marshal (weekly) for keeping his accounts	0	1	6
From the Knight Marshal for the like, (yearly) ..	5	5	0
For every odd writ over the dozens, accounted for in the week's return	0	1	6

Allowed by the Knight Marshal (weekly) towards office expences	0	9	2
Allowed by the Steward of the Court (weekly) towards office expences	0	6	8
Allowed by the Prothonotary of the Court, for the like	0	6	8
Allowed by the Attornies (weekly) for the paper used on affidavits, *the odd pence* on their profit bills; that is, suppose a weekly bill £3:2:2 £3 3:0 is charged; and so in other cases, making an even sum.			
For assigning every bail-bond	0	0	8
For every rule for time to put in bail	0	0	4
For searching for a writ some years back, according to the trouble			
Discount on stamps.			
Affidavits sworn at court, either before it sits, or after it rises	0	1	0
For every certificate for the admission of an officer.	0	2	6
For every order made thereon	0	2	6
For an order to excuse an officer from waiting	0	2	6
For an order for an officer to allow an habeas corpus, writ of error, or return his writ	0	2	6
For an order to alter an officer's seal	0	2	6

VI —A TABLE OF THE DIVISION OF PROFITS AMONG THE JUDGES AND OTHER OFFICERS BELONGING TO THE COURT.

Court Charge		ITEMS	The Lord Marshal and Steward of the Court's fee against Defendant		Prothonotary's Fee		Deputy Prothonotary's fee		Crier's fee		Sub Marshal's fee		Judge's Clerk's fee		Deputy Prothonotary's Clerk's fee	
s	d		s	d	s	d	s	d	s	d	s	d	s	d	s	d
•	2	For every special bail	1	4	•	8	•	1	•	•	•	1	•	•	•	•
•	6	For every common bail (except out of custody)	1	4	•	8	2	6	•	•	•	1	•	•	•	•
	8	Declaration	1	4	0	•	•	•	•	4	•	•	•	•	•	•
1	4	Imparlance	1	•	•	•	•	4	•	•	•	•	•	•	•	•
•	10	Issue and imparlance (stamp 2d) if no rule before	2	4	•	•	•	4	•	•	•	•	•	•	•	•
2	6	Issue and imparlance (stamp 2d) if rule before	2	4	•	•	•	•	•	•	•	•	•	•	•	•
1	6	Issue (stamp 2d)	1	4	•	•	•	•	•	•	•	•	•	•	•	•
	4	Issue special	1	4	•	•	2	•	•	•	•	•	•	•	•	•
1		Imparlance special	•	•	•	•	1	•	•	•	•	•	•	•	•	•
4	4	Issue special and imparlance	•	4	•	•	2	•	•	•	•	•	•	•	•	•
2	8	Patria	1	4	1	•	•	•	•	•	•	4	•	•	•	•
•	8	Patria special	1	4	1	•	1	•	•	4	•	•	•	•	•	•
		Assets quando, cognovit et relicta verificatione	1	4	1	•	•	•	•	4	•	4	•	•	•	•
1		Remittitur of damages	•	•	•	•	1	•	•	•	•	•	•	•	•	•
		(stamp 2d)	•	8	•	2	•	1	•	2	•	•	•	•	•	•
•		Execution (stamp)	1	8	•	2	•	2	•	•	•	•	•	•	•	•

• See Act Her. 4, c. 23, in Appendix p 113

		ITEMS	Clerk of the Crown and Signet &c. Courts fee	Prothonotary's fee	Deputy Prothonotary's fee	Clerk's fee	Sub-Sheriff's fee	Judge's Clerk's fee	Deputy Prothonotary's Clerk's fee
			s d	s d	s d	s d	s d	s d	s d
4		Scire facias stamp ...	. .	. .	2 6	. .	. .	. .	. .
	4	Letter of every discontinuance	. .	. .	. 4	. .	. .	. .	. .
2		Repl. at or for p...	1 4	. .	2 1	. .	. .	. .	. .
1		Re... and every subsequent pleadi.	. .	. .	1 .	. .	. .	. .	. .
		Every plea to ...	. .	. .	1 .	. .	. .	. .	. .
		Every rec... it's deb. ... (... stamp)	1 6	1 2	. 2	2	. .	. .	. .
		P... the pl... off. ...	1 6	1 2	. 2	. 6	And 1s 6d to the Officer who executes the writ	. .	. .
		... pl... ... op...	2 .	. .	1 .	2	. .	. .	. .
2		Verdict and j... on verdict	3 4	. 9	. 3	And 1s to the waiting Officers.	. .	. .	. .
4		Verdict without j...	1 4	. 9	. 3	And 1s to the waiting Officers.	. .	. .	. .
		J... p... t	. 2	. .	. .	. .	. .	. .	. .
		Judgment re-continuer or d... record	. 2	. .	. .	. .	. .	. .	. .
		Satisfaction acknowledged	1 4	. 4	. 4	. .	. .	. .	. .
2		New entry	. .	. .	2 .	. .	. .	. .	. .
2		Nile... d motus	1 4	1 .	. 4	. 4	. .	. .	. .
4		Nisi prius qu... supersedeas or ... en informatus	1 4	. .	1 8	. .	. .	. .	. .
4	6	Execution renewed stamp 2s)	. .	. .	. 6	. .	. .	. .	. .
4	6	Subp... renewed (stamp 2s)	. .	. .	. 6	. .	. .	. .	. .
3		Execution against bail stamp 2s)	. .	. .	1 .	. .	. .	. .	. .

† See Act 2 Hen 4, c. 23, in Appendix.

Total Charge	ITEMS.	The Kes Marshal and Steward of the Court's Fees, upon an equal division.			Prothonotary's Fees.		Deputy Prothonotary's Fees		Crier's Fees		Sub-Marshal's Fees		Judges Clerk's Fees		Deputy Prothonotary's Clerk's Fees	
£ s d		£	s	d	s	d	s	d	s	d	s	d	s	d	s	d
. 3 .	Execution against bail renewed (stamp 2s.)	.	.	.	.	.	1	.	.	.	.	.	.	.	.	.
. . 6	Venire execution, or subpoena, (if poor)	.	.	.	.	.	.	6	.	.	.	.	.	.	.	.
. 2 .	Committitur	.	1	8	.	2	.	2	.	.	.	.	.	.	.	.
. 4 8	Habeas corpus	.	2	8	1	4	.	4	.	4	.	.	.	.	.	.
. 2 4	Procedendo	.	1	4	.	4	.	4	.	4	.	.	.	.	.	.
. 1 .	Returning an habeas corpus for every cause after the 1st	.	.	.	.	.	1	.	.	.	.	.	.	.	.	.
. 2 .	Returning the statute under £5, one cause	.	.	.	.	.	2	.	.	.	.	.	.	.	.	.
. 4 .	The like for two causes	.	.	.	.	.	4	.	.	.	.	.	.	.	.	.
. 6 .	The like for three causes	.	.	.	.	.	6	.	.	.	.	.	.	.	.	.
. 6 .	Returning the statute six weeks between return of writ and issue joined	.	.	.	.	.	6	.	.	.	.	.	.	.	.	.
. 6 .	The like habeas corpus, and procedendo before	.	.	.	.	.	6	.	.	.	.	.	.	.	.	.
. 5 .	The like on a render by bail, after a writ of error transcribed	.	.	.	.	.	5	.	.	.	.	.	.	.	.	.
. 4 6	Supersedeas on a writ of error (stamp 2s.)	.	.	.	.	.	2	6	.	.	.	.	.	.	.	.
1 2 .	For allowing a writ of error	1	.	.	.	.	2	.	.	.	.	.	.	.	.	.
. 2 4	Executio judici	.	1	4	.	.	1	.	.	.	.	.	.	.	.	.
. 2 8	Forejudging an officer	.	1	4	1	.	.	4	.	.	.	.	.	.	.	.
. . 6	Withdrawing the record	.	.	.	.	.	.	6	.	.	.	.	.	.	.	.

Total Charge			ITEMS	The King's Marshal and Steward of the Court's fees upon original Dividend		Prothonotary's fees		Deputy Prothonotary's fees		Crier's fees		Sub-Marshal's fees		Judge's Clerk's fees		Deputy Prothonotary's Clerk's fees	
£	s	d		s	d	s	d	s	d	s	d	s	d	s	d	s	d
.	2	4	Writ of privilege	1	4	.	4	.	4	.	4						
.	1	.	Supersedeas thereon					1	.								
.	2	.	Returning an habeas corpus, one cause in execution					2	.								
.	2	4	Returning a writ (if on the day the writ is returnable)	1	8	.	5					.	3				
.	2	6	If returned on the following day	1	8	.	5					.	3			.	2
.	5	.	For allowing an habeas corpus by a foreign attorney	2	8	1	4	.	4	.	4					.	4
.	1	.	For swearing every affidavit					.	5	.	2	And 5d to the Steward of the Court.					
1	1	. per doz.	For signing every writ 1s. 6d. (these are counted in dozens, fourteen to every dozen, which makes £1 1·0)	12	.	7	6	1	6								
.	1	6	For every trial					.	6	And 1s to the Keeper of the Prison.							
.	1	.	For every exhibit on a trial							1	.						
.	.	6	For every execution on a nonpros													.	6
.	1	4	For copy of a writ or plaint											1	.	.	4
.	1	.	For carrying a writ or affidavit to court											1	.		
.	.	4	For searching for a bail-bond													.	4
.	.	4	For searching for a rule of court													.	4
.	.	4	For searching for a return to a writ													.	4
.	1	.	For copy of a bail-bond											1	.		

Total Charge		ITEMS.	The Ld. Marshal and Steward of the Court's fees, upon an equal division.		Prothonotary's fees.		Deputy Prothonotary's fees.		Crier's fees.		Sub-Marshal's fees.		Judge's Clerk's fees.		Deputy Prothonotary's Clerk's fees.	
s	d		s	d	s	d	s	d	s	d	s	d	s	d	s	d
17	6	For every officer sworn in					2	6					10	.	5	.
		For copy of a record 4d. per sheet (to the Prothonotary's Clerk														
.	4	For copy of a rule of court														4
		If special rule, 4d. per sheet (to the Prothonotary's Clerk														
.	6	For entering an incipitur as of last week														6
1	4	For copy of an affidavit													1	4
		If special, 4d. per sheet (to the Prothonotary's Clerk)														6
.	6	For every writ made out after the office hours (extra)														6
2	6	If after ten o'clock at night (extra)													2	6
5	8	For swearing every affidavit out of office (extra)													5	8
.	6	Searching for a writ													.	6
4	6	Every writ at the suit of an officer (stamp 2s.)											2	.	.	6
3	6	If a copy (stamp 2s.)											1	.	.	6
1	.	Every discharge on special bail													1	.
.	6	Every discharge on common bail													.	6
1	.	Every discharge on lords' act											.	.	1	.
2	6	For expedition in returning an habeas corpus											.	.	2	6

Total Charge £ s d	ITEMS	The Knt Marshal and Steward of his Court's fees upon an equal Dividend (s d)	Prothonotary's fees (s d)	Deputy Prothonotary's fees (£ s d)	Crier's fees (s d)	Sub Marshal's fees (s d)	Judge's Clerk's fees (s d)	Deputy Prothonotary's Clerk's fees (s d)
. 1 6	For taking off an officer's suspension in a cause			. 6			1 .	
. 2 6	For not waiting			. 6			2 .	
. 1 6	For want of security			. 6			1 .	
	For transcribing a writ of error 6s. 8d. per press, every press to contain 42 lines			6 8				
. . 6	On the discharge of a complaint against an officer			. 6				
. . 4	Every rule of court			. 4				
. . 8	If against an officer on a complaint			. 8				
. . 8	If to assign an officer's security bond			. 8				
. 3 4	For rule to indemnify the Knight Marshal			3 4				
. 1 .	Stobas			1 .				
. . 8	For a rule to shew cause			. 8				
. . 6	For every bail acknowledged before the judge						6	
. 15 6	For a bill of sale on an execution, (stamp 5s. 1d.)			. 10 5				
1 1 .	Attending on a subpœna at Westminster, and carrying the patent, 10s. 6d. to the person attending						10 6	
. 1 6	Allowed by the Sub-Marshal (weekly) for keeping his accounts			. 1 6				
5 5 .	From the Knight Marshal (yearly) for the like			5 5 .				

Total Charge		ITEMS.	The Knt Marshal and Steward of the Court's fees, upon an equal dividend		Prothonotary's fee		Deputy Prothonotary's fee		Crier's fees		Sub-Marshal's fees		Judge's Clerk's fees		Deputy Prothonotary's Clerk's fee	
s	*d*		*s*	*d*	*s*	*d*	*s*	*d*	*s*	*d*	*s*	*d*	*s*	*d*	*s*	*d*
1	6	Odd writ over the dozens, each	.	.	.	.	1	6	.	.	.	.	.	.	.	.
9	2	Allowed by the Knight Marshal towards office expences, (weekly) . . . . . . }	.	.	.	.	9	2	.	.	.	.	.	.	.	.
6	8	The like by the Steward of the court (weekly) . .	.	.	.	.	6	8	.	.	.	.	.	.	.	.
6	8	The like by the Prothonotary, (weekly)	.	.	.	.	6	8	.	.	.	.	.	.	.	.
		Allowed by the Attornies for paper, &c. to the Deputy Prothonotary . . . . }	The odd pence on their weekly bills.		.	.			.	.	.	.	.	.	.	.
.	8	For assigning a bail-bond	.	.	.	.	.	8	.	.	.	.	.	.	.	.
.	4	For a rule for time to put in bail	.	.	.	.	.	4	.	.	.	.	.	.	.	.
.		For searching for a writ, (if some years back) the prothonotary's clerk's fee . . . . }	According to the trouble.				.	.			.	.				
		Discount on stamps to the Deputy Prothonotary .	.	.	.	.			.	.	.	.	.	.	.	.
1	.	Affidavit sworn either before or after the court sits .	.	.	1	.	.	.	.	.	.	.	.	.	.	.
2	6	For a certificate for the admission of an officer . .	.	.	.	.	.	.	.	.	.	.	2	6	.	.
2	6	For an order made thereon	.	.	.	.	.	.	.	.	.	.	2	6	.	.
2	6	For an order to excuse an officer from waiting at court	.	.	.	.	.	6	.	.	.	.	2	.	.	.
2	6	The like for an order to bring an habeas corpus or writ of error . . . . }	.	.	.	.	.	6	.	.	.	.	2	.	.	.
2	6	For an order to alter an officer's seal . .	.	.	.	.	.	.	.	.	.	.	2	6	.	.

N B The Stamps are charged on the different Bills of Costs, according to the old Rate of Duties, in order that no confusion might arise. Allowance must therefore be made for the Reduction of Duty upon Law Proceedings, made by the recent Act.

COSTS OF 1812.

For Plaintiff on an Arrest, where General Issue pleaded, Verdict for Plaintiff, and Execution sued out.

Instructions and warrant to sue	£0	9	6
Affidavit	0	7	0
Writ	0	8	6
Arrest	0	10	6
Rule for bail	0	2	8
Rule for better bail	0	2	8
Enquiring after bail	0	3	4
Attending court on justification	0	3	4
Fee on bail absolute	0	1	8
Instructions for declaration	0	3	4
Declaration	0	13	0
Perfect	0	6	0
Rule to plead	0	2	8
Fee on a week's time to plead	0	1	8
Issue	0	4	4
Summons	0	13	0
Subpœna and tickets	0	12	0

* The stamp duties on the proceedings of these bills are charged as they were prior to the repeal of the stamp duties on law proceedings.

	£	s	d
Entering proceedings	0	4	8
Instructions for brief	0	6	8
Briefs	0	13	4
Counsel	2	2	0
Court fees	0	18	2
Attending	0	3	4
Ca. sa.	0	12	0
Paid taxing	0	1	0
	10	6	4

For Plaintiff on Process, Debt 40s. or upwards, where Defendant does not appear, and Plaintiff files Bail according to the Statute, and Enquiry executed.

	Attorney's Charge.			Out of Pocket.		
	£	s	d	£	s	d
Warrant, and instructions to sue	0	9	8	0	5	0
Writ, copy, and entry	0	10	6	0	6	6
Affidavit of service, duty, and oath	0	7	4	0	3	4
Paid officer for service	0	5	0	0	5	0
Appearance	0	3	0	0	0	8
Searching for common bail	0	3	4	0	0	0
Common bail, duty, &c.	0	8	10	0	7	0
Instructions for declaration	0	3	4	0	0	0
Declaration, (Narr.)	0	13	6	0	9	0
Imparlance	0	4	0	0	1	4
Perfect	0	6	6	0	0	4
Rule to plead	0	2	8	0	0	8
Notice of declaration, copy, and service	0	3	0	0	1	0

	Attorney's Charge.			Out of Pocket		
	£	s	d	£	s	d
Judgment (Nild.)	0	5	4	0	3	0
Summons	0	15	0	0	10	0
Notice of enquiry, copy, and service	0	3	0	0	1	0
Instructions for brief	0	3	4	0	0	0
Briefs	0	6	8	0	0	0
Subpœna and copies	0	16	0	0	8	6
To counsel	1	1	0	1	1	0
Attending court	0	3	4	0	0	0
Court fees, &c.	1	0	0	0	10	6
Attending to tax	0	3	4	0	0	0
Fi. fa. or ca. sa.	0	15	0	0	8	0
Attending and instructing officer	0	3	4	0	0	0
Fee and letters	0	5	4	0	0	0
	10	1	4	5	1	10

For the Defendant, where the General issue is pleaded, and Verdict for the Defendant.

Instructions, and warrant to defend	£0	9	8
Appearance	0	2	8
Common bail	0	8	10
Fee on rule to declare	0	2	8
Imparlance, and copy of declaration	0	4	0
Fee on rule to plead	0	1	8
The like for further time	0	2	8
Instructions for plea	0	3	4
Issue	0	4	6
Fee on plaintiff's summons	0	1	8
Instructions for brief	0	6	8

Brief	0	13	8
Subpœna and tickets	0	12	0
Counsel	2	2	0
Attending court	0	8	4
Court fees	0	18	2
Bill of costs and copy	0	8	0
Letters and messengers	0	5	4
Paid taxing	0	1	0
	7	6	6

APPENDIX.

ACTS OF PARLIAMENT.

28 ED. 1, c. 3. A D. 1300

Of what Things only the Marshal of the King's House shall hold Plea. Which Coroners shall enquire of the Death of a Man slain within the Verge.

CONCERNING the authority of stewards and marshals, and of such pleas as they may hold, and in what manner (1), it is ordained, that from henceforth they shall not hold plea of freehold, neither of debt, nor of covenant, nor of any contract made between the king's people, but only of trespass done within the house, and of other trespasses done within the verge, and of contracts and covenants that one of the king's house shall have made with another of the same house, and in the same house, and none other where (2). And they shall plead no plea of trespass, other than that which shall be attached by them before the king depart from the verge where the trespass shall be committed; and sh..l plead them speedily from day to day, so that they may be ple..ded and determined before that the king depart out of the limits of the same verge where the trespass was done (3). And if it so be that they cannot be determined within the limits of the same verge, then shall the same pleas cease before the steward, and the plaintiffs shall have recourse to the common law. And from henceforth the steward shall not take cognizance of debts, nor of other things, but of people of the same

(1) By the preamble to this act, it appears that it was passed in affirmance of the common law, and to relieve the subject against the usurpations and encroachments of the steward and marshal 2 Inst. 548

(2) See a writ founded upon this clause in Fitzherbert's Natura Brevium, where both the parties are not of the household, 241 C , and here, if the debtor plead, and thereby affirm the jurisdiction of the Court, and the cause be adjudged against him, yet he shall have an action upon the statute against the plaintiff. F N B. 242 A. See also *Lucking v. Denning,* Salk 201, pl 5.

(3) For the writ where the party proceeds, although the cause is discontinued by the removal of the king, see F N. B. 241 D And *note,* that although "the king go out of the bounds of the verge for his recreation, as to hunt, with no purpose to rest, tarry, abide, or make his repose there, and his counsel and household continue where they were, this is no removing within this statute " 2 Inst. 548

house, nor shall hold none other plea by obligation made at the distress of the steward and of the marshals. And if the steward or marshals do any thing contrary to this ordinance, it shall be holden as void. And forasmuch as heretofore many felonies committed within the verge have been unpunished (4), because the coroners of the country have not been authorised to enquire of such manner of felonies done within the verge, but the coroner of the king's house, which never continueth in one place, by reason whereof there can be no trial made in due manner, nor the felons put in exigent, nor outlawed, nor any thing presented in the circuit, the which hath been to the great damage of the king, and nothing to the good preservation of his peace, it is ordained, that from henceforth in cases of the death of men, whereof the coroner's office is to make view and inquest, it shall be commanded to the coroner of the country, that he, with the coroner of the king's house, shall do as belongeth to his office, and enrol it (5). And that thing that cannot be determined before the steward, where the felons cannot be attached, or for other like cause, shall be remitted to the common law, so that exigents, outlawries, and presentments, shall be made thereupon in eyre by the coroner of the country, as well as of other felonies done out of the verge, nevertheless they shall not omit, by reason hereof, to make attachments freshly upon the felonies done.

(4) The following is the comment of Lord Coke upon the criminal jurisdiction of the Marshalsea, and which has been observed upon, *ante*, p. 17 n. "That of antient time the steward and marshal had general authority, as justices in eyre, and as vicegerents of the Chief Justice of England *within the verge*, at what time they held plea of all felonies within the verge, which power is now vanished, but as steward and marshal of the Court of Marshalsea of the king's household, the title of their court in criminal causes was *placita coronæ Aulæ hospitii Domini regis coram Seneschallo et Marischallo*, and always confined to felonies done within the circuit of the king's household, the bounds whereof are made certain by the stat 33 H 8 And by that act it is provided that this Court have no jurisdiction in criminal causes, but only within the circuit of the king's palace or house. And Staunford saith, that the steward and marshal, before the said act of 33 Hen 8, might have heard and determined all felonies, &c. perpetrate within the king's palace or house

And Lord Coke adduces a case, where "a robbery was committed in a town within the verge, and this appearing to the Court, yet the same was inquired of, heard, and determined in the King's Bench, and so it may be before justices of eyre and terminer, and justices of peace, because their jurisdiction is general through the whole county, but of an offence within the king's palace it shall be heard and determined according to the said act of 33 H. 8." 2 Inst. 549.

(5) On the jurisdiction of the coroner Lord Coke observes, that "hereby it appears, that by the common law the coroner of the county could not intermeddle within the verge, but the coroner of the verge, and that if he took an indictment of the death of man, it was not allowable in law, and so it is if the coroner of the king's house take an indictment of the death of a man out of the verge, it is void, and *coram non judice* And if an indictment of the death of a man being slain out of the verge, be taken before the coroner of the king's house, and the coroner of the county, and so entered of record, it is insufficient, because the coroner of the king's house joined with him, who had no authority." 2 Inst. 550

The following are the principal cases which have been decided upon the construction of this act—*Michelborn's* case, Paqch. 38 Eliz. B. R. 9 Co. 20 *b*.—A writ of error was brought upon a judgment in the Marshalsea, in an action of trover, where neither of the parties were of the household; and the judgment was reversed, for the statute declaring of what actions they shall hold plea amounts to an exclusion of all others. And see S. C. Cro. Eliz. 502, where it appears that the Court was divided in opinion whether the statute did intend to exclude such personal actions.

Cox v. *Gray*, Trin. 10 Jac. B. R. 1 Buls 207, *S P*. And *note*, that Croke, Williams and Yelverton, JJ agreed, that in all actions both parties ought to be of the household, but Fleming, C J. was of opinion, that in trespass it was sufficient if only one of the parties was of the household. *Ib*. 213.

The *Case of the Marshalsea*, Mich. 10 Jac C. B. 10 Co. 76, is said by Lord Coke "to open the windows of the greatest part of this act." It enters very copiously into the jurisdiction of the Court, and on this account has been styled the case of the Marshalsea. The case was briefly as follows·

Hall brought an action of trespass, assault, battery, wounding, and false imprisonment, in C. B. against Stanley, Richardson and Cante. The defendants, as to all but the trespass, assault, and imprisonment, pleaded not guilty; as to them justified under the process of the Marshalsea Court, viz. that Cante had there brought an action on the case against one Ownstead, for 80*l*.; and that the said Hall was one of his bail; and that the plaintiff had a verdict and judgment, and that a *capias* was awarded against the said Ownstead, and *non est inventus* returned, upon which, according to the custom of the Court, a *capias* was awarded against the said Hall, by virtue whereof he was arrested by the defendants Stanley and Richardson, being officers of the said Court. The plaintiff replied, that neither the said Cante, nor the said Ownstead, *tempore exhibitionis billæ prædictæ, fuit servus seu servi dicti domini regis, seu de hospitio suo præd existen.* to which the defendants demurred. And in this case it was resolved—

1st That the steward and marshal, as judges of the Marshalsea Court, had no jurisdiction of pleas of the crown, or of trespass *quare clausum fregit*, or of ejectment, or of any real or mixt action, or of any personal action, except debt, covenant, or trespass *vi et armis*, as for a battery or taking away goods, and not where a freehold may be brought in question.

2d. That their jurisdiction was also limited as to persons: for in debt or covenant both parties ought to be of the household; but in trespass it is sufficient that one of the parties be of the king's household.

3d It was also limited as to place, viz. twelve miles round the king's household.

4th. That this act of *Artic. super Chartas* was not therefore introductory of any new law, but declaratory only of the antient common law of England, and was made to reduce the Court of the Marshalsea to its antient and true institution.

5th That the conclusion of the act is, that if the steward or marshal doth any thing contrary thereto, it shall be esteemed as null and void.

6th. That no action is given by the statute to the party grieved, yet when any thing is prohibited by statute, the party who is sued contrary thereto may have his action.

7th. That this action will lie against the defendants. And a difference was taken where a court hath jurisdiction of a cause, though it proceeds erroneously, no action will lie against the party who sues, or the officer who executes the process of the Court, but where the Court hath no jurisdiction of the cause, there the whole proceedings are *coram non judice*, and an action will lie against them, and the precept or warrant will be no excuse, for the judge of the Court is then to be looked upon as a mere stranger, and not as a judge of the cause, and the officer need not obey his warrant.

8th That the declaration being only in general *quod cum indebitatus fuit*

I

5 ED. 3, c. 2. A D. 1331 —10 ED. 3, c. 1. A. D. 1336.

Of what People Inquests in the Marshal's Court shall be taken. Redressing of error there.

AND that in every case where inquests be to be taken before the steward and the marshal of the king's house, that inquests be taken by men of the country thereabout, and not by men of the king's house, except it be of contracts, covenants, or trespasses made by men of the king's house of the one part and of the other, and that in the same house, according to another statute thereof made in the time of the said Edward the grandfather. And in case where any will complain of error made before the said steward and marshal, the plaintiff shall have a writ to remove the record and the process before the king in his place, and there the error shall be redressed. And likewise shall it be done in every other case where any man will complain him of error done before the same steward and marshal of the king's house.

---

27 ED 3, c. 5. A. D. 1353.

EXCLUDES the Marshalsea from taking cognizance of things belonging to the staple.

---

9 RIC. 2, c. 5 A. D. 1385.

The Fees of Priests taken in the Marshalsea of the King's House.

ITEM, for the reverence of God and of holy church, it is accorded and established, that priests and other people of holy church, taken in the Marshalsea of the king's house, shall pay such fees as lay-people pay, reasonably, and no more.

---

13 RIC 2, c. 3. A D. 1389

The Limits of the Steward's and Marshal's Court of the King's House.

ITEM, it is accorded and assented, that the Court of the steward and marshal of the king's house, nor also the jurisdiction thereof, shall not pass the space of twelve miles, to be counted from the lodging of our said lord the king.

in such a sum, without shewing the cause of the debt, was insufficient; yet if the Court had jurisdiction of the cause, no action would lie against the defendants, because then the proceedings would not be void, but voidable by error. *Note,* Sir Francis Bacon was at this time judge of the Marshalsea

A private act for the city of London is cited in Michelbourne's case and the case of the Marshalsea, as being in the Treasury, but not printed. It enacts—"That where before the steward and marshal, the Court being many times near the city of London, some inquests are taken of trespasses and other things done within the said city, betwixt some of the same city only, and betwixt them and foreigners jointly, or betwixt foreigners, and the conusance of which trespasses and other things belongs to the steward and marshal by reason of the verge, all such inquests shall be taken within the city of London, and not elsewhere."

2 HEN. 4, c. 23 A. D. 1400.

The Fees of the Marshal of the Marshalsea of the King's House.

"ITEM, Whereas the marshal of the Marshalsea of the Court of our lord the king's house, in the time of king Edward, grandfather of our lord the king that now is, and before, was wont to take the fees which do hereafter follow; that is to say, of every person that cometh by *capias* to the said Court, four pence, and if he be let to mainprise till his day, two pence more, and of every person which is impleaded of trespass, and findeth two mainpernors to keep his day till the end of the plea, to take for that cause two pence of the defendant; and of every person committed to prison by judgment of the steward, in whatsoever manner the same be, four pence; of every person delivered of felony, and of every felon let to mainprise by the court, four pence; which fees were wont to be taken and paid in full court, as the king hath well perceived by the complaint of the said commons thereof made in the said parliament." The same our lord the king, to avoid all such wrongs and oppressions to be done to his people, against the good customs and usages made and used in the time of his progenitors, by the advice and assent of the lords spiritual and temporal, and at the supplication of the said commons, hath ordained and established, that if the said marshal, or his officers under him, take other fees than above are declared, that the said marshal, and every of his said officers, shall lose their offices, and pay treble damages to the party grieved, and that the party grieved have his suit before the steward of the said Court for the time being

II Also it is ordained and established, that no servitor of bills that beareth a staff of the same Court, shall take for every mile from the same Court to the same place where he shall do his service, any more than 1d. and so for twelve miles 12d. and for to serve a *Venire facias xii homines &c.* or a *distringas* out of the same Court, the double and if any of the said servitors of bills do the contrary, he shall be punished by imprisonment, and make a fine to the king after the discretion of the steward of the same Court, and also be forejudged the Court.   And the same steward shall have power to make proclamation at his coming to the said Court, in every country, from time to time, of all the articles aforesaid, and thereof to execute punishment as afore is said.

---

11 HEN. 6, c 1. A D 1431.

They that dwell at the Stews, in Southwark, shall not be impanelled in juries, nor keep any inn or tavern but there

By this statute it is enacted—"That if any such person be returned by the sheriff, bailiff, or other minister of our said sovereign lord the King, in the said county of Surry, or by any officer before the Steward and Marshal of our sovereign lord the King's house, as well for the King as for the party, at all times from henceforth he may be challenged, and the challenge in that part allowed

15 HEN. 6, c. 1. A. D. 1436.

Where, in a suit before the marshal, the defendant may plead, that the plaintiff or he are not of the king's house.

" FIRST, because that the steward and marshal of the king's house and their deputies before this time have holden before them pleas of debt, detinue, or other pleas personal moved betwixt people which were not of the same house, making mention in their records, that the plaintiffs and defendants of the same pleas were of the said house, and do not allow to the parties defendants in the same pleas their challenges and exceptions by them alleged, that they themselves, or the plaintiffs in the same suits, be not of the same houses, against the laws and statutes before this time had and made, whereby many of the king's liege people, in his Court holden before the said steward and marshal, oftentimes against the law be grievously vexed and troubled, to their great damage and hindrance." ' Our said lord the king considering the premises, hath ordained by authority of the same parliament, that in every suit [surety] from henceforth against the said defendants to be taken, they shall not be estopped by such record, to say that themselves, or the plaintiffs in the same record specified, were not, at the time of the said plea or suit thereof commenced, of the king's house, as by the same record is supposed (1); but the defendants shall have their averment to say, that they themselves, or the said plaintiffs, were not of the same house at the time of such plea or suit commenced, the said record or other matter within the same contained notwithstanding.

(1) By the records in which they made mention that the parties were of the household, perhaps is meant, the recognizances of bail, for, it was usual to mention it in the plea roll; and Lord Coke, 10 Rep 73 *a*, (Case of the *Marshalsea*), says, it was not necessary. The stat. seems to be misprinted in the words—" *en chescun seurte desore enavaunt pur les defts &c* "

This act gives an exception to the defendant, which, if it had been always used, would effectually have destroyed the jurisdiction of the Court. But, whether it was from the general respect anciently paid to the prerogative, or from the Court not being so odious as afterwards, it still continued to exercise its usurped jurisdiction.

---

3 HEN. 7, c. 14. A. D. 1486.

Conspiring to destroy the king, or any lord councellor, or great officer, shall be felony.

ITEM, forasmuch as by quarrels made to such as have been in great authority, office, and of council with kings of this realm, hath ensued the destruction of the kings, and the undoing of this realm, so as it hath appeared evidently, when compassing of the death of such as were of the king's true subjects was had, the destruction of the prince was imagined thereby, and for the most part it hath grown and been occasioned by envy and malice of the king's own household servants, as now of late such a thing was likely to have ensued; and forasmuch as by the law of this land, if actual deeds be not had, there is no remedy for such false compassings, imaginations, and confederacies had against any lord, or any of the king's

council, or any of the king's great officers in his household, as steward, treasurer, and comptroller, and so great inconveniencies might ensue if such ungodly demeaning should not be straightly punished before that actual deed were done therefore it is ordained by the king, the lords spiritual and temporal, and the commons, of the said parliament assembled, and by authority of the same, that from henceforward the steward, treasurer, and comptroller of the king's house for the time being, or one of them, have full authority and power to enquire by twelve sad and discreet persons, of the cheque roll of the king's honourable household, if any servant admitted to be his servant in his house sworn, and his name put into the cheque-roll of his household, whatsoever he be, serving in any manner, office, or room, reputed, had, and taken under the state of a lord, make any confederacies, compassings, conspiracies, or imaginations, with any person or persons, to destroy or murder the king, or any lord of this realm, or any other person sworn to the king's council, or steward, treasurer, or comptroller of the king's house, that if it be found before the said steward for the time being, by the said twelve sad men, that any such of the king's servants as is above said, hath confedered, compassed, conspired, or imagined, as is above said, that he so found by that inquiry be put thereupon to answer, and the steward, treasurer, and comptroller, or two of them, have power to determine the same matter, according to the law and if he put him in trial, that then it be tried by other twelve sad men of the same household, and that such mis-doers have no challenge but for malice, and if such mis doers be found guilty by confession or otherwise, that the said offence be judged felony; and they to have judgment and execution as felons attainted ought for to have by the common law.

---

27 HEN. 8, c. 24. A. D. 1535.

An Act for recontinuing Liberties in the Crown

AND over this it is ordained by authority aforesaid, that in all such places wheresoever the king's highness in his own most royal person shall come to rest, tarry, abide, or make his repose within this realm or any his dominions, within liberty or without, there and within the verge limited and accustomed to his grace's court, during the time of his abode, his grace's steward, marshal, coroner, and all other his ministers, shall and may keep their courts for justice, and exercise their offices, as shall appertain to them, according to the laws, statutes and customs of this realm, as well within liberties as without.

---

32 HEN. 8, c 39. A D 1540

THE great master of the king's house shall have all authority that the lord steward had —[Repealed by 1 Mar sess 3, c. 4. re-establishing the name, office, and authority of the Lord Steward.]

33 HEN. 8, c 12. A. D. 1541.

The bill for the Household.

WHERE treasons, misprisions of treasons, murders, manslaughters, and other malicious strikings, by reason whereof blood is or shall be shed, against the king's peace, been often and many times done and committed within the limits of the king's palace or house, or other house or houses, where and when his Majesty is there demurrant and abiding in his own most royal person, which offences, when they be done, be best known by his highness's officers and ministers of his most honourable household, and by his Majesty's servants of the chequer-roll, and if his Majesty shall happen to remove from such his palace or house, or other house or houses, where such offences were done, before the trial or determination thereof, then such offences might not lawfully be tried, heard and determined by and before the said officers, but be remitted to be tried and determined by the order of ' _ common laws of this realm, by reason whereof, the punishm _ (of the said offenders in such cases hath been long delayed, and sometimes their offences forgotten and not remembered, and so escape unpunished. Be it therefore enacted by the King our sovereign lord, with the assent of the lords spiritual and temporal, and the Commons, in this present Parliament assembled, and by the authority of the same, that all treasons, misprisions of treasons, murders, manslaughters, bloodsheds and malicious strikings, by reason whereof blood is or shall be shed against the king's peace, which hath been done since the feast of All saints last past, or hereafter shall be done, within any the palaces or houses of his highness or his heirs, or any other house or houses, at such time as his Majesty hath been since the said feast of All-saints, or hereafter shall happen to be then demurrant or abiding in his royal person, shall be from thenceforth inquired of, tried, heard and determined within any the king's palaces or houses, or other house or houses where his Majesty or his heirs shall hereafter repair unto, or be abiding, in manner and form following, that is to say, before the lord great master, or lord steward for the time being, of the king's most honourable household, and of his heirs and successors, and in the absence of the said lord great master, or lord steward of the household, before the treasurer and comptroller for the time being of the king's most honourable household, and of his heirs and successors, and steward of the Marshalsea for the time being, or two of them, whereof the steward of the Marshalsea for the time being to be one, by virtue of their offices, without any commission or other authority or power, other than by the authority of this present act, to be given unto them or any of them, which steward of the Marshalsea shall be for ever from time to time assigned and appointed by writing under the seal of the said lord great master, or lord steward for the time being. And whether the king's majesty or his heirs, hath, or at any time hereafter shall be, removed from the palace, house or houses, where such offences were or shall be done, or not removed before they be enquired of, tried, heard and determined, yet such offences shall, by the authority of this act, always from henceforth be enquired of, tried, heard and determined before the

king's Majesty and his heirs, officers and ministers of his household before named, or two of them as is aforesaid, by the inquisition and verdict of his highness' and his heirs' household servants, in his or their check-roll, in manner and form as before and hereafter is expressed in this present act, and at such palace, house or houses, where his Majesty or his heirs shall be at any time hereafter demurrant or abiding.

II. And that all such returns of process, and all executions and judgments concerning the premises, shall be had and done by the officers before and hereafter expressed, and in manner and form as before and hereafter in this present act is contained.

III. And that all inquisitions upon the view of persons slain, or hereafter to be slain, within any of the king's said palaces or houses, or other house or houses aforesaid, shall be, by authority of this act, had and taken hereafter for ever by the coroner for the time being of the household of our sovereign lord the king or his heirs, without any adjoining or assisting of any other coroner of any shire within this realm, by the oath of twelve or more of the yeomen officers of the kings' and his heirs' most honourable household, returned by the two clerks comptrollers, the clerks of the check, and the clerks marshals, or one of them, for the time being, of the said household, to whom the said coroner of the same household shall direct his precept, which coroner of our said sovereign lord the king's household shall be from time to time named, appointed and assigned by the said lord great master, or lord steward for the time being, and that the said coroner of the said household shall, from time to time for ever, without delay, certify under his seal and the seals of such persons as shall be sworn before him, all such inquisitions, indictments and offices, upon the view of all dead bodies being slain at any time since the feast of All-saints aforesaid, or which hereafter shall be slain within any the king's said palaces or houses, or other house or houses aforesaid, before the said lord great master, or lord steward, and, in his absence, before the treasurer, comptroller and steward, of the Marshalsea aforesaid, or before two of them, whereof the said steward of the Marshalsea to be one, and that such inquisitions and offices so certified, shall be deemed, adjudged and taken for ever, as good and effectual in the law to all intents, constructions and purposes, as any inquisition taken upon the view of the body of any person being dead, by any coroner of any county of this realm, hath been or shall be adjudged or taken.

IV. And be it further enacted by the authority aforesaid, that the said two clerks comptrollers, clerks of the check, and clerks marshals for the time being of the king's said household, and of his heirs, or one of them for ever, upon a precept to them, or to any of them hereafter to be made by the said lord great master or lord steward, or, in the absence of the said lord great master or lord steward, by the said treasurer and comptroller of the king's most honourable household, and the said steward of the Marshalsea, or by two of them, whereof the said steward of the said Marshalsea to be one, shall have full power to summon, warn and return the names of twenty-four persons, being yeomen officers of the king's said household, and of his heirs, in the said check-roll, to enquire of such

treasons, misprisions of treasons, murders, manslaughters, and other malicious strikings, by reason whereof blood is or shall be shed, against the king's peace, before the said lord great master or lord steward, and, in his absence, before the said treasurer, comptroller, and steward of the Marshalsea, or before two of them at the least, whereof the steward to be one.

V. And that it shall be lawful to the said lord great master or lord steward, and, in his absence, to the said treasurer, comptroller, and the said steward aforesaid, or two of them, whereof the said steward to be one, before whom such returns shall be so made as is aforesaid, to cause such number of the said twenty four persons so returned, above the number of twelve persons, as to him or them shall seem expedient, to enquire of such treasons, misprisions of treasons, murders, manslaughters and other malicious strikings, by reason whereof blood is or shall be shed, against the king's peace within the said palaces or houses, or other the said house or houses, since the said feast of All saints, or at any time hereafter shall be committed or done within the said palace or house, or other the said house or houses.

VI. And if any person or persons be indicted by the said jury, so sworn before them as is aforesaid, or by inquisition before the said coroner of the said household, and certified before the said lord great master or lord steward, or in the absence of the said lord great master or lord steward, before the said treasurer, comptroller and steward, or before two of them, whereof the said steward to be one as is aforesaid, that then immediately without delay the said lord great master or lord steward, and, in his absence, the said treasurer, comptroller and steward, or two of them, whereof the said steward to be one, before whom the said presentment, inquisition or indictment shall so be found or certified by the said coroner of the same household, shall arraign before them all and every such person and persons so indicted according to the course of the common law of this realm, and forthwith, after issue joined between the king our sovereign lord, his heirs or successors, and the prisoner so arraigned, the same day and place, or any other day and place, at the pleasure of the said lord great master, lord steward, and, in his absence, at the pleasure of the said treasurer, comptroller and steward of the Marshalsea, or two of them as is aforesaid, shall make another precept to the said clerks comptrollers, clerks of the check, and clerks marshals for the time being of the said household, or to one of them, to summon and return one other jury of twenty-four persons, to appear before the said lord great master or lord steward, and in his absence, before the said treasurer, comptroller and steward of the Marshalsea, or before two of them, whereof the same steward to be one, at such day, time and place, and upon such pain, as shall be then limited and appointed, of the servants and gentlemen officers of the king's chamber, his heirs and successors, and of the said households, which now take or hereafter shall take, wages by the king's chequer-roll, and that the said lord great master or lord steward (if he be there present) or in his absence the said treasurer, comptroller and steward of the said Marshalsea, or two of them, whereof the same steward to be one, before whom such jury shall be so returned, shall cause twelve

of the same jury to be sworn, without any manner of challenge to be had or allowed for any manner of cause, to any of the said jury (malice only excepted) truly to be tried between our said sovereign lord the king and his heirs, and such person and persons as shall be so indicted and arraigned of such treasons, misprisions of treasons, murders, manslaughters and other malicious strikings, by reason whereof blood is or shall be shed, against the king's peace, or any of them; and if any such person or persons, so indicted and arraigned, be found guilty of any treason, misprision of treason, murders or manslaughters, that then all and every such person and persons so found guilty, shall have judgment of life and member, and suffer such pains of death, and shall forfeit all their manors lands, tenements, goods and chattels, in like manner and form, as if the same person and persons had been found guilty of any the said offences by the order of the common laws of this realm, without allowing to any such person or persons so found guilty of any of the same offences, the benefits of his or their clergy, or privilege of any sanctuary.

VII. And if any person or persons so arraigned be found guilty for malicious striking, by reason whereof blood is, hath been, or shall be shed, against the king's peace, within the said palace or house, or any other house, or any other the said house or houses; that then every such person or persons shall from henceforth have judgment by the said lord great master or lord steward, (if he be present) and in his absence by the other afore named, before whom such person and persons shall be so found guilty, to have his right hand striken off before the said lord great master, or lord steward, if he be there present, and in his absence before the said treasurer, comptroller and steward of the Marshalsea, or two of them at the least, whereof the said steward to be one, and at such place or time as he or they before whom such person or persons shall be so found guilty, shall appoint execution to be done; and the same execution to be done by such person as the said lord great master, or lord steward, if he be there present, and in his absence as the said treasurer, comptroller and steward of the Marshalsea, or two of them, whereof the steward to be one, shall name or appoint, and also shall have judgment to have perpetual imprisonment during his life, and shall pay fine and ransom at the king's majesty's pleasure, his heirs and successors.

VIII. And for the further declaration of the solemn and due circumstance of the execution appertaining, and of long time used and accustomed, to and for such malicious strikings, by reason whereof blood is, hath been, or hereafter shall be shed, against the king's peace· it is therefore enacted by the authority aforesaid, that the sergeant or chief surgeon for the time being, or his deputy, of the king's household, his heirs and successors, shall be ready at the time and place of execution as shall be appointed, as is aforesaid, to sear the stump, when the hand is stricken off.

IX. And the sergeant of the pantry for the time being of the same household, or his deputy, shall be also then and there ready to give bread to the party that shall have his hand so stricken off.

X. And the sergeant of the cellar for the time being of the same household, or his deputy, shall also be then and there ready with

a pot of red wine, to give the same party drink, after his hand is
so stricken off, and the stump seared.

XI. And the sergeant of the ewry for the time being of the same
household, or his deputy, shall also be then and there ready with
clothes sufficient for the surgeon to occupy about the same execution

XII. And the yeoman of the chandry for the time being of the
same household, or his deputy, shall also be then and there, and
have in readiness seared clothes, sufficient for the surgeon to occupy
about the same execution.

XIII And the master cook for the time being of the same household, or his deputy, shall also be then and there ready, and bring
with him a dressing knife, and shall deliver the same knife at the
place of execution to the serjeant of the larder for the time being
of the same household, or to his deputy, who shall be also then
and there ready, and hold upright the dressing knife till execution
be done.

XIV. And the serjeant of the poultry for the time being of the
same household, or his deputy, shall be also then and there ready
with a cock in his hand, ready for the surgeon to wrap about the
same stump when the hand shall be so stricken off.

XV. And the yeoman of the scullery for the time being of the
same household, or his deputy, to be also then and there ready, and
prepare and make at the place of execution a fire of coals, and
there to make ready searing irons against the said surgeon or his
deputy shall occupy the same.

XVI. And the sergeant or chief ferror for the time being of the
same household, or his deputy, shall be also then and there ready,
and bring with him the searing-irons, and deliver the same to the
same serjeant or chief surgeon, or to his deputy, when they be hot.

XVII. And the groom of the salcery for the time being of the
same household, or his deputy, shall be also then and there ready
with vinegar and cold water, and give attendance upon the said
surgeon or his deputy, until the same execution be done.

XVIII And the sergeant of the wood-yard for the time being
of the same household, or his deputy, shall bring to the said place
of execution a block, with a beetle, a staple, and cords, to bind the
said hand upon the block, while execution is in doing.

XIX. And be it further enacted by the authority aforesaid, that
if any person or persons so indicted of treason, misprision of treason, murder, manslaughter, or other malicious striking, by reason
whereof blood is, hath been, or shall be shed, against the king's
peace, as is aforesaid, and thereof be arraigned, and obstinately refuse to answer directly to the same offences whereof he or they be
so indicted; or if such person or persons so indicted and arraigned,
stand mute, and will not speak, then such person and persons so
refusing to answer, or standing mute, shall be convicted, judged and
deemed guilty of the thing whereof he or they is or shall be so indicted and arraigned, and shall have judgment to have like pains
of death, and other pains, punishments, executions, forfeitures,
losses, and seizures of lands, tenements, goods and chattels for the
same, as he or they ought or should have had for such like offences
if he or they were or should be found guilty thereof by the verdict

of twelve men. And be it further enacted by the authority aforesaid, that the said clerks comptrollers, clerks of the check, and clerks marshal, or one of them, for the time being, shall from time to time name, assign, and appoint a crier to make proclamations, and to call the juries, and to do other things as becometh a crier of a court to do belonging to that office.

XX. Provided always, and be it enacted by the authority aforesaid, that this act before rehearsed, concerning malicious strikings, by reason whereof blood is, hath been, or shall be shed, against the king's peace, nor the pains and forfeitures before rehearsed for the punishment of the same, shall not in any ways extend nor be prejudicial or hurtful to any nobleman, nor to any other person or persons, that shall happen to strike his or their servants within the said palaces or houses, or any other house or houses aforesaid, or within the limits of the same, with his or their hands or fists, or with any small staff or stick, for correction and punishment for any offences committed and done or to be committed and done, nor to any of the king's officers or servants that shall strike any person within the same palace or house, or any other house or houses as aforesaid, although by reason of the said stroke or strokes there happen to be any blood shed of such person as shall be so stricken, except the person so stricken do die of the same stroke within one year next after the same stroke so given. Provided also, and be it enacted by the authority aforesaid, that the trial of peers of this realm, for committing or doing any offences in this act before mentioned, shall be as it hath been used in times past; any thing in this act contained to the contrary notwithstanding.

XXI. Provided also that the liberty and jurisdiction of the Marshalsea Court and circuit of the verge shall be in all points, privileges and authorities, used by the ministers and officers of the same, in as full and as ample a manner as hath been heretofore lawfully used, for murders, felonies, offences, and all trespasses, contracts and other suits, whatsoever they be; any thing in this act to the contrary notwithstanding.

XXII. And forasmuch as before this time one Richard Staverton of Lincoln's-inn, gentleman, was commanded and appointed by the king's majesty to occupy the office of the coroner of his said house, by force whereof he has continued officer in the same by the space of sixteen years or more. be it enacted by the authority aforesaid, that the said Richard Staverton shall have, occupy and enjoy the said office of coroner during his life, together with all such profits and commodities as before this time have been due and appertaining in any wise to the same, and after his decease, the said coroner always to be made, assigned and appointed by the said lord great master, or lord steward for the time being.

XXIII. And for that hereafter it might be doubted, how far the limits and bounds of the said house or houses should extend or be taken, within which limits or bounds any of the said offences which have been committed or done since the said feast of All-saints, or hereafter shall be committed or done, for the which all and every person and persons so offending, should have and suffer the pains, penalties and forfeitures as is aforesaid, for plain declaration thereof, and for the avoiding of all doubts and questions which may hereafter happen to arise of, for, or upon the same

XXIV. Be it enacted by the authority aforesaid, that the limits and bounds of the said house and houses, within which any of the offences aforesaid, now committed or done since the said feast of All-saints, or hereafter to be committed and done, shall be punished as is aforesaid, shall extend and be taken within these places ensuing, and in none other, that is to say, within any edifices, courts, places, gardens, orchards, or houses within the porter's ward, of any of the house or houses above rehearsed, or within any gardens, privy walks, orchards, tilt-yards, wood-yards, tennis-plays, cock-fights, bowling-alleys near adjoining to any of the houses above rehearsed, and being part of the same, or within two hundred feet of the standard of any outward gate or gates of any of the houses above rehearsed, commonly used for passage out or from any of the house or houses above rehearsed.

XXV. Provided always, that this act shall not take effect, or be put in execution, till from and after the first day of May next ensuing, except only for murders and manslaughters; for the which offences of murder and manslaughter, the same to take effect from the feast of All-saints last past, according to the tenor and effect of the said act.

XXVI. Provided always, and be it enacted by the authority aforesaid, that this act before rehearsed concerning malicious strik-ings, by reason whereof blood is, hath been, or shall be shed, against the king's peace, nor the pains and forfeitures before re-hearsed for the punishment of the same, shall not in any wise ex-tend, or be prejudicial or hurtful to any nobleman, nor to any other person or persons, that shall happen to strike his or their servants within the said palace or house, or any other house or houses, place or places aforesaid, or within the limits of the same, with his or their hands or fists, or with any small staff or stick, for correction and punishment for any offences committed and done, or to be com-mitted and done; nor to any of the king's officer or officers, that in executing of his or their office shall strike any person or persons with his or their hands or fists, or with any small staff or stick, or with any staff commonly called a tip-staff, within the same palace or house, or any other palaces or houses or places aforesaid; nor to any other person or persons, that in doing service at any triumph, or any other time of service, by the king's commandment, or of any of his grace's council, or other his grace's head officers, shall hap-pen, for the executing of their said service, to strike any person or persons with his or their hands or fists, or with any small staff or stick, or with any staff commonly called a tip staff, within the same palace or house, or any other palaces or houses, or place or places aforesaid, although by reason of the same stroke or strokes there happen to be any blood shed of such person as shall be so stricken, except the person so stricken do die of the same stroke within one year next after the stroke so given.

XXVII. And also be it further enacted by the authority afore-said, that if any person or persons shall, from the first day of April next coming, steal or feloniously take away any plate, jewels or other goods of our said sovereign lord the king, his heirs or successors, kings, of the value of 1s. or above, or break or enter into any the king's houses, to the intent to steal any of the king's goods, his

hears or successors, kings, though his Majesty be absent, or any
other house, while it shall fortune the same his Majesty to be lodged
or abiding therein, every such offence to be deemed felony; and
the person or persons so offending, their abettors, procurers, counsellors and receptors, thereof lawfully convicted, to suffer like penalties, forfeitures, and pains of death, as appertaineth to felons, without having the benefit of their clergy or sanctuary, and every such
offender being apprehended within the verge of the king's house
to be arraigned and tried by men of the country, as other offenders
for offences done within the verge, before the steward of the said
Marshalsea, and other unto him associated, are to be arraigned and
tried within the same precinct (1).

(1) On this act Coke (Inst. 549.) observes—" That if a man strike in the
king's palace, where his royal person is resiant, unless blood be shed, he los-
eth not his hand; but in Westminster-hall, when the king's courts sit, or before the justices of assise sitting in their place, if any man strike another, although he draw no blood, yet shall he lose his right hand, so great honour
and reverence do laws give to the king's courts: for, in judgment of law, the
king himself is always present to minister justice, by his judges, in those
courts of justice, according to his kingly office, to all his subjects, *secundum
legem et consuetudinem Angliæ* "

The only instance that has been met with of a conviction upon this statute, is *Burket's case*, (Mich. 15 & 16 El Rot. 2). Burket, while a prisoner
in the Tower, struck his keeper, John Longworth, with a billet, by which
blood was shed, and he died *instanter*, it being without provocation it was
adjudged murder, of which he was attainted. And before his execution,
which was in the Strand, over against Somerset-house, his right hand was
first struck off, for it was held, that the Tower was one of the queen's houses
or standing palaces. 3 Inst. 140. 6 Mod. 76.

8 ELIZ. c. 2. A. D 1565.

*An act for the avoiding of wrongful vexation touching the writ of
Latitat.*

SECT. 3, provides, that if any person be attached or arrested in
the Marshalsea in any action personal, and the plaintiff do not
within three days after bail or appearance, unless further day be
given by special direction of the Court, exhibit his bill or declaration against the defendant, or on discontinuance or nonsuit, the
judge shall give the defendant his costs, to be recovered by action
of debt in any court of record.

43 ELIZ. c. 4. A. D 1600

APPOINTS the same allowance from the several counties to be paid
to the prisoners of the Marshalsea as to those of the King's Bench

49 GEO. 3, c. 126. A. D. 1809
An act to prevent the Sale of Offices.

CONTAINS a provision that the act is not to extend to the sale
of offices in the Marshalsea or Palace Court

LETTERS PATENTS, &c.

9 JAMES I.

JAMES, by the grace of God, King of England, Scotland, France and Ireland, Defender of the Faith, &c —To all our loving subjects within the verge of the household of us, our heirs and successors greeting—Whereas we have been informed of some complaints and griefs concerning the Court of Marshalsea, made as well in parliament as otherwise, and thereupon have been moved to give direction, that the grounds of such complaints should be examined and considered, and thereby have discovered that they have not arisen so much out of the nature of the jurisdiction, where the suitors have speedy justice from day to day, and have likewise the benefit of special bails and speedy trials, as in respect partly of the fee commonly called the Knight Marshal's Fee, which is great, and laid upon the defendants, and yet nevertheless is the ancient fee which hath been time out of mind used, and partly through some courses of vexation in the exercise of that jurisdiction, as arrests in time of progress, when the suitor cannot by any possibility have the effect of his suit, by reason of the removes of the court· And likewise by the not awarding of costs to the full against the plaintiff, where the suit appears to be but upon vexation, and also by the multitude of the Knight Marshal's men that make a gain upon arrests, by stirring of suits upon malice or frivolous causes And whereas the jurisdiction of the said ancient Court of Marshalsea is defective in power to hold plea of many personal actions, so as our loving subjects within the verge cannot there have the like ease in their suits as the inhabitants of other inferior liberties have—We have thought it the most expedient way, by these our Letters Patents, chiefly for the ease of our said loving subjects within the verge, by consent of the said Knight Marshal, to abate in great part his fee, and, by special ordinance and provision, to repress all those points which have, and may make the said ancient Court of Marshalsea grievous, and by other letters patents, of the date of these presents, to erect a New Court within the verge for personal actions which concern persons, not being, or which hereafter shall not be of our household, to be before the said Knight Marshal and some fit person learned in the law, and therein to grant the said Knight Marshal such fees as may be easy for the subject to bear, and yet, in some measure, by reason of the said actions countervail his loss of fees abated as aforesaid; and therefore have ordained, constituted, and decreed for us, our heirs, and successors, as followeth, viz

1. *Imprimis.* That upon any arrest by process issuing either out of the ancient Court of the Marshalsea, or out of the New Court of the verge, now newly erected by our letters patents, and bearing

date with the date of these presents, the Knight Marshal for the time being, nor any of the Knight Marshal's men, shall not at any time hereafter take any fee or fees to the use of any such Knight Marshal other than three shillings and sixpence, besides other officers' fees.

2. *Item.* That the judges of the ancient Court of Marshalsea, for the time being, shall not take any other fees for any thing doing in their office, than of ancient time the judges of the same court have lawfully and usually taken. And that the judges of the said New Court for the verge for the time being, or hereafter to be, and their deputies, every one of them, having but one only deputy, shall not take any other fees for any thing doing in their offices than are allowed unto them, and are set down expressly in a schedule to the patent thereof annexed (being in substance agreeable to the ancient fees of the ancient Court of Marshalsea in all points except in some particulars abated. And that every of the said judges and their deputies shall, before he or they, or any of them, be admitted to execute their offices, take a corporal oath before some such persons as we, our heirs, or successors, shall appoint to take the same, and shall swear that they shall well and truly, according to their learning, knowledge, and judgment in the law, speedily, without any unnecessary delay, administer justice in their places, according to the laws and statutes of this realm: and such oath for this present shall be taken before the treasurer and comptroller of our household, or one of them.

3. *Item.* That the said Marshal and other judges of the said several courts, every one of them, by himself in person, or by his sufficient and only deputy, sworn and admitted as aforesaid, shall duly and diligently attend the seats of justice in each of the said courts, every court day from the time of the beginning or proclaiming of the said courts and every of them, until the end and adjournment over of every of them unto a further day, and that no other person, nor any person unsworn and admitted especially thereunto, shall take upon him, or be suffered hereafter to sit in either of the said seats of justice in either of the said courts.

4. *Item.* That in every case whereas any defendant is by the statutes of this realm to recover his costs against any plaintiff in any action in either of the said courts, the said judges and every of them, and every of their deputies, shall from henceforth from time to time adjudge and allow unto every such defendant in each of the said courts their full charges by them truly and justly expended in that behalf.

5. *Item.* That the clerk of the papers and his deputies, the counsellors, the attornies, the crier and his deputy, the keepers and porters of the ancient prison of the Marshalsea and their deputies, all the Marshal's men, bearers of the verge, and other the officers of the ancient Court of Marshalsea, shall not take or exact any other fees for any thing concerning any of their offices, other than they or the like officers of ancient time lawfully and severally have taken; nor that they or any of them shall directly or indirectly stir up any suits or arrests; and that the prothonotary or his deputies, the counsellors, attornies, the crier, and his deputy, the under-marshal, keeper, and porter, of the new prison of the Marshalsea for the verge, all the marshal's men, bearers of the verge, and other

the officers of the new court for the verge, shall not take or exact any other fees for any thing concerning any of their offices, other than are allowed unto them, and are set down in the said schedule unto the said letters patents of the said new court annexed, being in substance agreeable unto the ancient fees of the ancient court of Marshalsea in all points; and that the said prothonotary and his deputies, the counsellors, attornies, and crier and his deputy, the under-marshal, keepers, and porters of the prisons aforesaid and their deputies, and all the said marshal's men, and other the officers of each of the said courts at such time as they are to take upon them the execution of their said offices, shall for ever from henceforth from time to time take upon them and each of them a corporal oath before some of the judges of the said several courts, or their deputies, honestly and lawfully to execute their offices

6. *Item.* That if it shall appear that the debt for which any person shall be arrested into either of the said courts is under ten shillings, that the defendant may tender the just debt the first court day, and thereupon be discharged, in which case he shall have the knight's fee repaid, but if the plaintiff will aver his debt to be more than ten shillings, if upon trial it fall out his due debt was under ten shillings, the defendant shall recover all his costs and damages against the plaintiff for them.

7. *Item* In time of any progress of us, our heirs, and successors, when it shall appear by our jests that we are not to continue at any place the full space of one month, that during such progress there shall be no suits or arrests commenced or made into either of the said courts, nor that the said courts, or either of them, shall in any wise follow the royal court of us, our heirs, and successors   And this our order shall be a sufficient dispensation of the service and attendance of the said officers; as well of the officers and ministers of the said ancient Court of Marshalsea as of the new Court of the Verge, for that our subjects in such speedy progress cannot have the effect of their suits, and nevertheless are troubled and charged with arrests and payments.

8. *Item* That the number of the knight marshal's men, bearers of the verge, shall be restrained to the number of twenty, which shall not hereafter be exceeded.

And we do by these presents straightly charge and command all and every the knight-marshals, judges, counsellors, prothonotary, attornies, and all and every other officers and ministers of the said courts, that they and every of them do duly observe and perform all the ordinances of the said courts according to these presents, upon peril of forfeiture of their said offices, and such further penalty as by the laws and statutes of this realm may be inflicted upon them. In witness whereof, &c   Witness ourself at Westminster, the 8th day of June.

Per Breve de Privato Sigillo

9 *JAC.* 1.

REX omnibus ad quos, &c. salutem   CUM nobis expediens et
necessarium videtur, quod omnes et singuli subditi nostri et personæ quæcunque infra virgam hospitii nostri residentes, inhabitantes,
contrahentes, seu negotiantes, in omnibus et omnimodis actionibus,
placitis, et querelis suis personalibus celeriorem haberent justitiam,
eo quod ipsi in negotiis et servitiis nostris majorem in modum quam
alii subditi nostri in remotioribus Angliæ partibus commorantes,
occupantur et implicantur   CUMQUE Curia Marescaltiæ Hospitii Regum Angliæ sit antiqua curia, ordinata pro bona conservatione
et custodia pacis infra hospitium regum Angliæ ac infra virgam eidem pertinentem, ac pro determinatione diversarum actionum et
querelarum personalium infra hospitium et virgam prædictam
emergentium, prout per leges et statuta hujus regni Angliæ liquet
et apparet   Ac nihilominus diversæ quæstiones et dubia modo
mota et facta sunt et indies oriuntur, tangentia jurisdictionem prædictæ curiæ, per quæ subditi nostri propter incertitudinem juris-
dictionis gravantur et molestantur. CUMQUE insuper ad notitiam
nostram regiam pervenerint nonnullæ querelæ, tam de feodis quæ
in curia prædicta usitata fuerunt de antiquo, quam de compluribus
abusibus et gravaminibus quæ intra procedenda ejusdem curiæ irrepserunt, quibus nos per ordinationes quasdam nuper sub magno
sigillo nostro factas et constitutas subvenimus et debito modo re
medium apposuimus   SCIATIS igitur nos, de gratia nostra speciali, certa scientia et mero motu nostris, fecisse, creasse, ordinasse, et
constituisse, et per præsentes, pro nobis, heredibus et successoribus
nostris, facere, creare, ordinare, et constituere aliam curiam pro
virga hospitii nostri, heredum et successorum nostrorum, pro admi
nistratione justitiæ omnibus et singulis personis de hospitio nostro
non existentibus, vel quæ non fuerint de hospitio nostro, heredum
seu successorum nostrorum, infra virgam illam de tempore in tempus existentibus, venientibus, confluentibus, negotiantibus, commorantibus, contrahentibus, sive quoquo modo intromittentibus, et
pro terminatione omnium et omnimodorum actionum, placitorum,
et querelarum personalium deinceps inter personas prædictas motorum sive movendorum, dependentium sive dependendorum in omnibus parochiis, villis, hamletis, libertatibus, franchesiis, et locis
infra virgam prædictam hospitii nostri, heredum et successorum nostrorum, limitatis, consuetis, seu pertinentibus, ac in quibuscunque comitatibus et locis infra præcincta virgæ hujusmodi hospitii nostri, ubi
nos nunc sumus, vel ubicurque aliquo tempore vel aliquibus temporibus, ac toties quoties imposterum nos, heredes et successores nostri
erimus, venerimus, transibimus vel remanebimus infra hoc regnum
nostrum Angliæ, exceptis tantum civitatibus, burgis, villis, et aliis
libertatibus, et franchesiis, in quibus aliqui subditi nostri sive ali-

9 JAMES I

JAMES, by the grace of God, of England, Scotland, France, and Ireland, King, Defender, &c , to all to whom these present letters shall come, greeting

Whereas, it appears unto us expedient and necessary, that all and singular our subjects and persons whatsoever, residing, inhabiting, contracting, or trafficking within the virge of our household, should have more speedy justice in all and all manner of their personal actions, pleas, and plaints, because they are more occupied and engaged in our business, than others of our subjects residing in more remote parts of England

And whereas, the Court of the Marshalsea of the household of the kings of England is an ancient Court, constituted for the good preservation and keeping of the peace within the household of the kings of England, and within the virge pertaining to the same, and for determining divers actions and personal plaints arising within the household and verge aforesaid, as by the laws and statutes of this realm of England is clear and evident. And, nevertheless, divers questions and doubts are now agitated and made and daily arise, touching the jurisdiction of the aforesaid court, by means whereof our subjects are vexed and troubled, on account of the uncertainty of the jurisdiction And whereas, besides, some complaints have come to our royal knowledge, as well concerning the fees which have been anciently used in the aforesaid court, as concerning many abuses and grievances which have crept into the proceedings of the said court, which we have in due manner relieved and remedied by certain ordinances under our great seal, lately made and constituted Know ye, therefore, that we, of our special grace, certain knowledge and mere motion, have made, created, ordained, and constituted, and by these presents, for us, our heirs, and successors, do make, create, ordain, and constitute another court for the verge of our household, our heirs' and successors', for the administration of justice to all and every persons not being of our household, or who shall not have been of the household of us, our heirs or successors, from time to time being, coming, resorting, carrying on business, sojourning, contracting, or in any manner entering within that virge , and for determining all and all manner of actions, pleas, and personal plaints hereafter commenced, or to be commenced, pending, or to be pending between the aforesaid persons, in all parishes, towns, hamlets, liberties, franchises, and places within the aforesaid virge of the household of us, our heirs or successors, prescribed, accustomed or pertaining, and in all counties and places within the precincts of the virge of this our household, where we now are, or where, at any time, or at any times, and as often as, hereafter we, our heirs, and successors shall be, come, pass through, or remain within this our kingdom of England, excepting only the cities, boroughs, towns, and other liberties and franchises in which any our subjects or subject have

K 2

quis subditus noster habent seu habet vel habere debent seu debet
potestatem et authoritatem tenendi, audiendi, et terminandi talia
actiones, placita, et querelas personales, per aliquam priorem legalem concessionem, consuetudinem, vel præscriptionem.   Ipsamque
fore curiam de recordo, ac appellari Curiam Virgæ Hospitii prædicti, et habere commune sigillum, et communem prisonam ad aliquem locum certum infra virgam hospitii prædicti ; ac eandem curiam et placita prædicta in eadem curia inter personas prædictas
movenda sive dependentia, tenenda fore de die in diem coram marescallo nostro hospitii nostri, heredum et successorum nostrorum,
pro tempore existente, et aliqua alia persona habili et erudita in
lege, per nos, heredes et successores nostros de tempore in tempus
nominandis et appunctuandis, judicibus ejusdem curiæ per has literas constitutis, aut eorum legitimis et sufficientibus deputatis, ad
aliquem locum certum infra virgam hospitii nostri prædicti, de
tempore in tempus per marescallum nostrum et personam prædictam, aut eorum legitimos et sufficientes deputatos appunctuandum
et assignandum, per præsentes ordinamus et constituimus.   Et easdem actiones per ipsos judices aut legitimos et sufficientes deputatos eorum versus aliquam personam in custodia marescalli mares-
calliæ hospicii nostri prædicti existentem, vel aliter qualitercunque
ad dictam curiam virgæ prædictæ legitime arrestatam seu arrestan-
dam per aliquod breve dictæ curiæ virgæ, secundum leges et consuetudines regni nostri Angliæ audiendas et terminandas similiter volumus
et ordinamus per præsentes. SALVIS nobis heredibus et successoribus nostris amerciamentis, tam in quadam scedula præsentibus annexa mentionatis, quam aliis quibuscunque in dicta curia virgæ limitandis, imponendis seu assessandis   AC ulterius de gratia nostra
speciali, certa scientia et mero motu nostris, pro nobis, heredibus et
successoribus nostris, nominamus, ordinamus, appunctuamus, et
constituimus dilectum servientem nostrum Thomam Vavasor, militem, marescallum hospitii nostri, ac Franciscum Bacon, militem,
solicitatorem nostrum generalem, fore præsentes et modernos judices curiæ nostræ virgæ prædictæ, ac Thomam Petre, armigerum,
fore modernum clericum et prothonotarium curiæ virgæ nostræ
prædictæ, ad scribenda, facienda, et irrotulanda omnia et singula
brevia et retorna brevium, manucaptiones sive ballia, billas, narrationes, responsiones, replicationes, rejunctiones, surrejunctiones, exitus, warianta attornati, veredicta, judicia, et alia processus, et recorda quæcunque ejusdem curiæ virgæ prædictæ, ac ad custodienda brevia, rotulos, et recorda quæcumque ejusdem curiæ virgæ
prædictæ.   Habendum, tenendum, et exercendum officia prædicta
cuilibet eorum respective per se, vel per sufficientem deputatum
suum sive deputatos suos, pro terminis vitarum eorum et cujuslibet eorum respective, quolibet eorum et deputato suo sacramentum præstante in dicta curia virgæ prædictæ ad officium
suum honeste et fideliter exercendum   AC ulterius de gratia
nostra speciali ac ex certa scientia et mero motu nostris concedimus pro nobis, heredibus et successoribus nostris, præfato marescallo hospitii nostri pro tempore existente, immediate post
mortem, discontinuationem, sive legalem et judicialem amotionem
prothonotarii dictæ curiæ pro tempore existente ab officio illo,
potestatem et authoritatem nominandi, ordinandi, et constituen-

or hath, or ought to have the power and authority of holding, hearing, and determining such personal actions, pleas, and plaints by any former lawful grant, custom, or prescription.   And by these presents we ordain and constitute, that the said court be a court of record, and called the Court of the Virge of the Household aforesaid, and have a common seal, and a common prison at some certain place within the virge of the household aforesaid and that the said court, and the aforesaid pleas in the said court between the persons aforesaid, to be commenced or pending, should be holden from day to day before our marshal of the household of us, our heirs and successors, for the time being, and some other fit person learned in the law (to be nominated and appointed by us, our heirs, and successors, from time to time), by these letters constituted the judges of the said court, or their lawful and sufficient deputies, at some certain place within the virge of our household aforesaid, to be from time to time appointed and assigned by our marshal and the person aforesaid, or their lawful and sufficient deputies And by these presents we likewise will and ordain that the said actions against any person being in the custody of the marshal of the marshalsea of our household aforesaid, or in any manner howsoever before the said Court of the virge aforesaid, lawfully arrested or to be arrested by any writ of the said Court of the virge, be heard and determined by the said judges or their lawful and sufficient deputies according to the laws and customs of our realm of England

Saving to us, our heirs, and successors, as well the amerciaments mentioned in a certain schedule annexed to these presents, as all others whatsoever, to be defined, imposed, or assessed in the said court of the virge

And moreover, of our special grace, certain knowledge, and mere motion, for ourselves, our heirs, and successors, we nominate, ordain, appoint, and constitute our beloved servant, Thomas Vavasor, Knight, Marshal of our Household, and Francis Bacon, Knight, our Solicitor-General, to be the presiding and present judges of our court of the virge aforesaid; and Thomas Petre, Esquire, to be the present Clerk and Prothonotary of our court of the virge aforesaid, to write, make, and enrol all and every the writs, and returns of writs, mainprizes or bails, bills, declarations, answers, replications, rejoinders, surrejoinders, issues, warrants of attorney, verdicts, judgments, and other processes and records whatsoever of the said court of the virge aforesaid, and to keep all writs, rolls, and records whatsoever of the said court of the virge aforesaid   To have, hold, and perform the offices aforesaid to each of them respectively, by themselves, or by their sufficient deputy or deputies, for the terms of their lives, and of each of them respectively, every one of them and his deputy making oath in the said court of the virge aforesaid, to perform their offices honestly and faithfully

And moreover, of our special grace, and of our certain knowledge and mere motion, we grant for ourselves, our heirs, and successors, to the aforesaid marshal of our household for the time being, immediately after the death, discontinuance, or lawful and judicial removal of the prothonotary of the said court, for the time being, from that office, the power and authority of nominating, ordaining, and constituting one other fit person, for the term of his life, from

di unam aliam idoneam personam pro termino vitæ suæ, de tem
pore in tempus, in locum et officium cujuslibet talis prothonotarii
sic mortui, discontinuati, sive amoti. AC etiam damus et concedimus pro nobis, heredibus et successoribus nostris, de eadem
gratia nostra speciali, certa scientia, et mero motu nostris, præfatis judicibus pro tempore existente plenam potestatem nominandi, ordinandi, admittendi, et constituendi quatuor personas consiliarios eruditos in lege fore consiliarios, et sex alias idoneas personas
fore attornatos in dicta curia virgæ, pro termino vitæ cujuslibet talis personæ, ad prosequenda et defendenda omnia et singula actiones, placita, et querelas in eadem curia mota sive movenda, quolibet eorum in eadem curia sacramentum præstante ad officium suum honeste et fideliter faciendum, et quod judices dictæ curiæ
virgæ pro tempore existente, immediate post mortem, discontinuationem, sive legalem et judicialem amotionem alicujus eorum consi-
liariorum et attornatorum dictæ curiæ virgæ, potestatem et auctoritatem habeant nominandi, ordinandi, admittendi, et constituendi
unam aliam idoneam personam, de tempore in tempus, in locum
et officium cujuslibet talis consiliarii sic ut præfertur mortui, discontinuati sive amoti. AC etiam damus et concedimus de gratia
nostra speciali, certa scientia et mero motu nostris, pro nobis, heredibus et successoribus nostris, marescallo hospitii nostri, heredum
et successorum nostrorum, pro tempore existente, plenam potestatem
et auctoritatem nominandi, ordinandi, admittendi, et constituendi
unam idoneam personam fore submarescallum marescaltiæ hospitii prædicti, ac custodem prisonæ curiæ prædictæ, et unam aliam
idoneam personam fore janitorem ejusdem prisonæ, ac unam aliam
personam idoneam fore proclamatorem dictæ curiæ virgæ, pro termino vitæ cujuslibet talis personæ, ad officia illa per se vel per
sufficientes deputatos suos exercenda; dicto custode prisonæ, jani-
tore, et proclamatore, et deputatis suis, sacramentum præstantibus
ad officia sua honeste et fideliter exercenda. Et quod marescallus
hospitii nostri, heredum et successorum nostrorum, pro tempore
existente, immediate post mortem, discontinuationem, sive legalem
et judicialem amotionem alicujus talis custodis prisonæ, janitoris
prisonæ, sive proclamatoris dictæ curiæ virgæ, potestatem et auctoritatem habeat nominandi, ordinandi, admittendi, et constituendi
unam aliam idoneam personam, de tempore in tempus, in locum et
officium cujuslibet talis custodis prisonæ, janitoris prisonæ, sive proclamatoris, sic ut præfertur mortui, discontinuati, sive amoti. Ita
quod in eadem curia, ad aliquod tempus, sint tantum unus prothonotarius, quatuor consiliarii, sex attornati, unus custos prisonæ,
unus janitor prisonæ, et unus proclamator dictæ curiæ virgæ prædictæ, quibus feoda in dicta curia virgæ allocata fuerint, pro causis prosequendis et defendendis, seu aliis rebus agendis in eadem
curia et prisona prædicta. Ac quod prædictus marescallus hospitii nostri, heredum et successorum nostrorum, pro tempore existente, habeat potestatem et auctoritatem faciendi, nominandi, admittendi et constituendi, de tempore in tempus, tot et tales portatores
virgarum, communiter vocatos Anglice *Marshal's Men*, fore officiarios curiæ virgæ nostræ prædictæ, heredum et successorum nostrorum, ad exequenda omnia et singula mandata, brevia, et processus
a dicta curia virgæ nostræ prædictæ emanentia, quot et quales

time to time, to the place and office of every such prothonotary so deceased, discontinued, or removed.

And also we give and grant, for ourselves, our heirs, and successors, of our said same special grace, certain knowledge, and mere motion, to the aforesaid judges, for the time being, the full power of nominating, ordaining, admitting, and constituting four persons, counsellors learned in the law, to be *counsel*, and six other fit persons to be *attornies* in the said court of the virge, for the term of the life of every such person, to prosecute and defend all and every actions, pleas, and plaints, commenced or to be commenced in the said court; each of them making oath in the said court to perform his duty honestly and faithfully: and that the judges of the said court of the virge, for the time being, immediately after the death, discontinuance, or lawful and judicial removal of any of those counsel and attornies of the said court of the virge, may have the power and authority of nominating, ordaining, admitting, and constituting one other fit person, from time to time, to the place and office of every such counsel so as aforesaid deceased, discontinued, or removed

And also we give and grant, for ourselves, our heirs, and successors, of our said special grace, certain knowledge, and mere motion, to the marshal of the household of us, our heirs and successors, for the time being, the full power and authority of nominating, ordaining, admitting, and constituting one fit person to be sub-marshal of the marshalsea of the household aforesaid and keeper of the prison of the court aforesaid, and one other fit person to be turnkey of the said prison, and one other fit person to be crier of the said court of the virge, for the term of the life of every such person, to perform those offices by themselves, or their sufficient deputies, the said keeper of the prison, turnkey, and crier, and their deputies, making oath to perform their duties honestly and faithfully.

And that the marshal of the household of us, our heirs and successors, for the time being, immediately after the death, discontinuance, or lawful and judicial removal of any such keeper of the prison, turnkey of the prison, or crier of the said court of the virge, may have the power and authority of nominating, ordaining, admitting, and constituting one other fit person, from time to time, into the place and office of every such keeper of the prison, turnkey of the prison, or crier, so as aforesaid deceased, discontinued, or removed   So that, in the same court, at any time, there be only one prothonotary, four counsel, six attornies, one keeper of the prison, one turnkey of the prison, and one crier of the said court of the virge aforesaid, to whom the fees in the said court of the virge shall be allowed for causes prosecuted and defended, or other business done in the said court and prison aforesaid.   And that the aforesaid marshal of the household of us, our heirs and successors, for the time being, may have the power and authority of making, nominating, admitting, and constituting, from time to time, so many and such *portatores virgarum* (bearers of the rods), commonly called, in English, Marshal's Men, to be the officers of the court of the virge aforesaid of us, our heirs and successors, to execute all and every the orders, writs, and processes issuing from the said court of our

præfato marescallo hospitii nostri prædicti pro tempore existente
expediens et necessarium videbitur; quolibet eorum sacramentum
præstante in dicta curia virgæ prædictæ ad officium suum honeste et
fideliter exercendum. AC ulterius ex uberiori gratia nostra speciali,
certa scientia, et mero motu nostris, concessimus et allocavimus, ac
pro nobis, heredibus et successoribus nostris, concedimus et allocamus in perpetuum præfatis judicibus, prothonotario, consiliariis, attornatis, proclamatori, custodi ac janitori prisonæ prædictæ ac quibuscunque aliis officiariis et ministris dictæ curiæ virgæ nostræ
prædictæ, et eorum cuilibet, ac successoribus eorum et cujuslibet
eorum, in eorum separalibus officiis respective, omnia et singula
talia et consimilia feoda et regarda in quadam scedula his præsentibus annexata. Et quod ipsi et eorum quilibet habeant, capiant, et
percipiant, de tempore in tempus, de omnibus et singulis personis in
dicta curia virgæ prædictæ quoquo modo negotiantibus, prædicta
separalia feoda et regarda, ut præfertur fore debita et allocata per
præsentes respective cuilibet eorum pro exercitio officiorum suorum in qualibet re, et per quemlibet eorum respective agendum,
aut ratione officiorum suorum vel alicujus eorum, et non alia neque
plura feoda seu regarda pro præmissis seu aliqua inde parcella.
VOLUMUS ulterius, quod hæ literæ nostræ patentes erunt in
omnibus firmæ, validæ et effectuales in lege, non obstante [non]
nominando aliquam concessionem de præmissis seu de aliqua inde
parcella per nos vel aliquem progenitorum seu prædecessorum nostrorum præantea factam, et non obstante male nominando, male
recitando, vel non nominando seu non recitando, vel non vere nominando præmissa vel aliquam inde parcellam· ac statuto in parliamento domini Edwardi nuper regis Angliæ primi, anno regni sui
tertio, statuto in parliamento domini Henrici nuper regis Angliæ
quarti, anno regni sui secundo; ac statuto in parliamento domini
Henrici nuper regis Angliæ sexti, anno regni sui vicesimo tertio,
editis seu provisis; seu aliquo alio statuto, lege, seu consuetudine in
contrarium inde non obstante. PRÆCIPIMUS denique omnibus
et singulis justiciariis nostris ad pacem, vicecomitibus, custodibus
gaolarum et prisonarum, balivis, constabulariis, et aliis officiariis
nostris, ac quibuscunqe subditis nostris infra virgam ubicunque &c.
tam infra libertates quam extra, quod sint dictis judicibus nostris
dictæ curiæ virgæ nostræ, et mandatis cujuslibet eorum, obedientes, et eorum cujuslibet præcepta et mandata diligenter et firmiter
perimplere et custodire, ac perimplenda et custodienda causare,
et ministris curiæ virgæ prædictæ in executione officiorum suorum
fore intendentes et auxiliantes, sub violatoris mandati nostri pœnam
periculo incurrendi. IN cujus rei testimonium, &c. teste rege apud
Westmonasterium octavo die Junii

Per breve de Privato Sigillo.

virge aforesaid, as it shall appear expedient and necessary to the aforesaid Marshal of our Household aforesaid, for the time being; every one of them making oath in the said court of the virge aforesaid, to perform his duty honestly and faithfully.

And we moreover, of our more abundant special grace, certain knowledge, and mere motion, have granted and allowed, and for ourselves, our heirs, and successors, do grant and allow for ever to the aforesaid judges, prothonotary, counsel, attornies, crier, keeper and turnkey of the prison aforesaid, and to all the other officers and ministers whatsoever of our court of the virge aforesaid, and to each of them, and to the successors of them and of each of them, in their several offices respectively, all and every such and the like fees and perquisites in a certain schedule to these presents annexed.   And that they, and every one of them, may have, take, and receive, from time to time, of all and singular the persons having any manner of business in the said court of the virge aforesaid, the aforesaid several fees and perquisites, as is above stated to be due and allowed by these presents to each of them respectively, for the exercise of their offices in any business, and by whomsoever of them respectively it is done, or in respect of their own offices, or of any one of them, and no other or greater fees or perquisites than according to the premises, or any parcel thereof

We will, moreover, that these our letters patent shall be firm, valid, and effectual in law, in all things, notwithstanding the not naming any grant touching the premises, or any part thereof, by us or any of our ancestors or predecessors heretofore made, and notwithstanding the mis-naming or mis-reciting, or not naming or not reciting, or not correctly naming the premises, or any parcel thereof. And notwithstanding the Act of Parliament of Lord Edward the First, late King of England, passed or provided in the third year of his reign, the Act of Parliament of Lord Henry the Fourth, late King of England, in the second year of his reign, and the Act of Parliament of Henry the Sixth, late King of England, in the twenty-third year of his reign, or any other statute, law, or custom to the contrary hereof.

Lastly, we command all and several our justices of the peace, sheriffs, keepers of gaols and prisons, bailiffs, constables, and other our officers, and all our subjects whatsoever, wheresoever, &c. within the virge, as well within liberties as without, that they be obedient to our said judges of our said court of the virge, and to the commands of each of them, and diligently and firmly to fulfil and keep, and cause to be fulfilled and kept, the precepts and commands of either of them, and to be aiding and assisting the officers of the court of the virge aforesaid in the execution of their offices, under the peril of incurring the punishment of a violator of our command   In witness whereof, &c   Witness the King at Westminster, the 8th day of June,

By the writ of Privy Seal.

DE SCEDULA EARUNDEM LITERARUM ANNEXA.

Feoda ordinaria Curiæ Virgæ ex parte Querentis solvenda.

	s.	d.
Pro quolibet breve sive præcepto curiæ de capias vel attachiamento, judicibus, inter eos equaliter dividendum	..	xij
Pro scribendo cujuslibet eorundem brevium, et cujuslibet alias et pluries inde, prothonotario	..	ij
Pro feodo portatoris virgæ pro executione cujuslibet talis brevis		xvj
Pro feodo attornati super quamlibet narrationem exitus, venire facias, et habeas corpora juratorum		xx
Pro warranto attornati, prothonotario		iiij
Pro faciendo cujuslibet narrationis et ingrossatione inde, clericis suis		xij
Pro feodo curiæ super qualibet narratione exitus et cognitione satisfactionis, judicibus, inter eos equaliter dividendum		xvj
Pro annotatione et affilatione cujuslibet narrationis et intratione cujuslibet satisfactionis, prothonotario		viij
Pro feodo prothonotarii pro intratione cujuslibet exitus, et cujuslibet veredicti et judicii		xij
Pro feodo proclamatoris super quolibet exitu		iiij
Pro quolibet breve de venire facias, habeas corpora, distringas juratores, et breve de executione, et quolibet alio breve, judicibus, inter eos equaliter dividendum		xx
Pro scribendo cujuslibet eorum, prothonotario		iiij
Pro retorno cujuslibet eorum, prothonotario	..	xij
Pro executione cujuslibet venire facias, portatori virgæ	ij	..
Pro executione cujuslibet habeas corpora et distringas juratores, portatori virgæ		xviij
Pro feodo proclamatoris pro summonitione juratorum		vj
Pro quolibet veredicto et judicio superinde, judicibus, inter eos dividendum	iiij	iiij
Pro custodiendo cujuslibet juratæ marescallo, portatori virgæ	..	xij
Pro quolibet feodo consiliarii ad legem	v	.
Pro feodo proclamatoris pro proclamatione cujuslibet juratæ	.	vj
Pro qualibet billa custagii, clerico attornato	.	viij

Feoda ordinaria ex parte Defendentis solvenda

Pro feodo militis marescalli super qualibet arresto	iiij	iiij
Pro feodo prothonotarii superinde		x
Pro feodo custodis prisonæ superinde		iiij
Pro feodo janitoris prisonæ superinde		iiij

THE SCHEDULE ANNEXED TO THE SAID LETTERS PATENT.

The Ordinary Fees of the Court of the Virge, to be paid by the Plaintiff.

	l.	s	d
For every writ or precept of court, of capias, or attachment, to the judges, to be equally divided between them	0	1	0
For writing each of the said writs, and of every alias and pluries thereon, to the prothonotary	0	0	2
For officer's fee for executing every such writ	0	1	4
For attorney's fee on every declaration of issue, venire facias, and habeas corpora juratorum	0	1	8
For warrant of attorney, to the prothonotary	0	0	4
For drawing every declaration and engrossing thereof, to his clerks	0	1	0
For court fee, on every declaration of issue, and acknowledgment of satisfaction, to the judges, to be equally divided between them	0	1	4
For filling up and filing every declaration and entering every satisfaction, to the prothonotary	0	0	8
For the prothonotary's fee for entering every issue, and every verdict and judgment	0	1	0
For the crier's fee on every issue	0	0	4
For every writ of venire facias, habeas corpora, distringas juratores and writ of execution, and every other writ, to the judges, to be equally divided between them	0	1	8
For writing each of them, to the prothonotary	0	0	4
For the return of each of the said writs, to the prothonotary	0	1	0
For the execution of each venire facias, to the officer	0	2	0
For the execution of each habeas corpora and distringas juratores, to the officer	0	1	6
For the crier's fee for summoning the jurors	0	0	6
For every verdict and judgment thereon, to the judges, to be divided between them	0	3	4
For keeping by the marshal of every jurat, to the officer	0	1	0
For counsel's fee	0	5	0
For crier's fee, for calling each jurat	0	0	6
For every bill of costs, to the attorney's clerk	0	0	8

Ordinary Fees to be paid by the Defendant

	l.	s	d
For knight-marshal's fee on every arrest	0	3	4
For prothonotary's fee thereon	0	0	10
For the keeper of the prison's fee thereon	0	0	4
For turnkey's fee thereon	0	0	4

Pro qualibet ballia in curia, et pro qualibet licentia
loquendi, judicibus, inter eos dividendum .... xvj
Pro intratione cujuslibet ballii, prothonotario v
Pro feodo custodiæ prisonio superinde .... j
Pro feodo attornati super qualibet h. lo. exitu, venire
facias, et habeas corpora juratorum xx
Pro copia cujuslibet narrationis, prothonotario .... xij
Pro qualibet exitu ex parte defendentis, judicibus,
inter eos dividendum .... xvj
Pro quolibet warranto attornati pro defendente super-
inde, prothonotario ... . iiij

Feoda accidentia

Pro qualibet regula curiæ, prothonotario ... ... iiij
Pro tractatione cujuslibet narrationis, placiti, replicationis, rejunctionis, surrejunctionis, et morationis in
lege, pro quolibet folio, clericis prothonotarii .... .. iiij
Pro irrotulatione cujuslibet folii inde, prothonotario .. ·. viij
Pro quolibet breve de subpœna, judicibus, inter eos
dividendum .... ij ..
Pro scribendo inde, et cujuslibet decem tales, et pro
quolibet retraxit, prothonotario .... vj
Pro allocatione cujuslibet brevis de procedendo, judicibus, inter eos dividendum xx
Pro intratione inde ac cujuslibet inde continuationis ac
assignationis obligationis comparentiæ de recordo,
prothonotario .... viij
Pro executione cujuslibet brevis de scire facias, pro-
clamatori .... xij
Pro copia cujuslibet recordi pro quolibet folio inde,
prothonotario .... iiij
Pro feodo proclamatoris super quolibet nonpros .... .. iiij
Pro quolibet venire facias, habeas corpora, seu distrin-
gas juratores per proviso judicibus, inter eos divi-
dendum xx
Pro scribendo inde, prothonotario ... . iiij
Pro executione inde, proclamatori .. . . ij ..
Pro retorno inde, prothonotario .. . . xij
Pro custodiendo juratæ inde, proclamatori ....
Pro quolibet nonpros, ac qualibet allocatione cujus-
libet brevis de habeas corpora, brevis de privile-
gio, supersedeas, et cujuslibet alii talis brevis, judicibus, inter eos dividendum xx
Pro intratione cujuslibet eorum de recordo, prothono
tario .... viij
Pro retorno cujuslibet talis brevis, judicibus, inter eos
dividendum .. ·· .... xvj
Pro scribendo retornum inde, pro qualibet actione,
prothonotario .... xij
Pro allocatione cujuslibet brevis de errore, judicibus,
inter eos dividendum .... xx ·

For every bail in court, and for every imparlance, to the judges, to be divided between them	0	1	4
For entering every bail, to the prothonotary	0	0	5
For the fee of the keeper of the prison thereon · · ··	0	0	1
For attorney's fee on every imparlance, issue, venire facias, and habeas corpora juratorum	0	1	8
For copy of every declaration, to the prothonotary ····	0	1	0
For every issue on the part of the defendant, to the judges, to be divided between them	0	1	4
For every warrant of attorney for defendant thereon, to the prothonotary	0	0	4

Extra Costs

For every rule of court, to the prothonotary ···· ···	0	0	4
For drawing every declaration, plea, replication, rejoinder, surrejoinder, and demurrer, for every folio, to the prothonotary's clerks ···· .. .. ···	0	0	4
For enrolling every folio thereof, to the prothonotary ··	0	0	8
For every writ of subpœna, to the judges, to be divided between them · ··· .. .. ·	0	2	0
For writing thereof and of every decem tales, and for every retraxit, to the prothonotary	0	0	6
For the allowance of every writ of procedendo, to the judges, to be divided between them · · ··· ···	0	1	8
For entry thereof, and of every continuance thereof, and assignment of the bond of appearance of record, to the prothonotary	0	0	8
For the executing of every writ of scire facias, to the crier ..... ·· · ···· ·· · · · ·············	0	1	0
For copy of every record, for every folio thereof, to the prothonotary ...... · · · · .. ··	0	0	4
For crier's fee on every nonpros ·· ··	0	0	4
For every venire facias, habeas corpora, or distringas juratores by proviso, to the judges, to be divided between them · · .... · · ··	0	1	8
For writing thereof, to the prothonotary	0	0	4
For the execution thereof, to the crier....	0	2	0
For the return thereof, to the prothonotary ·· ····	0	1	0
For keeping the jurat thereof, to the crier··· · ··· ··	0	1	0
For every nonpros, and for every allowance of every writ of habeas corpora, writ of privilege, supersedeas, and every other such writ, to the judges, to be divided between them ··· .... · · ·· ··· ····	0	1	8
For entry of every one of them of record, to the prothonotary .... · ·· ····	0	0	8
For the return of every such writ, to the judges, to be divided between them ··· .. ···· ··· .. ····	0	1	4
For writing the return thereof, for every action, to the prothonotary ·· ···· ·· ..... · · ··	0	1	0
For the allowance of every writ of error, to the judges, to be divided between them · ··· · · ·· ····	1	0	0

Pro intratione inde, prothonotario · ·   ·   ij   ·

Pro quolibet breve de supersedeas · · ····· ·   ij   vj

Pro certificatione recordi, pro quolibet rotulo perga-
mem, et pro scribendo inde, prothonotario · · ·   vj   viij

Pro feodo correctionis cujuslibet prisonaru in executione, custodi prisonæ ·   · ·   ··· ···   ·   xviij

Pro feodo clerici prothonotarii superinde   ·· ·   xviij

Pro feodo janitoris prisonæ superinde   ··· ·   xvj

Pro feodo clerici prothonotarii pro intratione causæ
onerationis et exonerationis cujuslibet prisonarii ··   ··   iiij

Pro qualibet obligatione comparentiæ prisonaru,
eidem clerico   ··· ··   ··   ·   ·   ··   vj

Amerciamenta Domino Regi

De quolibet defendente qui dedicit factum suum ····   ··   xij

De quolibet querente pro falso clamore amerciandum   vj

De quolibet defendente in misericordia ·   · ·····   xij

De qualibet parte fore capta per judicium curiæ, pro
fine regis ·· ··· ·   ·   ··   ·   ·   ʌ ʌ   xij

---

22 *JAC* I

REX omnibus ad quos, &c salutem. CUM nos per literas nos
tras patentes, gerentes datum apud Westmonasterium octavo die
Junii, anno regni nostri Angliæ, Franciæ, et Hiberniæ nono, ac
Scotiæ quadragesimo quarto, pro considerationibus in eisdem literis
nostris patentibus specificatis, fecerimus, creaverimus, ordinaveri
mus, et constituerimus quandam curiam pro virga hospitii nostri,
heredum et successorum nostrorum, pro administratione justitiæ
omnibus et singulis personis de Hospitio nostro tunc non existenti
bus, vel quæ non essent de Hospitio nostro, heredum et successorum
nostrorum infra virgam illam de tempore in tempus existentibus,
venientibus, confluentibus, negotiantibus, commorantibus, contrahentibus, seu quoquo modo intromittentibus, et pro terminatione
omnium et omnimodorum actionum, placitorum, et querelarum
personalium deinceps inter personas prædictas tunc motorum seu
movendorum, dependentium seu dependendorum in omnibus parochiis, villis, hamletis, liberiatibus, franchesiis, et locis infra virgam
prædictam hospitii nostri, heredum et successorum nostrorum,
limitatis, consuetis, sive pertinentibus, ac in quibuscunque civitatibus et locis infra præcincta virgæ hujusmodi hospitii nostri, ubi
nos tunc eramus, vel ubicunque nos, heredes, et successores nostri
essemus, viremus, transiremus, vel remanaremus, infra regnum

For the entry thereof, to the prothonotary	0	2	0
For every writ of supersedeas	0	2	6
For certificate of record, for every roll of parchment, and for writing thereof, to the prothonotary	0	6	8
For fee of safe custody of every prisoner in execution, to the keeper of the prison	0	1	6
For the prothonotary's clerk's fee thereon	0	1	6
For the turnkey's fee thereon	0	1	4
For the prothonotary's clerk's fee for entry of every cause of charge and discharge of every prisoner	0	0	4
For every bond for prisoner's maintenance, to the prothonotary's clerk	0	0	6

Amerciaments to our Lord the King.

Of every defendant who denies his own deed	0	1	0
Of every plaintiff to be fined for a false claim	0	0	6
Of every defendant in mercy	0	1	0
Of each party to be taken by judgment of the court for the king's fine	0	1	0

22 JAMES I.

JAMES the First, by the grace of God, of England, Scotland, France, and Ireland, King, &c to all to whom these letters shall come, greeting

Whereas we did, by our letters patent, bearing date at Westminster, the eighth day of June, in the ninth year of our reign of England, France, and Ireland, and the forty-fourth of Scotland, for the considerations in our said letters patent specified, make, create, ordain, and constitute a certain court for the virge of the household of us, our heirs and successors, for the administration of justice to all and singular the persons then not being of our household, or who might not be of the household of us, our heirs and successors, within that virge from time to time being, coming, resorting, carrying on business, sojourning, contracting, or in any manner entering; and for the determination of all and all manner of personal actions, pleas, and plaints hereafter between the aforesaid persons then moved or to be moved, pending or to be pending in all parishes, towns, hamlets liberties, franchises and places within the aforesaid virge of the household of us, our heirs and successors limited, accustomed or pertaining, and in whatsoever cities and places within the precincts of the said virge of our household, where we then were, or wherever we, our heirs and successors

nostrum Angliæ, exceptis prout in eisdem literis patentibus excipitur. Ac per easdem literas nostras patentes eandem curiam fore curiam de recordo et appellari Curiam Virgæ Hospitii prædicti, ac habere commune sigillum, et communem prisonam, et coram marescallo hospitii nostri heredum et successorum nostrorum pro tempore existente, et aliqua alia persona habili et erudita in lege, per nos, heredes et successores nostros de tempore in tempus nominandis, de die in diem tenendam, ordinaverimus et constituerimus Et quod virtute earundem literarum nostrarum patentium diversi officiarii pro serviciis ejusdem curiæ necessarii et idonei de tempore in tempus eligentur, et ad officia illa respective bene et fideliter exequenda sacramenta corporalia respective præstarent necnon multas alias potestates et authoritates tam judicibus curiæ illius quam officiariis prædictis ibidem attendendas per prædictas literas nostras patentes dederimus et concesserimus prout per easdem literas nostras patentes plenius liquet et apparet Cumque nobis jam nuper satis constat quod in erectione et institutione curiæ prædictæ aliqui defectus præter expectationem nostram irrepserunt, per quos subditi nostri iterum conquerentes non possint in sectis suis tempestiva illa remedia habere quæ nos in fundatione ejusdem curiæ illis gratiose intendebamus SCIATIS igitur quod nos pro diversis bonis causis et considerationibus nos ad præsens specialiter movendis, revocavimus, cassavimus, et annihilavimus, et per præsentes pro nobis, heredibus et successoribus nostris, revocamus, cassamus et annihilamus prædictas literas nostras patentes gerentes datum prædicto octavo die Junii anno regni nostri Angliæ nono superdicto. Necnon easdem literas nostras patentes, et omnia in eisdem concessa, contenta, vel specificata, vacua, irritata, frustrata et determinata fore et esse, declaramus et adjudicamus per præsentes In cujus rei, &c. T. R. apud Westmonasterium, quartodecimo die Februarii

Per breve de Privato Sigillo

might be, come, pass through, or remain within our kingdom of England, except as in the said letters patent is excepted   And we did, by our said letters patent, ordain and constitute the same court to be a court of record, and to be called The Court of the Virge of the Household aforesaid, and to have a common seal and common prison, and be holden from day to day before the Marshal of the Household of us, our heirs and successors for the time being, and some other fit person and learned in the law, to be from time to time nominated by us, our heirs and successors   And that by virtue of our said letters patent, divers officers were to be elected from time to time, necessary and fit for the different duties of the said Court, and they were respectively to take a corporal oath, well and faithfully to perform their respective offices.   We did also, by our aforesaid letters patent, give and grant many other powers and authorities to be observed as well by the judges of that court as by the officers aforesaid, as by the same our letters patent is evident and manifest   And whereas it is already sufficiently apparent unto us, that in the erection and institution of the court aforesaid some defects, contrary to our expectation, have crept in, by which our subjects are complaining that they cannot obtain in their suits those salutary remedies, which in the foundation of the said court we graciously intended for them   KNOW ye, therefore, that we, for divers good causes and considerations us to these presents specially moving, have revoked. cancelled, and annulled, and by these presents for us, our heirs and successors, do revoke, cancel, and annul our aforesaid letters patent, bearing date on the aforesaid eighth day of June, in the aforesaid ninth year of our reign of England   And also by these presents we do declare and adjudge our said letters patent, and all things granted, contained, or specified therein to become and to be void, of no avail, null and determined   In witness whereof, &c.   Witness the king, at Westminster, the fourteenth day of February

By the writ of Privy Seal.

22 *JAC.* 1.

REX omnibus ad quos, &c. salutem   CUM nobis expediens et necessarium videtur, quod omnes et singuli subditi nostri et personæ quæcunque infra virgam hospitii nostri residentes, inhabitantes, confluentes, contrahentes, negotiantes, seu existentes, in omnibus et omnimodis actionibus, placitis, et querelis suis personalibus celeriorem haberent justitiam, eo quod ipsi tam in negotiis et servitiis nostris quam in occasionibus officiariorum et famulorum hospitii nostri multo magis ac sæpius quam alii subditi nostri in remotioribus partibus Angliæ commorantes, occupantur et implicantur. CUMQUE Curia Marescalciæ Hospitii Regum Angliæ sit antiqua curia, ordinata pro bona conservatione et custodia pacis infra hospitium regum Angliæ ac infra virgam ejusdem hospitii, ac pro determinatione diversarum actionum et querelarum personalium infra hospitium et virgam prædictam emergentium, prout per leges et statuta hujus regni nostri Angliæ liquet et apparet   Ac nihilominus, prædicti subditi nostri infra præcincta virgæ prædictæ inhabitantes, confluentes aut commorantes, non autem de hospitio nostro existentes, in eadem curia nostra marescalciæ hospitii nostri, in legitimis actionibus et querelis suis aliquam certam prosecutionem ob dubia quædam nuper suborta jurisdictionem curiæ illius concernentia, non habuerunt   CUMQUE insuper ad notitiam nostram pervenerit, quod nonnulli tam servitorum et famulorum hospitii nostri prædicti, quam aliorum subditorum nostrorum infra virgam ejusdem hospitii commorantium, de feodis et expensis curiæ prædictæ ab ipsis modo receptis, licet ibidem de antiquo debitis et usitatis, conquerantur· SCIATIS igitur, quod nos, ex cura nostra regia festinum in hac parte remedium adhiberi cupientes, ut omnia hospitium nostrum concernentia pro communi bono et relevamine omnium inhabitantium et aliorum contrahentium et confluentium infra virgam ejusdem melius tractentur et expediantur, de gratia nostra speciali, ac ex certa scientia et mero motu nostris, fecimus, creavimus, ereximus, ordinavimus, et constituimus, ac per præsentes, pro nobis, heredibus et successoribus nostris, facimus, creamus, erigimus, ordinamus, et constituimus aliam curiam pro virga hospitii nostri, heredum et successorum nostrorum, pro administratione justitiæ omnibus et singulis personis infra virgam hospitii nostri, heredum vel successorum nostrorum, de tempore in tempus existentibus, venientibus, confluentibus, negotiantibus, commorantibus, contrahentibus, sive quoquo modo intromittentibus, in omnibus locis infra virgam prædictam hospitii nostri, heredum et successorum nostrorum, existentibus, ac in quibuscunque comitatibus et locis infra præcincta virgæ hujusmodi hospitii nostri, heredum vel successorum nostrorum, ubi nunc sumus, vel ubicunque aliquo tempore vel aliquibus temporibus, ac toties quoties imposterum nos, heredes et successores nostri erimus, transibimus vel remanebimus infra hoc regnum nostrum Angliæ,

22 JAMES I

JAMES, &c, to all to whom, &c. greeting —Whereas, it appears unto us expedient and necessary, that all and singular our subjects and persons whatsoever residing, inhabiting, resorting, contracting, trafficking or being within the virge of our household, should have more speedy justice in all and all manner of their personal actions, pleas, and plaints, because they are much more and more frequently occupied and engaged, is well in our business and service as in the emergencies of our officers and domestics, than other our subjects residing in more remote parts of England

And whereas the Court of the Marshalsea of the Household of the kings of England is an ancient Court, constituted for the good preservation and keeping of the peace within the household of the kings of England, and within the virge of the said household, and for determining divers personal actions and plaints arising within the household and virge aforesaid, as by the laws and statutes of this our realm of England is clear and evident And, nevertheless, our subjects aforesaid, inhabiting, resorting, or tarrying within the precincts of the virge aforesaid, but not being of our household, have had no determinate prosecution of their lawful actions and plaints in our said court of the Marshalsea of our household, on account of certain doubts which have lately arisen concerning the jurisdiction of that court. And whereas, it hath also come to our knowledge, that some, as well of the servants and domestics of our household aforesaid, as of other our subjects residing within the virge of the said household, complain of the fees and expenses of the court aforesaid by them now received, although antiently there due and accustomed Know ye, therefore, that we, of our royal care, being desirous that a speedy remedy in this behalf should be applied, so that all things concerning our household may be better managed and facilitated for the common good, and for the relief of all persons inhabiting, and of others contracting and resorting within the virge of the said [household]—We of our special grace, and of our certain knowledge and mere motion, have made, created, erected, ordained, and constituted, and by these presents, for us, our heirs, and successors, do make, create, erect, ordain, and constitute another court for the virge of the household of us, our heirs and successors, for the administration of justice to all and every the persons from time to time being, coming, resorting, trafficking, sojourning, contracting, or in any manner entering within the virge of the household of us, our heirs or successors, in all places being within the aforesaid virge of the household of us, our heirs and successors; and in all counties and places whatsoever within the precincts of the said virge of the household of us, our heirs and successors, where we now are, or wheresoever, at any time or times, and as often as, hereafter we, our heirs, and successors shall be, pass through, or remain within this our kingdom of

(exceptis tantum civitatibus, burgis, villis, et aliis libertatibus
et franchesiis, in quibus alii subditi nostri sive aliquis subditus
noster habent seu habet vel habere debent vel debet potestatem
et authoritatem audiendi et terminandi talia actiones, placita, et querelas personales, per aliquam priorem legalem concessionem, consuetudinem, vel præscriptionem, qualia in prædicta
curia facta et erecta per has literas nostras patentes terminari valeant); et curiam illam de cætero erig. et constitui volumus per
præsentes. VOLUMUS etiam, ac per præsentes pro nobis, heredibus et successoribus nostris, concedimus, ordinamus et constituimus, quod curia illa sit appellata et nuncupata Curia virgæ
hospitii domini regis, et sic curia de recordo coram senescallo
hospitii nostri, heredum et successorum nostrorum pro tempore existente, vel ejus deputato sufficiente, et in vacatione ejusdem officii
senescalli hospitii prædicti coram marescallo ejusdem hospitii pro
tempore existente, vel deputato suo sufficiente, de die in diem qualibet septimana per annum, tenenda et continuanda, excepta die
Dominica et diebus festis Natalis Domini, Circumcisionis Domini,
Epiphaniæ, Purificationis et Annunciationis Beatæ Mariæ Virginis,
Parasceves, Ascensionis Domini, Sancti Michaelis Archangeli, et
Omnium Sanctorum. Et quod idem, senescallus hospitii prædicti
vel ejus deputatus, et in vacatione officii illius marescallus dicti
hospitii vel ejus deputatus, pro tempore existente, habeant et habebunt plenam potestatem et authoritatem, de tempore in tempus,
audiendi et terminandi in dicta curia per querelam in eadem curia
levandam, omnes et omnimodas actiones, debita, computationes
conventiones, contractus, transgressiones vi et armis seu aliter in
contemptu nostri, heredum et successorum nostrorum factas vel
fiendas, transgressiones super casum, conventiones, detentiones, con-
temptus, deceptiones, et alias res, actiones et placita quæcunque
personalia, infra virgam hospitii prædicti seu limittas vel præcincta ejusdem, exceptis præexceptis, quovismodo emergentia
sive emergenda, contingentia sive contingenda, exceptis omnibus
hujusmodi actionibus, placitis, et querelis personalibus, in quibus
tam querens vel querentes quam defendens vel defendentes sint
vel fuerint, sit vel fuerit de hospitio nostro, heredum vel successorum nostrorum, et omnibus aliis actionibus de transgressionibus
vi et armis, in quibus vel querens vel defendens sit vel fuerit de
hospitio prædicto. Et quod idem senescallus hospitii prædicti vel
ejus deputatus, et in vacatione officii illius marescallus dicti hospitii vel ejus deputatus pro tempore existente, super hujusmodi
querimoniis, placitis, querelis et actionibus, habeant et habebunt
potestatem et authoritatem personas defendentes, versus quas hujusmodi querelæ, placita, sive actiones in prædicta curia virgæ
hospitii levari vel moveri contigerint, in placitum deducere per
summonitiones, attachiamenta et districtiones, secundum consuetudinem in curia prædicta marescalciæ hospitii prædicti antehac
usitatam, vel per leges et consuetudines regni nostri Angliæ approbatam, portatoribus virgarum hospitii prædicti et aliis ministris
curiæ illius per senescallum hospitii prædicti vel ejus deputatum,
et in vacatione officii illius per marescallum dicti hospitii vel ejus
deputatum pro tempore existente, deputandis, vel eorum alicui vel
aliquibus, dirigenda. Et pro defectu catallorum et terrarum hu-

England, (except only the cities, boroughs, towns, and other liberties and franchises in which any our subjects or subject have or
hath, or ought to have the power and authority of hearing and determining such personal actions, pleas, and plaints by any former lawful grant, custom, or prescription, as can be determined in the court
aforesaid, made and erected by these our letters patent), and we
will, by these presents, that the said court from henceforth be erected and constituted.

We also will, and we do by these presents, for us, our heirs, and
successors, grant, ordain, and constitute, that the said court be
called and named the court of the virge of the household of the
lord the king, and so a court of record before the steward of the
household of us, our heirs, and successors, for the time being, or
his sufficient deputy, and in the vacancy of the said office of the
steward of the household aforesaid, before the marshal of the said
household for the time being, or his sufficient deputy, to be holden
and continued from day to day, every week throughout the year,
excepting the Lord's-day and Christmas-day, the day of the Circumcision of our Lord, the Epiphany, the Purification and Annunciation of the blessed Virgin Mary, Good Friday, the Ascension
of our Lord, St Michael the Archangel, and the day of All Saints
And that the said, the steward of the household aforesaid, or his deputy, and in the vacancy of that office the marshal of the said household, or his deputy, for the time being, may and shall have full power
and authority, from time to time, of hearing and determining in the
said court, by plaint, to be levied in the said court, all and all manner of actions, debts, accounts, covenants, contracts, trespasses, *vi et
armis*, or otherwise committed or to be committed in contempt of
us, our heirs and successors, trespasses on the case, covenants, de-
tainers, contempts, frauds, and other matters, personal actions and
pleas whatsoever, within the virge of the household aforesaid, or the
limits or precincts of the same, except as before excepted, in any
manner arising or to arise, happening or to happen, except all such
personal actions, pleas and plaints, in which, as well the plaintiff or
plaintiffs, as the defendant or defendants, may be or have been, is or
hath been of the household of us, our heirs or successors, and all other
actions of trespasses *vi et armis*, in which either the plaintiff or defendant may be or hath been of the household aforesaid   And that the
said steward of the household aforesaid, or his deputy, and in the vacancy of that office, the marshal of the said household, or his deputy
for the time being, upon such complaints, pleas, plaints, and actions,
may and shall have power and authority of bringing into plea, by
summonses, attachments, and distresses, (to be directed to the bearers
of the rods of the household aforesaid and the other officers of the
said court, to be named by the steward of the household aforesaid,
or his deputy, and in the vacancy of that office, by the marshal of
the said household, or his deputy, for the time being, or to any or
either of them), the persons of the defendants, against whom such
plaints, pleas, or actions shall happen to be levied or moved in
the aforesaid court of the virge of the household, according to the
custom heretofore used in the aforesaid court of the marshalsea of the
household aforesaid, or sanctioned by the laws and customs of our
realm of England   And for deficiency of chattles and lands of such

jusmodi defendentium infra virgam prædictam, libertates, limittas vel præcincta ejusdem (exceptis præexceptis), ubi sive per quæ summoniri, attachiari, vel distringi possint, per attachiamenta aut captionem corporum suorum, et actiones, querelas et placita superdicta omnia et singula (exceptis in casibus præexceptis) separatim audire et determinare, et per consimilia processus, judicia, et executiones judiciorum deducere et terminare, per quæ et in tam amplis modo et forma prout consimilia placita in prædicta antiqua curia marescaltiæ hospitii prædicti, vel per leges et consuetudines regni nostri Angliæ, deducuntur et terminantur · Executionesque processuum et judiciorum per prædictos portatores virgæ hospitii prædicti, et alios ministros prædictos fiant et habeantur. SALVIS nobis, heredibus et successoribus nostris, finibus et amerciamentis inde provenientibus, tam in quadam schedula præsentibus annexa mentionatis, quam aliis quibuscunque in dicta curia virgæ hospitii prædicti limitandis, imponendis, taxandis seu assidendis VOLUMUS etiam, ac per præsentes pro nobis, heredibus et successoribus nostris, concedimus, ordinamus et constituimus, quod sit in perpetuum in curia prædicta commune sigillum, ab aliis sigillis curiarum nostrarum discrepans et diversum, pro brevibus, attachiamentis, et aliis processubus curiæ illius sigillandis, et pro causis et negotiis ejusdem curiæ quibuscunque peragendis et expediendis, deserviturum

Et quod sit de cætero infra virgam prædictam, libertates et præcincta ejusdem, una prisona sive gaola pro conservatione, retentione, et salva custodia omnium et singulorum prisonariorum, infra præcincta sive jurisdictionem curiæ prædictæ attachiatorum seu attachiandorum pro quacunque causa, quæ in curia prædicta audiri vel determinari poterit, ibidem moraturi donec et quousque legitimo modo deliberantur

Et pro meliori executione prædictæ voluntatis et concessionis nostræ, assignavimus, nominavimus, constituimus et fecimus, ac per præsentes pro nobis, heredibus et successoribus nostris, assignamus, nominamus, constituimus et facimus prædilectum et perquam fidelem consanguineum et consiliarium nostrum, Jacobum Marchionem Hamilton, modo senescallum hospitii nostri, fore et esse primum et modernum unicum judicem curiæ nostræ virgæ prædictæ per se vel per sufficientem deputatum suum satis habilem et eruditum in lege exequendum Assignavimus etiam ac per præsentes pro nobis, heredibus et successoribus nostris, assignamus, ordinamus, et constituimus prædilectum et fidelem servientem nostrum Edwardum Zouch, militem, modo marescallum hospitii nostri, necnon marescallum hospitii nostri, heredum et successorum nostrorum pro tempore existente, fore et esse assistentem senescallo hospitii nostri, heredum et successorum nostrorum, pro tempore existente, in curia prædicta. Quiquidem assistens cum hujusmodi judice locum assidendi in curia prædicta et consulendi habeat, non autem ullam potestatem dirigendi vel adjudicandi in aliquibus causis ibidem dependentibus vel dependendis.

Assignavimus etiam, ac per præsentes pro nobis, heredibus, et successoribus nostris, assignamus, constituimus, et ordinamus quod in omnibus temporibus futuris, quandocunque et quotiescunque prædictum officium senescalli hospitii nostri vacare con-

defendants within the virge aforesaid, the liberties, limits or precincts
of the same, (except as before excepted), where or by which they
may be summoned, attached, or distrained by attachment or
capias; and all and singular the actions, plaints and pleas aforesaid, (except in the cases before excepted), separately to hear and
determine, and to bring to an end and terminate by the like processes, judgments, and executions of judgments, by which, and in
as ample manner and form as the like pleas in the aforesaid ancient
court of the marshalsea of the household aforesaid, or by the laws
and customs of our realm of England, are brought to an end and
terminated   And the executions of the processes and judgments,
be done and had by the aforesaid bearers of the rod of the virge
of the household aforesaid, and the other officers aforesaid

Saving to us, our heirs, and successors, as well the fines and
amerciaments thereby arising, mentioned in a certain schedule annexed to these presents, as all others whatsoever, to be defined,
imposed, taxed, or assessed in the said court of the virge of the
household aforesaid.

We also will, and we do by these presents, for us, our heirs and
successors grant, ordain, and constitute, that there be for ever in
the court aforesaid, a common seal, varying and differing from
other seals of our courts, to be used for sealing the writs, attachments, and other processes of the same court, and for performing and
dispatching all causes and business whatsoever of the said court.

And that there be from henceforth, within the virge aforesaid,
the liberties and precincts of the same, one prison or gaol, for the
keeping, retaining, and safe custody of all and singular the prisoners within the precincts or jurisdiction of the court aforesaid, attached or to be attached for any cause whatsoever, which shall be
heard or determined in the court aforesaid, there to be detained
until they shall be lawfully discharged.

And for the better execution of our aforesaid will and grant,
we have appointed, nominated, constituted, and made, and by these
presents we do, for us, our heirs and successors, appoint, nominate,
constitute and make our well beloved and very faithful cousin and
counsellor, James, Marquis of Hamilton, now steward of our
household, to become and be the first and present sole judge of
our court of the virge aforesaid, to act by himself or by his sufficient deputy, well skilled and learned in the law.

We have also appointed, and we do by these presents, for us, our
heirs and successors, appoint, ordain and constitute, our well beloved and faithful servant Sir Edward Zouch, Knight, now marshal of our household, and also the marshal of the household of us,
our heirs and successors, for the time being, to become and be
assisting to the steward of the household of us, our heirs and successors, for the time being, in the court aforesaid   which said as-
sistant may sit with and advise such judge, in the court aforesaid,
but not to have power of ruling or giving judgment in any causes
there pending or to be pending.

We have also appointed, and we do by these presents for us, our
heirs and successors, appoint, constitute and ordain, that in all future times, whensoever and as oftensoever as the aforesaid office
of steward of our household shall happen to be vacant, the afore-

tigerit, prædictus Edwardus Zouch, miles, marescallus hospitii nostri prædicti, et marescallus ejusdem hospitii nostri prædicti, heredum et successorum nostrorum pro tempore existente, sit et erit unicus judex curiæ prædictæ per se vel per sufficientem deputatum suum satis habilem et eruditum in lege, ad omnia et omnimoda placita, processus, et causas prædictas, tempore vacationis officii senescalli hospitii prædicti accidentia, dependentia, sive emergentia, audiendum et terminandum.

Assignavimus etiam, ac per præsentes, pro nobis heredibus et successoribus nostris, assignamus, ordinamus, et constituimus Johannem Hooker, armigerum, fore primum et modernum prothonotarium curiæ virgæ prædictæ, ad scribendum, faciendum et irrotulandum omnia et singula brevia, retornas brevium, manucaptiones sive ballia, bilias, narrationes, responsiones, replicationes, rejunctiones, surrejunctiones, exitus, warranta attornati, veredicta, judicia, et alia processus et recorda quæcunque ejusdem curiæ virgæ prædictæ, et ad custodiendum brevia, rotulos, et recorda quæcunque ejusdem curiæ virgæ prædictæ. Habendum, tenendum, exercendum, et exequendum dictum officium prothonotarii curiæ virgæ prædictæ, eidem Johanni Hooker, per se, vel per sufficientem deputatum suum sive deputatos suos sufficientes, durante vita naturali ejusdem Johannis. VOLUMUS etiam, ac per præsentes, pro nobis, heredibus et successoribus nostris, ordinamus et constituimus, quod præfatus Jacobus Marchio Hamilton, modo senescallus hospitii nostri prædicti et senescallus hospitii nostri, heredum et successorum nostrorum, pro tempore existente, qui per præsentes judices curiæ virgæ prædictæ appunctuantur, necnon prædictus Edwardus Zouch, miles, marescallus hospitii nostri, et marescallus hospitii nostri, heredum et successorum nostrorum, pro tempore existente, qui, durante aliqua vacatione officii senescalli hospitii prædicti similiter per præsentes judices ejusdem hospitii prædicti respective appunctuantur; antequam ad officium illud exequendum admittantur, vel eorum aliquis respective admittatur, coram cancellario Angliæ vel custode magni sigilli Angliæ, et coram marescallo Angliæ, camerario hospitii regis, thesaurario et contrarotulatori hospitii nostri prædicti, heredum vel successorum nostrorum, vel coram eorum aliquo vel aliquibus, in loco publico, ubi curia prædicta tunc respective tenebitur, sacramentum corporale super sancta Dei evangelia, ad officium illud judicis curiæ virgæ prædictæ recte, bene, juste, et fideliter exequendum, et ad plenam et celerem justitiam populo suo ibidem litiganti et litigando, juxta eorum sanam discretionem et meliorem scientiam, intellectum, et judicium suum, administrandum, et omnia alia officio judicis prædicti in aliquo spectantia vel pertinentia, observandum, præstabunt, et quilibet eorum respective præstabit. QUARE VOLUMUS, ac per præsentes pro nobis, heredibus et successoribus nostris, damus et concedimus cancellario Angliæ, custodi magni sigilli Angliæ, marescallo Angliæ, camerario hospitii regis, thesaurario et contrarotulatorio hospitii prædicti, tam præsentibus quam futuris, et quibuslibet et cuilibet eorum pro tempore existente, vel temporibus existentibus, plenam potestatem et auctoritatem dandi et administrandi sacramentum corporale super sancta Dei evangelia, tam modernis judicibus curiæ prædictæ in præsentibus

said Sir Edward Zouch, Knight, marshal of our household aforesaid, and the marshal of the said household of us, our heirs and
successors, for the time being, may and shall be the only judge
of the court aforesaid, by himself, or by his sufficient deputy, well
skilled and learned in the law, to hear and determine all and
all manner of pleas, processes and causes aforesaid, happening,
pending, or arising in the time of the vacancy of the office of the
steward of the household aforesaid.

We have also appointed, and we do by these presents, for us,
our heirs, and successors, appoint, ordain, and constitute John
Hooker, Esq to be the first and present Prothonotary of the
court of the virge aforesaid, to write, draw, and enrol all and every the writs, returns of writs, mainprizes or bails, bills, declarations, answers, replications, rejoinders, surrejoinders, issues,
warrants of attorney, verdicts, judgments, and other processes and
records whatsoever of the said court of the virge aforesaid, and to
keep all writs, rolls, and records whatsoever of the said court of the
virge aforesaid, To have, hold, exercise and perform the said office
of Prothonotary of the court of the virge aforesaid to the said John
Hooker, by himself, or by his sufficient deputy or sufficient deputies, for the natural life of the said John [Hooker].

We will also, and we do by these presents, for us, our heirs and
successors, ordain and constitute, that the aforesaid James, Marquis
of Hamilton, now steward of our household aforesaid, and the steward of the household of us, our heirs and successors, for the time
being, who are by these presents appointed judges of the court of
the virge aforesaid, And also, the aforesaid Sir Edward Zouch,
Knight, marshal of our household, and the marshal of the household of us, our heirs and successors, for the time being, who, during any vacancy of the office of steward of the household aforesaid,
are likewise by these presents respectively appointed the judges of
the said household, before they are admitted, or each of them respectively is admitted, to perform that office, they, and every one
of them respectively shall take their corporal oath on the Holy
Gospels of God, before the Chancellor of England, or the Keeper
of the Great Seal of England, and before the Marshal of England,
the Chamberlain of the king's household, the Treasurer and Comptroller of the aforesaid household of us, our heirs and successors,
or before any or either of them, in a public place, where the
court aforesaid shall then be respectively holden, rightfully, well,
justly, and faithfully to perform the said office of judge of the court
of the virge aforesaid, and to administer full and speedy justice
to his people there litigating or to litigate, according to their sound
discretion and best skill, understanding and judgment, and to observe all other things, in any manner belonging or appertaining to
the office of the aforesaid judge   Wherefore we will, and we do by
these presents, for us, our heirs and successors, give and grant to the
Chancellor of England, the Keeper of the Great Seal of England, the
Marshal of England, the Chamberlain of the king's household, the
Treasurer and Comptroller of the household aforesaid, as well present as future, and to every one and each of them for the time being, full power and authority of giving and administering a corporal
oath, upon the holy gospels of God, as well to the present judges
of the court aforesaid, in these presents named, as to all other judges

nominatis, quam omnibus aliis judicibus ejusdem curiæ deinceps in
perpetuum futuris, pro vera et fideli executione officii illius in omnibus, et per omnia officium illud tangentia, modo et forma prædictis,
et hoc absque aliqua commissione vel ulteriori warranto a nobis,
heredibus, vel successoribus nostris, in ea parte procurando vel obtinendo

Cumque senescallus hospitii prædicti, ratione officii illius ma-
joris in aula regia eminentiæ, sit necessario in grandiori servitio hujus regni vel concernenti personam nostram, heredum
et successorum nostrorum, sæpius impensurus, et marescallus
etiam dicti hospitii, ratione officii sui, multis aliis occasionibus
ejusdem hospitii sæpenumero erit impeditus, ita quod neuter
eorum possit satis intendere prædicto officio judicis curiæ virgæ
prædictæ pro expeditione causarum ioidem dependentium vel
dependendarum, prout requisitum fuerit, Nos igitur volumus et per
præsentes de ampliori gratia nostra speciali, ac ex certa scientia et
mero motu nostris, pro nobis, heredibus et successoribus nostris,
concedimus præfato Jacobo Marchioni Hamilton, senescallo hospitii nostri, et senescallo hospitii nostri, heredum et successorum
nostrorum, pro tempore existente, plenam potestatem et authoritatem nominandi, eligendi, deputandi, et assignandi unum probum et discretum virum, in legibus Angliæ eruditum., in loco
ejusdem senescalli, fore judicem prædictæ curiæ virgæ, ad omnia
illo officio judicis ejusdem curiæ pertinentia in absentia prædicti
senescalli præstandum et exequendum Quodque judex curiæ
illius sic eligendus et deputandus, antequam ad officium illud exequendum admittatur, sacramentum corporale super sancta Dei
evangelia, coram senescallo hospitii prædicti, ad officium illud judicis curiæ illius, secundum ejus scientiam, in omnibus, et per omnia officium illud tangentia sive concernentia, bene et fideliter exequendum, et plenam justitiam in curia illa administrandum,
præstabit. Ac idcirco senescallo hospitii prædicti, pro tempore
existente, hujusmodi sacramentum de tempore in tempus, judici
curiæ prædictæ in forma prædicta deputando, administrandi plenam potestatem et authoritatem, pro nobis, heredibus et successoribus nostris, damus et concedimus per præsentes. Ac etiam præfato
Edwardo Zouch, militi, modo marescallo hospitii nostri, et marescallo hospitii nostri, heredum et successorum nostrorum, pro
tempore existente, consimilem potestatem et authoritatem per præsentes damus et concedimus, in tempore vacationis officii senescalli
hospitii prædicti, quandocunque et quoties acciderit, nominandi, eligendi, deputandi, et assignandi, unum probum et discretum
virum, in legibus Angliæ eruditum, in loco ejusdem marescalli,
et in tempore vacationis officii prædicti senescalli hospitii nostri,
heredum et successorum nostrorum, fore judicem prædictæ curiæ
virgæ, ad omnia illa ad officium judicis ejusdem curiæ spectantia,
in absentia prædicti marescalli, et in tempore vacationis officii
prædicti senescalli hospitii prædicti præstandum et exequendum Quodque judex curiæ illius sic eligendus et deputandus, antequam ad officium illud exequendum admittatur, sacramentum
corporale super sancta Dei evangelia, coram marescallo hospitii
prædicti pro tempore existente, ad officium illud judicis curiæ
illius, secundum ejus scientiam, in omnibus et per omnia officium
illud tangentia sive concernentia, bene et fideliter exequendum,

of the said court, from henceforth for ever, for the true and faithful execution of that office, in and by all things touching the said office, in manner and form aforesaid: And this, without any commission or further warrant from us, our heirs and successors, in that behalf to be procured or obtained.

And whereas the steward of the household aforesaid, by reason of that office of very great eminence in the royal palace, is, of necessity, very frequently engaged in the more important services of this kingdom, or concerning the person of us, our heirs and successors; and also the Marshal of the said household, by reason of his office, will be frequently hindered by the many other emergencies of the said household; so that neither of them can sufficiently attend to the aforesaid office of judge of the court of the virge aforesaid, as will be requisite for the quick dispatch of causes there pending or to be pending: We therefore will, and we do by these presents, of our more abundant special grace, and of our certain knowledge and mere motion, for us, our heirs and successors, grant to the aforesaid James, Marquis of Hamilton, steward of our household, and to the steward of the household of us, our heirs and successors, for the time being, full power and authority of nominating, choosing, deputing, and appointing one honest and discrete man, learned in the laws of England, in place of the said steward, to be the judge of the aforesaid court of the virge, to perform and execute, in the absence of the said steward, all things relating to the said office of judge of the said court: And that the judge of the said court, so to be chosen and deputed, before that he be admitted to execute that office, shall take a corporeal oath, on the holy gospels of God, before the steward of the household aforesaid, well and faithfully to execute the said office of judge of the said court, according to his knowledge, in and by all things touching or concerning the said office, and to administer full justice in the said court: And therefore, for us, our heirs and successors, we give and grant, by these presents, to the steward of the household aforesaid, for the time being, full power and authority of administering such oath, from time to time, to the judge of the court aforesaid, in form aforesaid to be deputed.

And also, by these presents, we do give and grant to the aforesaid Edward Zouch, Knight, now marshal of our household, and to the marshal of the household of us, our heirs and successors, for the time being, in the time of the vacancy of the office of steward of the household aforesaid, whenever, and as often as it shall happen, the like power and authority of nominating, choosing, deputing and appointing one honest and discrete man, learned in the laws of England, in place of the said marshal, and in the time of the vacancy of the said office of steward of the household of us, our heirs and successors, to be the judge of the aforesaid court of the virge, to perform and execute all those things belonging to the office of judge of the said court, in the absence of the aforesaid marshal, and in the time of the vacancy of the office of the aforesaid steward of the household aforesaid. And that the judge of the said court, so to be chosen and deputed, before that he be admitted to execute that office, shall take a corporal oath, on the holy gospels of God, before the marshal of the aforesaid household for the time being, well and faithfully to execute the said office of judge of the said court, according to his knowledge, in and by all things touching or concerning the said

et ad plenam justitiam omnibus personis in curia illa coram ipso litem habentibus administrandum, præstabit. Et ideo marescallo hospitii prædicti pro tempore existente, hujusmodi sacramentum de tempore in tempus, tali judici curiæ prædictæ, in forma prædicta deputando, administrandi plenam potestatem et authoritatem, pro nobis, heredibus et successoribus nostris, damus et concedimus per præsentes. Volumus etiam, ac per præsentes pro nobis, heredibus et successoribus nostris, concedimus, quod de tempore in tempus, et ad omnia tempora post mortem prædicti Johannis Hooker, aut postquam officium illud prothonotarii curiæ prædictæ per resignationem, amotionem, vel cessionem prædicti Johannis Hooker, aut alio modo vacari contigerit, ac sic deinceps toties quoties casus sic acciderit, bene liceat et licebit marescallo hospitii nostri, heredum et successorum nostrorum, pro tempore existente, nominare et eligere unum alium virum discretum et idoneum fore et esse prothonotarium curiæ virgæ prædictæ. Quiquidem prothonotarius sic nominatus et electus per marescallum hospitii prædicti, per senescallum ejusdem hospitii, et in vacatione [officii] hujusmodi senescalli per marescallum prædictum, ad officium illud exequendum de tempore in tempus admissus erit. Et quod ille qui sic in officium prothonotarii curiæ virgæ prædictæ de tempore in tempus nominatus, electus et admissus fuerit, officium illud habeat et exerceat durante vita sua naturali, per se vel per sufficientem deputatum suum, sive deputatos suos sufficientes, exequendum.

Damus insuper, et pro nobis, heredibus et successoribus nostris concedimus per præsentes, præfato senescallo et marescallo hospitii nostri, heredum et successorum nostrorum, pro tempore existente, et in tempore vacationis officii illius senescalli hospitii prædicti, marescallo ejusdem hospitii soli, plenam potestatem et authoritatem nominandi, ordinandi, constituendi, et admittendi quatuor personas consiliarios eruditos in lege, fore consiliarios; et sex alias idoneas personas fore attornatos in dicta curia virgæ, pro termino vitæ cujuslibet talis personæ, ad prosequendum et defendendum omnia et singula actiones, placita, et querelas in eadem curia mota sive movenda. Ac etiam damus, et pro nobis, heredibus et successoribus nostris concedimus marescallo hospitii nostri, heredum et successorum nostrorum, pro tempore existente, plenam potestatem et authoritatem nominandi, ordinandi, constituendi et admittendi, unam aliam personam fore submarescallum curiæ prædictæ, ac custodem prisonæ curiæ prædictæ, ac unam aliam idoneam personam fore janitorem ejusdem prisonæ; necnon unam aliam personam idoneam fore præconem vel proclamatorem dictæ curiæ virgæ, pro termino vitæ cujuslibet talis personæ, ad omnia et singula eisdem officiis, pro meliori servitio curiæ illius et expeditione causarum ibidem dependentium et dependendarum, in aliquo spectantia vel pertinentia, præstandum et exequendum. Quodque præfatus prothonotarius, quatuor consiliarii, sex attornati, submarescallus, janitor, et proclamator, antequam ad loca sive officia illa exequendum respective admittantur, seu eorum aliquis admittatur, sacramentum corporale super sancta Dei evangelia, coram prædicto senescallo hospitii, seu coram prædicto [marescallo], eorumve unius deputato pro tempore existente, in curia prædicta, ad loca et officia illa respective bene et fideliter exequendum, et in eisdem respective se bene gerendum, præstabunt, et quilibet eorum præ-

office, and to administer full justice to all persons having any action before him in the said court   And therefore, for us, our heirs and successors, we give and grant, by these presents, to the marshal of the household aforesaid, for the time being, full power and authority of administering such oath from time to time, to such judge of the court aforesaid, in form aforesaid to be deputed.

We also will, and we do by these presents, for us, our heirs and successors, grant, that, from time to time, and at all times after the death of the aforesaid John Hooker, or after that the said office of prothonotary of the court aforesaid shall happen to be vacant, by the resignation, removal, or cession of the aforesaid John Hooker, or by any other means, and so hereafter as often as the case shall so happen, it may and shall be lawful for the marshal of the household of us, our heirs and successors, for the time being, to nominate and choose one other discrete and fit person to become and to be the prothonotary of the court of the virge aforesaid, which prothonotary, so nominated and chosen by the marshal of the household aforesaid, shall be admitted by the steward of the said household, and in the vacancy [of the office] of such steward, by the marshal aforesaid, from time to time, to execute that office. And that he who shall be, from time to time, so nominated, chosen, and admitted into the office of prothonotary of the court of the virge aforesaid, may, during his natural life, have and exercise the said office, to be executed by himself, or by his sufficient deputy or deputies.

We also give, and we do, by these presents, for us, our heirs and successors, grant to the aforesaid steward and marshal of the household of us, our heirs and successors, for the time being, and during the vacancy of the said office of steward of the household aforesaid, to the marshal of the said household alone, the full power and authority of nominating, ordaining, constituting and admitting, four persons, counsellors learned in the law, to be counsel, and six other fit persons to be attornies in the said court of the virge, for the term of the life of every such person, to prosecute and defend all and every actions, pleas, and plaints, commenced or to be commenced in the said court   And we also give, and we do by these presents, for us, our heirs and successors, grant to the marshal of the household of us, our heirs and successors, for the time being, the full power and authority of nominating, ordaining, constituting, and admitting one other person to be sub-marshal of the court aforesaid and keeper of the prison of the court aforesaid, and one other fit person to be turnkey of the said prison, and also one other fit person to be crier or proclamator of the said court of the virge, for the term of the life of every such person, to perform and execute all and singular the duties to the said offices in any wise belonging or pertaining, for the better service of the said court, and the despatch of causes there pending or to be pending   And that the aforesaid prothonotary, the four counsellors, six attornies, submarshal, turnkey and crier, before that they or any one of them respectively be admitted to execute the said places or offices, they and every one of them shall take a corporal oath, on the holy gospels of God, before the aforesaid steward of the household, or before the aforesaid [marshal], or the deputy of one of them for the time being, in the aforesaid court, well and faithfully to execute the said places and offices respectively, and well to conduct themselves in the same respectively.   To which said

stabit Quibus quidem senescallo et marescallo ac deputato et
eorum cuilibet pro tempore existente, hujusmodi sacramentum de
tempore in tempus eisdem prothonotario, consiliarus, attornatis,
submarescallo, janitori, et proclamatori, et cuilibet et quibuslibet
eorum administrandi plenam potestatem et authoritatem, pro nobis, heredibus et successoribus nostris, damus et concedimus per
præsentes. Ita quod in eadem curia, ad aliquod tempus, sint tantum unus prothonotarius, quatuor consiliarii, sex attornati, unus
custos prisonæ, unus janitor prisonæ, et unus proclamator curiæ
virgæ prædictæ, quibus feoda in dicta curia virgæ allocata fuerint,
pro causis prosequendis et defendendis, seu aliis rebus agendis
in eadem curia et prisona prædictis

Damus ulterius, et per præsentes pro nobis, heredibus, et successoribus nostris, concedimus marescallo hospitii nostri, heredum
et successorum nostrorum pro tempore existente, plenam potestatem et auctoritatem nominandi, constituendi et admittendi, de
tempore in tempus, viginti portatores virgarum nostrarum, fore
officiarios curiæ virgæ nostræ prædictæ, heredum et successorum nostrorum, ad exequendum mandata, brevia, et processus
a dicta curia virgæ emanantia Quodque quilibet eorundem
portatorum virgarum, antequam ad officium illud exequendum
admittatur, sacramentum corporale super sancta Dei evangelia,
coram judice curiæ prædictæ pro tempore existente, ad semet-
ipsos in officio illo bene gerendum præstabit, cui quidem judici
hujusmodi sacramentum de tempore in tempus administrandi plenam potestatem, pro nobis, heredibus, et successoribus nostris, damus et concedimus per præsentes Et quod iidem portatores virgæ
prædictæ, [qui] sic de tempore in tempus nominati, præfecti et jurati
fuerint, officia et loca illa habeant et exerceant, et quilibet eorum
habeat et exerceat, quamdiu se bene gesserit et gesserint in eodem
et eisdem. VOLUMUS item, ac per præsentes, pro nobis, heredibus, et successoribus nostris, firmiter injungendo præcipimus senescallo hospitii nostri, heredum et successorum nostrorum, pro
tempore existente, et in tempore vacationis officii illius marescallo
dicti hospitii pro tempore existente, quod uterque eorum non omittat per se, vel per sufficientem deputatum suum, in forma prædicta
assignandum et jurandum, personaliter attendere in curia prædicta
de die in diem, ad causas ibidem dependentes vel dependendas secundum leges et consuetudines regni nostri Angliæ audiendum et
terminandum, et quod iidem judices in omnibus hujusmodi causis,
actionibus, placitis et querelis, coram eis vel eorum aliquo dependentibus, in quibus pars defendens vel partes defendentes debet
vel debent, per legem terræ, habere custagia et expensas sectarum suarum, ipsis defendentibus et eorum cuilibet custagia et expensas sua ad plenas denariorum summas circa sectas illas respective per ipsos vel eorum aliquem expensas, taxent et assidant, et
eorum quilibet taxet et assidat. Et si forte acciderit aliquem vel
aliquos in curia prædicta implacitari super aliquam actionem de-
biti, ubi revera debitum illud non excedat decem solidos legalis
monetæ Angliæ, quod in omni hujusmodi casu defendens sic
implacitatus et ad primam curiam post ipsius summonitionem
vel arrestationem debitum illud satisfacere se præbens, idem defendens habeat allocationem exinde de feodis per ipsum super sum-

steward and marshal and deputy, and to each of them for the time being, we do by these presents, for us, our heirs and successors, give and grant full power and authority of administering such oath from time to time to the said prothonotary, counsellors, attornies, submarshal, gaoler and crier, and to each and every of them So that, in the same court, at any time, there be only one prothonotary, four counsellors, six attornies, one keeper of the prison, one turnkey of the prison, and one crier of the court of the virge aforesaid, to whom the fees in the said court of the virge shall be allowed for causes prosecuted and defended, or other business done in the said court and prison aforesaid

We give moreover, and we do by these presents, for us, our heirs and successors, grant to the marshal of the houschold of us, our heirs and successors, for the time being, full power and authority of nominating, constituting, and admitting, from time to time, twenty bearers of our rods, to become the officers of the court of the virge aforesaid of us, our heirs and successors, to execute the orders, writs, and processes issuing from the said court of the virge. And that every one of the said bearers of the rods, before that he be admitted to execute that office, shall take a corporal oath, on the holy gospels of God, before the judge of the said court for the time being, to behave himself well in the said office, to which judge we give and grant, by these presents, for us, our heirs and successors, the full power of administering such oath from time to time And that the said bearers of the rods of the virge aforesaid, who have so from time to time been nominated, made, and sworn, they and each of them may have and exercise the said offices and places, as long as they and each of them shall well behave themselves in the same

We also will, and we do by these presents, for us, our heirs and successors, firmly enjoin and command the steward of the household of us, our heirs and successors, for the time being, and, in the time of the vacancy of that office, the marshal of the said household for the time being, that neither of them omit, by himself or by his sufficient deputy, in the form aforesaid appointed and sworn, personally to attend in the court aforesaid, from day to day, to hear and determine the causes there pending or to be pending, according to the laws and customs of our realm of England And that the said judges, in all such causes, actions, pleas, and plaints, depending before them or any one of them, in which the party defendant or parties defendants ought, by the law of the land, to have the costs and expenses of their suits, they and each of them tax and assess to the said defendants, and to each of them, their costs and expenses, to the full sum expended by them or any of them in their respective suits And if by chance it shall happen, that any one or more be impleaded in the said court on any action of debt, where in truth the said debt may not exceed ten shillings of lawful money of England, that, in every such case the defendant so impleaded, and offering himself at the first court after his summons or arrest to satisfy the said debt, the said defendant may have an allowance from that time of the fees by him expended on the

monitionem illam vel arrestationem expensis, et residuum solvens in placito hujusmodi, ad respondendum ulterius non coarctetur. Et si in illo casu querens, debitum illud majus esse asserens, ulterius versus eundem defendentem prosequi velit, si deinceps, super legalem examinationem et triationem inde per formam curiæ illius, aliter apparebit, defendens ille recuperet versus dictum querentem omnia et omnimoda custagia sua circa sectam illam apponerit, secundum veram denariorum summam per ipsum defendentem in secta illa expensam. AC ulterius, de uberiori gratia nostra speciali, ac ex certa scientia, et mero motu nostris, concessimus et allocavimus, ac per præsentes pro nobis, heredibus et successoribus nostris, concedimus et allocamus præfatis judicibus, prothonotario, consiliariis, attornatis, submarescallo, janitori, proclamatori, et portatoribus virgarum prædictis, et aliis officiariis et ministris curiæ virgæ prædictæ, pro tempore existente, quod bene liceat et licebit eis et eorum cuilibet, de tempore in tempus, capere, percipere, et habere de omnibus et singulis personis in curia virgæ prædictæ negotiantibus, talia et consimilia feoda et vada qualia in schedula his præsentibus annexa continentur et specificantur, secundum veram intentionem nostram in eadem schedula declaratam, et non alia neque plura feoda et regarda MANDAMUS etiam, ac pro nobis, heredibus et successoribus nostris, firmiter injungendo præcipimus omnibus et singulis justiciariis, vicecomitibus, custodibus gaolarum et prisonarum, ballivis, constabulariis, et aliis officiariis, et subditis nostris quibuscunque, infra virgam hospitii prædicti, tam infra libertates quam extra, quod sint prædictis judicibus curiæ virgæ prædictæ, et mandatis cujuslibet eorum, infra tenorem et veram intentionem harum literarum nostrarum patentium in omnibus obedientes, et eorum cujuslibet præcepta et mandata diligenter et firmiter perimplere et custodire, ac perimpleri et custodiri causare, ac omnibus officiariis et ministris curiæ virgæ prædictæ in executione officiorum suorum fore intendentes et auxiliantes, sub violatoris mandati nostri regii periculo incurrendi. VOLUMUS denique, et per præsentes pro nobis, heredibus et successoribus nostris concedimus, quod hæ literæ nostræ patentes, et omnia in eisdem contenta et specificata, sint et erunt in omnibus et per omnia firmæ, validæ et effectuales in lege, non obstante non nominando aliquam concessionem de præmissis seu de aliqua inde parcella, per nos vel aliquem progenitorum sive prædecessorum nostrorum antehac factam, ac non obstante male nominando, male recitando, vel non nominando vel non recitando, vel non recte nominando præmissa vel aliquam inde parcellam ac non obstante statuto in parliamento domini Edwardi nuper regis Angliæ primo, anno regni sui tertio, tento edito. Ac non obstante statuto in parliamento domini Henrici nuper regis Angliæ quarti, anno regni sui secundo, tento edito. Et non obstante statuto in parliamento domini Henrici nuper regis Angliæ sexti, anno regni sui vicesimo tertio, tento edito; aut aliquo alio statuto, actu, ordinatione, provisione, constitutione, vel restrictione, aut aliqua alia causa vel materia quacunque in contrarium inde non obstante. IN cujus rei testimonium, &c teste rege apud Westmonasterium, quintodecimo die Februarii, &c

Per breve de Privato Sigillo.

said summons or arrest, and paying the residue shall not be compel-
ed to answer further in such plea   And if in that case the plaintiff, avowing that the said debt is greater, wish to proceed further
against he said defendant, if afterwards, upon the lawful examination and trial thereof by the form of the said court, it shall appear
otherwise, the said defendant may recover against the said plaintiff
all and all manner his costs laid out concerning the said suit, according to the true sum by him the defendant in the said suit expended

And further, of our more abundant special grace, and of our
certain knowledge, and mere motion, we have granted and allowed, and by these presents, for us, our heirs and successors, do grant
and allow to the aforesaid judges, prothonotary, counsel, attornies,
sub-marshal, turnkey, crier, and bearers of the rods aforesaid, and
to the other officers and ministers of the court of the virge
aforesaid for the time being, that it may and shall be lawful for
them, and every one of them, from time to time, to take, receive,
and have, of all and singular the persons having business in the
court of the virge aforesaid, such and the like fees and dues, as in
the schedule to these presents annexed are contained and specified,
according to our true intent in the said schedule declared, and no
other or greater fees and rewards

We also command, and we do for us, our heirs and successors,
strictly enjoin and order all and singular our justices, sheriffs,
keepers of gaols and prisons, bailiffs, constables, and other our officers and subjects whatsoever, within the virge of the household
aforesaid, as well within liberties as without, that they be obedient
in all things to the aforesaid judges of the court of the virge
aforesaid, and to the commands of each of them, within the tenor
and true intent of these our letters patent, and diligently and firmly fulfil and keep, and cause to be fulfilled and kept, the precepts
and commands of each of them, and be aiding and assisting to all
the officers and ministers of the court of the virge aforesaid in the
execution of their offices, under the peril of incurring [the punish-
ment] of a violator of our royal command.

We lastly will, and we do by these presents, for us, our heirs
and successors, grant, that these our letters patent, and all things
contained and specified therein, may and shall be firm, valid, and
effectual in law, in and by all things, notwithstanding the not naming any grant touching the premises, or any parcel thereof, by us,
or any of our ancestors or predecessors heretofore made, and notwithstanding the mis-naming, mis-reciting, or not naming or not
reciting, or not correctly naming the premises, or any parcel thereof
And notwithstanding the statute enacted in the Parliament of Lord
Edward the First, late King of England, held in the third year
of his reign, and notwithstanding the statute enacted in the Parliament of Lord Henry the Fourth, late King of England, held in the
second year of his reign, and notwithstanding the statute enacted
in the Parliament of Lord Henry the Sixth, late King of England,
held in the twenty-third year of his reign, or any other statute, act,
ordinance, provision, constitution or restriction, or any other cause
or matter whatsoever to the contrary hereof notwithstanding

In witness whereof, &c   Witness the King at Westminster, the
15th day of February, &c

By writ of Privy Seal,

M

6 *CAR. I.*

———

REX omnibus ad quos, &c salutem CUM nobis expediens et necessarium visum fuerit, ut omnes et singuli subditi nostri et personæ
quæcunque infra duodecem leucas seu milliaria circumquaque a palatio nostro de Westmonasterio, in comitatu nostro Middlesexiæ, ubi
nos plerumque et concilium nostrum sæpius atque magis quam alius
in palatiis nostris residere consuevimus, quemadmodum etiam progenitores nostri reges Angliæ et concilia sua olim consueverunt, residentes, inhabitantes, confluentes, commorantes, contrahentes, negotiantes, seu existentes, in omnibus et omnimodis actionibus, placitis, et querelis suis personalibus celeriorem haberent justitiam, eo
quod ipsi tam in negotiis et servitiis nostris quam in occasionibus officiariorum et famulorum nostrorum et charissimæ consortis nostræ
et concilii nostri multo magis ac sæpius quam alii subditi nostri in
remotioribus partibus Angliæ commorantes, occupantur et implicantur Quod ideo imprimis evenit, quia quoties et quandocunque
ad alias ædes seu palatia nostra alibi sita ad libitum nostrum secedere nobis contingere solet, reditus noster ad dictum palatium nostrum de Westmonasterio citius contingit, unde etiam residentes, inhabitantes, confluentes, et commorantes, infra dictas duodecem leucas, eam ob causam maxime, tam durante præsentia nostra ad
dictum palatium nostrum quam dum absumus, contractibus atque
aliis negotiis ad provisionem in reditum nostrum et servitia nostra
alia spectantibus perpetuo involvuntur, et præ cæteris subditis nostris onerantur. CUMQUE Curia Marescaltiæ Hospitii Regum
Angliæ sit antiqua curia, ordinata pro bona conservatione et custodia pacis infra hospitium regum Angliæ, ubicunque pro tempore fuerit, ac pro determinatione diversarum actionum et querelarum personalium infra hospitium et virgam hospitii prædicti emergentium,
prout per leges et statuta hujus regni nostri Angliæ liquet et appa-
ret· Ac nihilominus subditi nostri infra præcincta virgæ prædictæ
inhabitantes, confluentes aut commorantes, non autem de hospitio
nostro existentes, in eadem curia marescaltiæ hospitii nostri, in diversis legitimis actionibus et querelis suis aliquam certam prosecutionem [tam] ob dubia quædam nuper suborta jurisdictionem curiæ illius concernentia, quam alias ob causas, non habuerunt Ac præterea
placita et querelæ in eadem curia inchoata et antequam nos ex limitibus virgæ ejusdem hospitii discesserimus non finita et determinata,
secundum leges et statuta hujus regni nostri Angliæ per discessionem nostram ex dictis limitibus cessare solent, adeo etiam ut sæpenumero infra dictas duodecem leucas seu milliaria justitia in placitis et querelis ibi ut præfertur inchoatis, et per nostram ut præfertur discessionem cessantibus, non sine gravi et multa dilatione exhibeatur CUMQUE insuper ad notitiam nostram pervenerit, quod
nonnulli tam servitorum et famulorum hospitii nostri prædicti, quam
aliorum subditorum nostrorum infra virgam ejusdem hospitii commorantium, de feodis et expensis curiæ prædictæ ab ipsis modo receptis, licet ibidem de antiquo debitis et usitatis, conquerantur.——

CHARLES, &c., to all to whom, &c. greeting —Whereas, it hath appeared unto us expedient and necessary, that all and singular our subjects and persons whatsoever residing, inhabiting, resorting, tarrying, contracting, trafficking or being within twelve miles, every way, from our palace of Westminster, in our county of Middlesex, (where we most commonly, and our council oftener and more than in our other palaces have been accustomed to reside, as also the kings of England, our progenitors, and their councils have formerly been accustomed), should have more speedy justice in all and all manner of their personal actions, pleas, and plaints, because they are much more and more frequently occupied and engaged, as well in our affairs and service as in the business of our officers and domestics, and of our most dear consort and of our council, than other our subjects residing in more remote parts of England which happens on this account especially, because as often and whensoever at our pleasure we are accustomed to retire to our other houses or palaces situated elsewhere, we sooner return to our said palace of Westminster, whence also the persons residing, inhabiting, resorting, and tarrying within the said twelve miles, on that account especially, as well during our presence at our said palace as while we are absent, are constantly engaged in contracts and other businesses relating to the providing for our return and our other services, and are more burthened than the rest of our subjects:

And whereas the Court of the Marshalsea of the Household of the kings of England is an ancient Court, constituted for the good preservation and keeping of the peace within the household of the kings of England, wheresoever for the time it shall be, and for determining divers personal actions and plaints arising within the household and the virge of the household aforesaid, as by the laws and statutes of this our realm of England is clear and evident And, nevertheless, our subjects inhabiting, resorting, or tarrying within the precincts of the virge aforesaid, but not being of our household, have had no determinate prosecution of their various lawful actions and plaints in the said court of the Marshalsea of our household, on account of certain doubts which have lately arisen concerning the jurisdiction of that court, as well as for other causes And besides, the pleas and plaints commenced in the same court, and not finished and determined before we shall have departed from the limits of the virge of the same household, according to the laws and statutes of this our kingdom of England are accustomed to abate on account of our departure out of the said limits, so that oftentimes within the said twelve miles justice cannot be administered without grievous and great delay in the pleas and plaints there (as above mentioned) commenced, and abating (as above mentioned) by our departure And whereas, it hath also come to our knowledge, that some, as well of the servants and domestics of our household aforesaid, as of other our subjects residing within the virge of the said household, complain of the fees and expenses of the court aforesaid by them now received, although anciently

SCIATIS igitur, quod nos, ex cura regia nostra festinum in hac
parte remedium adhibere cupientes, et ut omnes et omnimodæ actiones, placita et querelæ personales omnium et singulorum subditorum nostrorum et personarum quarumcunque residentium, inhabitantium, confluentium, contrahentium, negotiantium, seu existentium, infra predictas duodecem leucas seu milliaria circumquaque a
dicto palatio nostro de Westmonasterio extensa celerius tractentur
et expediantur, de gratia nostra speciali, ac ex certa scientia et mero motu nostris, fecimus, creavimus, ereximus, ordinavimus, et constituimus, ac per præsentes, pro nobis, heredibus et successoribus
nostris, facimus, creamus, erigimus, ordinamus, et constituimus
unam curiam de recordo coram justiciarius infra scriptis duobus vel
uno eorum, infra palatium Westmonasterii vel in aliquo alio loco publico et idoneo infra duodecim leucas seu milliaria ab eodem palatio
situato, in forma sequenti tenendam, quæ per nomen Curiæ Palatii
Regis Westmonasterii vocabitur et nuncupabitur, pro administratione et exhibitione justitiæ in actionibus, placitis et querelis personalibus, omnibus et singulis personis ibidem placitare volentibus, de
omnibus et omnimodis transgressionibus vi et armis, transgressionibus super casum, debitis, computis, detentionibus bonorum et
catallorum, deceptionibus et contractibus, et aliis causis, loquelis, et placitis personalibus quibuscunque, de quacunque summa, in omnibus locis infra duodecim leucas seu milliaria a palatio
Westmonasterii emergentibus, perpetratis, habitis, vel inhibitis, cujuscunque comitatus fuerint loca illa, (excepta civitate nostra Londini et exceptis etiam civitatibus, burgis, villis, et aliis libertatibus
et franchesiis, infra prædictas duodecem leucas seu milliaria, in quibus aliqui subditi nostri sive aliquis subditus noster habent sive
habet vel habere debent vel debet potestatem et authoritatem audiendi et terminandi talia actiones, placita, et querelas personales,
per aliquam priorem legalem concessionem, consuetudinem, vel
præscriptionem, qualia in prædicta curia facta et erecta per has literas nostras patentes terminari valeant, quoad actiones, placita et
querelæ ad summas tales attingentes unde prædicti alii subditi nostri in curiis suis cognoscere valeant et possint, et ibidem fuerint inchoata), et curiam illam de novo erigi et constitui volumus, ac erigimus et constituimus per præsentes. VOLUMUS etiam, ac per
præsentes pro nobis, heredibus et successoribus nostris, concedimus,
ordinamus et constituimus, quod curia illa per nomen Curiæ Palatii
Regis Westmonasterii nuncupabitur, et sit curia de recordo de die in
diem qualibet septimana per annum, [exceptis] die Dominico et diebus
festis Natalis Domini, Circumcisionis Domini, Epiphaniæ, Purificationis et Annunciationis Beatæ Mariæ Virginis, Parasceves, Ascensionis Domini, Sancti Michaelis Archangeli, et Omnium Sanctorum,
coram senescallo hospitii nostri, heredum vel successorum nostrorum, ac marescallo hospitii nostri, heredum et successorum nostrorum, et una alia persona in legibus Angliæ erudita, per nos, heredes et successores nostros nominanda et constituenda, qui senescallus Curiæ Palatii Regis Westmonasterii vocabitur et nuncupabitur, seu coram deputato suo sufficiente de tempore in tempus con-
stituendo, ac in absentia prædicti marescalli pro tempore existente,
seu hujusmodi marescallo non existente, coram prædicto senescallo
hospitii prædicti pro tempore existente, ac prædicto senescallo cu-

there due and accustomed. Know ye, therefore, that we, of our royal care, being desirous to apply a speedy remedy in this behalf, and that all and all manner of personal actions, pleas, and plaints of all and singular our subjects and persons whatsoever residing, inhabiting, resorting, contracting, trafficking, or being within the aforesaid twelve miles, extending every way from our said palace of Westminster, may be more quickly proceeded in and facilitated —We of our special grace, and of our certain knowledge and mere motion, have made, created, erected, ordained, and constituted, and by these presents, for us, our heirs and successors, do make, create, erect, ordain, and constitute one court of record to be holden in form following, before the two judges hereunder mentioned, or one of them, within the palace of Westminster, or in any other public and proper place situated within twelve miles from the same palace, which shall be called and named by the name of the Court of the Palace of the King at Westminster, for the administration and exhibition of justice in personal actions, pleas, and plaints, to all and every the persons desiring to plead there concerning all and all manner of trespasses vi et armis, trespasses upon the case, debts, accounts, detinues of goods and chattels, frauds and contracts, and other personal causes, plaints, and pleas whatsoever, of whatsoever sum, arising, done, had, or withheld, in all places within twelve miles from the palace of Westminster, of whatsoever county those places shall be, (except our city of London and except also the cities, boroughs, towns, and other liberties and franchises within the aforesaid twelve miles, in which any our subjects or subject have or hath, or ought to have the power and authority of hearing and determining such personal actions, pleas, and plaints by any former lawful grant, custom, or prescription, as can be determined in the court aforesaid, made and erected by these our letters patent, as far as the actions, pleas, and plaints are of such an amount as those our subjects aforesaid may and can have cognizance of in their courts, and shall there be commenced)· and we will that the said court be new erected and constituted, and by these presents we do erect and constitute it.

We also will, and do by these presents, for us, our heirs, and successors, grant, ordain, and constitute, that the said court shall be called by the name of the Court of the Palace of the King at Westminster, and be a court of record, from day to day, in every week throughout the year, [except] the Lord's day and the feast days of Christmas, Circumcision of our Lord, Epiphany, Purification and Annunciation of the blessed Virgin Mary, Good Friday, Ascension of our Lord, St Michael the Archangel, and All Saints, to be holden before the steward of the household of us, our heirs, or successors, and the marshal of the household of us, our heir and successors, and one other person learned in the laws of England, to be nominated and appointed by us, our heirs and successors, who shall be called and named the Steward of the Court of the Palace of the King at Westminster, or before his sufficient deputy from time to time to be appointed, and in the absence of the aforesaid marshal for the time being, or there being no such marshal, before the aforesaid steward of the household aforesaid for the time being, and the aforesaid steward of the court of the palace of the

riæ palatii regis Westmonasterii, vel deputato suo; et in absentia hujusmodi senescalli hospitii prædicti, seu hujusmodi senescallo non existente, coram marescallo hospitii prædicti pro tempore existente, ac prædicto senescallo curiæ palatii regis Westmonasterii, vel deputato suo pro tempore existente; ac in absentia hujusmodi senescalli hospitii prædicti ac marescalli, seu neutro eorum existente, coram prædicto senescallo curiæ palatii regis Westmonasterii, vel deputato suo pro tempore existente, tenenda· Et volumus ulterius quod thesaurarius et contrarotulator hospitii nostri pro tempore existente, si et quotiescunque ipsi vel eorum alteruter interesse voluerit vel voluerint, sint etiam judex sive judices in curia prædicta, simul cum judicibus superdictis, ita quod curia prædicta, quando et quotiescunque thesaurarius et contrarotulator hospitii nostri prædicti non interfuerint vel neuter eorum interfuerit, tenebitur coram senescallo et marescallo hospitii nostri prædicti et senescallo curiæ prædictæ, aut ejus deputato, respective, ut prædictum est.

Volumus etiam, pro nobis, heredibus et successoribus nostris, quod de cætero in perpetuum erit quoddam officium, quod officium senescalli curiæ palatii regis Westmonasterii vocabitur et nuncupabitur, ac officium senescalli curiæ palatii regis Westmonasterii facimus, creamus, et constituimus pro nobis, heredibus et successoribus nostris per præsentes VOLUMUS etiam, pro nobis, heredibus et successoribus nostris quod de cætero in perpetuum erit quidam officiarius, per nos, heredes et successores nostros de tempore in tempus nominandus et constituendus, qui senescallus curiæ palatii* regis Westmonasterii vocabitur et nuncupabitur Quodque erunt in perpetuum judices quidam, qui judices curiæ palatii regis Westmonasterii vocabuntur et nuncupabuntur, ad cognoscendum de omnibus et singulis placitis, actionibus, et querelis in his literis patentibus, secundum formam earum, specificatis, et omnia eadem placita, actiones et querelas ad audiendum et terminandum; qui, de tempore in tempus, respective audient et terminabunt in dicta curia per querelas in eadem curia levandas, omnes et omnimodas actiones, debita, computos, conventiones, contractus, transgressiones vi et armis seu aliter in contemptu nostri, heredum et successorum nostrorum factas vel fiendas, transgressiones super casum, detentiones, deceptiones, et alias res, actiones et placita quæcunque personalia, infra duodecem leucas prædictas, secundum modum et formam inferius in his literis patentibus respective præscripta (exceptis semper locis prædictis infra limites dictarum duodecem leucarum præexceptis) ut præmittitur quoad præexceptis, et prædicta civitate Londini excepta, ac exceptis omnibus hujusmodi actionibus, placitis, et querelis personalibus, in quibus tam querens vel querentes quam defendens vel defendentes sint vel fuerint, sit vel fuerit de hospitio nostro, heredum vel successorum nostrorum, et omnibus aliis actionibus de transgressionibus vi et armis, in quibus vel querens vel defendens sit vel fuerit de hospitio prædicto, tempore quo dictum palatium infra virgam hospitii nostri, heredum et successorum nostrorum, pro tempore existente fore contigerit VOLUMUS insuper et concedimus pro nobis heredibus et successoribus nostris quod senescallus hospitii nostri, heredum et successorum nostrorum, qui pro tempore fuerit, et senescallus curiæ palatii regis Westmonasterii, per se vel per sufficientem deputatum suum, secundum modum et

king at Westminster or his deputy, and in the absence of such steward of the household aforesaid, or there being no such steward, before the marshal of the household aforesaid for the time being, and the aforesaid steward of the court of the palace of the king at Westminster, or his deputy for the time being, and in the absence of such steward and marshal of the household aforesaid, or there being neither of them, before the aforesaid steward of the court of the palace of the king at Westminster, or his deputy for the time being. And we moreover will that the treasurer and comptroller of our household for the time being, if and as often as they or either of them shall be willing to be present, be also judge or judges in the Court aforesaid, together with the judges above-mentioned so that the court aforesaid, when and as often as the treasurer and comptroller of our household aforesaid, or either of them, shall not be present, shall be holden before the steward and marshal of our household aforesaid, and the steward of the court aforesaid, or his deputy, respectively, as is aforesaid.

We also will, for us, our heirs, and successors, that from henceforth for ever there shall be a certain office, which shall be called and named The Office of the Steward of the Court of the Palace of the King at Westminster, and we by these presents, for us, our heirs and successors, do make, create, and constitute the Office of the Steward of the Court of the Palace of the King at Westminster.

We also will for us, our heirs, and successors, that from henceforth for ever there shall be a certain officer, by us, our heirs, and successors from time to time to be nominated and appointed, who shall be called and named The Steward of the Court of the Palace of the King at Westminster and that there shall be for ever certain judges, who shall be called and named The Judges of the Court of the Palace of the King at Westminster, to take cognizance of all and singular the pleas, actions, and plaints in these letters patent specified, according to the form thereof, and to hear and determine all the said pleas, actions and plaints, who from time to time respectively shall hear and determine in the said court, by plaints to be levied in the said court, all and all manner of actions, debts, accounts, covenants, contracts, trespasses *vi et armis*, or otherwise committed or to be committed in contempt of us, our heirs and successors, trespasses on the case, detinues, frauds, and other personal causes, actions and pleas whatsoever, within the twelve miles aforesaid, according to the manner and form hereafter in these letters patent respectively prescribed, except always the places aforesaid within the limits of the said twelve miles before excepted, as is premised with respect to the exceptions before made, and except the aforesaid city of London, and except all such personal actions, pleas and plaints, in which, as well the plaintiff or plaintiffs, as the defendant or defendants, may or shall be of the household of us, our heirs or successors, and all other actions of trespass *vi et armis*, in which either the plaintiff or defendant may or shall be of the household aforesaid, at the time when the said palace shall happen to be within the virge of the household of us, our heirs and successors for the time being

We will moreover, and for us, our heirs, and successors, do grant, that the steward of the household of us, our heirs and successors for the time being, and the steward of the court of the palace of the king at Westminster, by himself or by his sufficient deputy, to be made and appointed according to the manner and form below

formam inferius praescripta faciendum et constituendum, erunt et sint judices conjunctim, et uterque et alteruter eorum sint et erunt, sit et erit judex divisim et separatim, in dicta curia; et quod quandocunque, quotiescunque, et quamdiu contigerit nullum senescallum hospitii nostri, heredum vel successorum nostrorum fore, tunc et tamdiu marescallus hospitii nostri, heredum et successorum nostrorum, qui pro tempore fuerit, et senescallus curiae palatii regis Westmonasterii, per se aut per deputatum suum, ut praedictum est, sint et erunt judices conjunctim, et uterque et alteruter eorum sit et erit judex divisim et separatim in eadem curia. Et quod iisdem modo et forma, ut praescriptum est, placita, querelae, et actiones teneantur, audiantur, et terminentur coram dictis senescallo et marescallo hospitii nostri, heredum et successorum nostrorum, et senescallo curiae palatii regis Westmonasterii, aut nomine et vice ejus coram deputato suo ut praefertur, respective, in dicta curia in perpetuum. Et quod dicti senescallus, marescallus, et senescallus curiae palatii regis Westmonasterii, qui pro tempore respective fuerit, per se vel per sufficientem deputatum suum, ut praefertur, et eorum quilibet, simul cum praefato thesaurario et contrarotulatore hospitii nostri pro tempore existente, si interesse voluerit vel voluerint, ut praedictum est, respective, in dictis placitis, actionibus, et querelis personalibus, ut praedictum est, habeant et habebunt potestatem et authoritatem personas defendentes, versus quas hujusmodi querelae, placita, sive actiones in praedicta curia levari vel moveri contigerint, in placita deducere per summonitiones, attachiamenta et districtiones, secundum consuetudinem in praedicta curia marescaliae hospitii nostri et progenitorum nostrorum antehac usitatam, vel per leges et consuetudines regni nostri Angliae approbatam, portatoribus virgarum hospitii praedicti et aliis ministris curiae praedictae, per marescallum hospitii praedicti, qui pro tempore fuerit, deputandis, vel eorum alicui vel aliquibus, dirigenda, et pro defectu caballorum et terrarum hujusmodi defendentium infra duodecim leucas praedictas, libertates, limittas vel praecincta earundem (exceptis praeexceptis), ubi sive per quae summoniri, attachiari, vel distringi possint, per attachiamenta aut captionem corporum suorum, actiones, querelas et placita superdicta omnia et singula (exceptis in casibus praeexceptis) prout et ad modum et formam quibus priores judices dictae antiquae curiae respective constituuntur et ordinantur audire et determinare, et per consimilia processus, judicia, et executiones judicii deducere et terminare, per quae et in tam amplis modo et forma prout consimilia placita, querelae, et actiones, in praedicta antiqua curia de recordo, vel per leges et consuetudines regni nostri Angliae, deducuntur et terminantur. Executionesque processuum, et judicia per praedictos portatores virgarum hospitii praedicti, et alios ministros praedictos fiant et habeantur · Salvis nobis, heredibus et successoribus nostris, finibus et amerciamentis inde provenientibus. AC insuper ut celeris justitia in curia praedicta fiat, ne scilicet defendens aliquis in querelis, placitis, aut actionibus praedictis, aut eorum aliquo, in dicta curia levatis aut institutis, placitando forinseca placita processum justitiae minime retardet, volumus et concedimus, et pro nobis, heredibus et successoribus nostris ordinamus et constituimus, quod nullus defendens in dicta curia admittatur ad placitandum

prescribed, shall and may be judges conjointly, and both and either of them may and shall be a judge severally and separately in the said court, and that whensoever and as often soever, and as long as it shall happen that there be no steward of the household of us, our heirs or successors, then and so long the marshal of the household of us, our heirs and successors, for the time being, and the steward of the court of the palace of the king at Westminster, by himself or by his deputy as is aforesaid, may and shall be judges conjointly, and both and either of them may and shall be judge severally and separately in the said court. And that in the same manner and form as is prescribed, pleas, plaints, and actions may be holden, heard, and determined before the said steward and marshal of the household of us, our heirs and successors, and the steward of the court of the palace of the king at Westminster, or in his name and stead before his deputy, as above mentioned, respectively, in the said court for ever. And that the said steward, the marshal, and the steward of the court of the palace of the king at Westminster respectively, for the time being, by himself or by his sufficient deputy, as is before mentioned, and any one of them, together with the aforesaid treasurer and comptroller of our household for the time being, if he or they respectively shall be willing to be present, as is aforesaid, in the said personal pleas, actions, and plaints, as is aforesaid, may and shall have power and authority of bringing into plea, by summonses, attachments, and distresses, (to be directed to the bearers of the rods of the household aforesaid and the other officers of the aforesaid court, to be deputed by the marshal of the aforesaid household, for the time being, or to any or either of them), the persons of the defendants, against whom such plaints, pleas, or actions shall happen to be levied or moved in the aforesaid court, according to the custom heretofore used in the aforesaid court of the marshalsea of the household of us and our ancestors, or sanctioned by the laws and customs of our realm of England, and for deficiency of chattels and lands of such defendants within the twelve miles aforesaid, the liberties, limits or precincts of the same, (except as before excepted), where or by which they may be summoned, attached, or distrained by attachment or *capias;* all and singular the actions, plaints and pleas aforesaid, (except in the cases before excepted), as and according to the manner and form in which the former judges of the said antient court are respectively appointed and ordained to hear and determine, and to bring to an end and terminate by the like processes, judgments, and executions of judgments, by which, and in as ample manner and form as the like pleas, plaints and actions in the aforesaid antient court of record, or by the laws and customs of our realm of England, are brought to an end and terminated, and that the executions of the processes and judgments be made and served by the aforesaid bearers of the rods of the household aforesaid, and the other officers aforesaid. Saving to us, our heirs, and successors, the fines and amerciaments thereby arising.

And moreover, that speedy justice may be done in the court aforesaid, to wit, that no defendant in the plaints, pleas, or actions aforesaid, or any of them, levied or instituted in the said court, may in the least retard the course of justice by pleading foreign pleas, we will and grant, and for us, our heirs, and successors, do ordain and constitute, that no defendant be admitted in the said court to plead

forinsecum placitum in aliqua querela, actione, sive placito in eadem curia levato, ibidem non triabili, nisi prius tactis sanctis evangeliis coram judice aliquo dictæ curiæ seu deputato suo prædicto, in ipsa curia sedente sacramentum suum præstiterit materiam placiti forinseci quod placitavit veram esse. Atque plenam potestatem et authoritatem, pro nobis, heredibus et successoribus [nostris], damus et concedimus unicuique judici prædicto respective, qui pro tempore fuerint, et deputato prædicto qui pro tempore fuerit, ad præstandum ejusmodi sacramentum, et juramento ejusmodi onerare quemlibet defendentem qui de tempore in tempus hujusmodi placitum forinsecum, ut præfertur, in curia prædicta placitaverit.

Volumus præterea, et pro nobis, heredibus et successoribus nostris, concedimus, ordinamus, et constituimus, quod de tempore in tempus senescallus curiæ palatii regis Westmonasterii, per nos, heredes, et successores nostros, ut prædictum est nominandus et assignandus, plenam potestatem habeat et authoritatem nominandi, eligendi, deputandi, et assignandi unum probum et discretum virum, in legibus hujus regni nostri Angliæ etiam eruditum, in loco et vice ejusdem senescalli, sic per nos, heredes sive successores nostros ut prædictum est nominandi et assignandi, atque ut deputatus ejus, de tempore in tempus, omnia quæ ad officium senescalli curiæ palatii regis Westmonasterii [pertinent], in absentia senescalli prædicti, de tempore in tempus præstabit et exequetur. Et quod quicquid in dicta curia factum aut præstitum fuerit ab ejusmodi probo et discreto viro, per prædictum senescallum de tempore in tempus nominando, eligendo, deputando, et assignando, ut vice seu loco ejusdem senescalli, et ut per deputatum ejusdem, ad omne ratum habebitur, et vim et effectum sortietur, ac si factum fuerit aut præstitum per ipsum senescallum per nos, ut præfertur, heredes, vel successores nostros nominandum et assignandum. VOLUMUS etiam, ac per præsentes pro nobis, heredibus et successoribus nostris concedimus, ordinamus, et constituimus, quod sit in perpetuum in curia palatii regis Westmonasterii prædicta quoddam officium, quod officium prothonotarii curiæ palatii regis Westmonasterii vocabitur et nuncupabitur, ac officium prothonotarii curiæ palatii regis Westmonasterii nominamus, facimus, creamus, et constituimus pro nobis, heredibus, et successoribus nostris. [Et] concedimus, quod sit in perpetuum in eadem curia quidam officiarius, qui prothonotarius curiæ palatii regis Westmonasterii vocabitur et nuncupabitur, ad scribendum, faciendum et irrotulandum omnia et singula brevia, processus, manucaptiones sive ballia, billas, narrationes, barras, responsiones, replicationes, rejunctiones, surrejunctiones, exitus, warranta attornati, veredicta, judicia, et alia processus et recorda quæcunque ejusdem curiæ palatii regis Westmonasterii prædictæ, et ad custodiendum brevia, rotulos, et recorda quæcunque ejusdem curiæ. VOLUMUS etiam, ac per præsentes pro nobis, heredibus et successoribus nostris, concedimus, ordinamus et constituimus, quod sit in perpetuum in curia palatii regis Westmonasterii prædicta commune sigillum, ab aliis sigillis curiarum nostrarum aliarum diversum, pro brevibus, attachiamentis, et aliis processibus curiæ illius sigillandis, et pro causis et negotiis ejusdem curiæ quibuscunque peragendis et expediendis, deserviturum. Et quod dictum commune sigillum fabricabitur et formabitur ad arbitrium dicti marescalli hospitii nostri.

a foreign plea in any plaint, action, or plea levied in the said court not triable there, unless he shall first, touching the holy gospels, make oath before some judge of the said court, or his deputy aforesaid, sitting in the said court, that the matter of the foreign plea which he hath pleaded is true   And for us, our heirs and successors, we do give and grant full power and authority to either judge aforesaid respectively for the time being, and the deputy aforesaid for the time being, to administer such oath, and to bind by such oath every defendant who from time to time shall plead such foreign plea as aforesaid, in the court aforesaid

We also will, and for us, our heirs and successors, do grant, ordain, and constitute, that from time to time the steward of the court of the palace of the king at Westminster, to be nominated and appointed as is aforesaid by us, our heirs and successors, may have full power and authority of nominating, choosing, deputing, and appointing one honest and discreet man, also learned in the laws of this our kingdom of England, in the place and stead of the said steward, so by us, our heirs, or successors as is aforesaid to be nominated and appointed, and that his deputy from time to time shall perform and execute, in the absence of the aforesaid steward from time to time, all things relating to the office of steward of the court of the palace of the king at Westminster.   And that whatever shall be done or performed in the said court by such honest and discreet man, from time to time to be nominated, elected, deputed and assigned by the steward aforesaid, as in the stead or place of the said steward, and as his said deputy, shall be held ratified in every thing, and have force and effect, as if it shall have been done or performed by the steward himself, by us, our heirs, or successors, as is aforesaid, to be nominated and appointed

We also will, and by these presents for us, our heirs, and successors, do grant, ordain, and appoint, that there be for ever, in the court of the palace of the king at Westminster aforesaid, a certain office, which shall be called and named The Office of the Prothonotary of the court of the palace of the king at Westminster, and we do nominate, make, create, and constitute, for us, our heirs, and successors, The Office of the Prothonotary of the Court of the Palace of the king at Westminster   [And] we grant that there be for ever in the same court a certain officer, who shall be called and named the Prothonotary of the Court of the Palace of the King at Westminster, to write, draw, and enrol all and singular the writs, processes, main prizes or bails, bills, declarations, bars, answers, replications, rejoinder, surrejoinders, issues, warrants of attorney, verdicts, judgment, and other processes and records whatsoever of the same court of the palace of the king at Westminster aforesaid, and to keep all writs, rolls, and records whatsoever of the same court

We also will, and we do by these presents, for us, our heirs and successors grant, ordain, and appoint, that there shall be for ever in the court of the palace of the king at Westminster aforesaid, a common seal, different from other seals of our other courts, to serve for sealing writs, attachments, and other processes of the same court, and for performing and dispatching the affairs and business whatsoever of the said court   And that the device and form of the said common seal shall be at the discretion of the said marshal of our household

Et quod sit de cætero infra duodecem leucas prædictas, una prisona sive gaola pro conservatione, retentione, et salva custodia omnium et singulorum prisonariorum, infra prædicta sive jurisdictionem curiæ prædictæ attachiatorum seu attachiandorum pro quacunque causa, quæ in curia prædicta audiri vel determinari, vel ibidem inchoari contigerit, ibidem moraturi donec et quousque legitimo modo deliberentur

Volumus etiam, ac pro nobis, heredibus, et successoribus nostris, concedimus, ordinamus et constituimus per præsentes, quod sit in perpetuum in curia palatii regis Westmonasterii prædicti, quidam submarescallus curiæ prædictæ, qui habeat custodiam prisonæ sive gaolæ prædictæ

Assignavimus etiam, ac per præsentes pro nobis, heredibus et successoribus nostris, appunctuamus, ordinamus, et constituimus Edmundum Verney, militem, modo marescallum hospitii nostri, [et marescallum hospitii nostri] heredum et successorum nostrorum, qui pro tempore imposterum fuerint respective, fore et esse judicem cum senescallo hospitii nostri, heredum et successorum nostrorum, pro tempore existente, et dicto senescallo curiæ palatii regis Westmonasterii per nos nominato aut nominando pro alio judice, ut prædictum est, in curia palatii regis Westmonasterii prædicti, quamdiu senescallum aliquem hospitii prædicti fore contigerit Qui quidem marescallus cum dicto senescallo hospitii prædicti et dicto senescallo curiæ palatii regis Westmonasterii, seu eorum alterutro, locum assidendi in curia prædicta et consulendi habeat, et potestatem seu suffragium dirigendi vel adjudicandi in omnibus causis ibidem dependentibus vel dependendis

Assignavimus etiam, ac per præsentes pro nobis, heredibus, et successoribus nostris, assignamus, constituimus, et ordinamus quod in omnibus temporibus futuris, quandocunque et quoties cunque prædictum officium senescalli hospitii nostri, heredum et successorum nostrorum, vacari contigerit, [quod] prædictus Edmundus Verney, miles, marescallus hospitii nostri prædicti, et marescallus ejusdem hospitii nostri, heredum et successorum nostrorum pro tempore existente respective, sit et erit judex curiæ palatii regis Westmonasterii prædictæ conjunctim cum senescallo curiæ palatii regis Westmonasterii, qui pro tempore fuerit, ut prædictum est, per nos nominato vel nominando, et uterque et alteruter eorum erit et sit judex divisim et separatim in eadem curia, ad omnia et omnimoda placita, processus, et causas prædictas, tempore vacationis officii senescalli hospitii prædicti audiendum et terminandum, secundum tenorem præsentium literarum nostrarum ut prædictum est

Assignavimus etiam, ac per præsentes, pro nobis, heredibus et successoribus nostris, assignamus, nominamus, et constituimus Edwardum Harbert, de Interiori Templo, Londini, armigerum, fore et esse primum et modernum senescallum curiæ palatii regis Westmonasterii ad omnia quæ ad senescallum curiæ palatii regis Westmonasterii pertinent faciendum et exequendum, Habendum, tenendum, exercendum, et exequendum dictum officium senescalli curiæ palatii regis Westmonasterii, eidem Edwardo Harbert, per se vel per sufficientem deputatum suum, ut præfertur deputandum, durante vita naturali ejusdem Edwardi Harbert

Assignavimus etiam, ac per præsentes, pro nobis, heredibus et successoribus nostris, assignamus, ordinamus, et constituimus Jo-

And that there be from henceforth, within the twelve miles aforesaid, one prison or gaol, for the keeping, retaining, and safe custody of all and singular the prisoners within the precincts or jurisdiction of the court aforesaid, attached or to be attached for any cause whatsoever, which shall happen to be heard or determined in the court aforesaid, or there to be commenced, there to be detained until they may be lawfully discharged We also will, and for us, our heirs, and successors, by these presents do grant, ordain, and constitute, that there be for ever in the court of the palace of the king at Westminster aforesaid, a certain submarshal of the court aforesaid, who may have the custody of the prison or gaol aforesaid

We have also appointed, and do by these presents, for us, our heirs, and successors, appoint, ordain and constitute, Sir Edmund Verney, Knight, now marshal of our household, [and the marshal of the household of us], our heirs and successors, who shall be for the time to come, respectively, to become and be judge with the steward of the household of us, our heirs and successors for the time being, and with the said steward of the court of the palace of the king at Westminster, by us nominated or to be nominated for another judge, as is aforesaid, in the court of the palace of the king at Westminster aforesaid, as long as there shall happen to be any steward of the household aforesaid which said marshal may, in the court aforesaid, sit with and advise the said steward of the household aforesaid, and the said steward of the court of the palace of the king at Westminster, or either of them, and have power or suffrage of ruling or giving judgment in all causes there pending or to be pending

We have also appointed, and we do by these presents for us, our heirs and successors, appoint, constitute and ordain, that at all future times, whensoever and as oftensoever as the aforesaid office of steward of the household of us, our heirs and successors, shall happen to be vacant, [that] the aforesaid Sir Edmund Verney, Knight, marshal of our household aforesaid, and the marshal of the said household of us, our heirs and successors, for the time being, respectively, may and shall be judge of the court of the palace of the king at Westminster aforesaid, conjointly with the steward of the court of the palace of the king at Westminster for the time being, as is aforesaid, by us nominated or to be nominated, and both and either of them shall and may be judge severally and separately in the said court, to hear and determine all and all manner of pleas, processes and causes aforesaid, in the time of the vacancy of the office of the steward of the household aforesaid, according to the tenor of our present letters, as is aforesaid We have also appointed, and by these presents we do, for us our heirs and successors, appoint, nominate, and constitute Edward Harbert, of the Inner Temple, at London, esquire, to become and be the first and present steward of the court of the palace of the king at Westminster, to do and execute all things which belong to the steward of the court of the palace of the king at Westminster, To have, hold, exercise, and execute the said office of steward of the court of the palace of the king at Westminster, to the said Edward Harbert, by himself or by his sufficient deputy, as is aforesaid to be deputed, during the natural life of the said Edward Harbert

We have also appointed, and we do by these presents, for us, our heirs, and successors, appoint, ordain, and constitute John

hannem Bert, armigerum, fore primum et modernum prothonotarium curiæ palatii regis Westmonasterii prædictæ ad omnia quæ ad
officium prothonotarii curiæ palatii regis Westmonasterii prædicta
pertinent, faciendum [et] exequendum, Habendum, tenendum, exercendum, et exequendum dictum officium prothonotarii curiæ palatii
regis Westmonasterii prædictæ, eidem Johanni Bert, per se, vel per
sufficientem deputatum suum sive deputatos suos sufficientes, durante vita naturali ejusdem Johannis Bert VOLUMUS etiam, ac per
præsentes, pro nobis, heredibus et successoribus nostris, ordinamus
et constituimus, quod senescalli hospitii nostri, heredum et successorum nostrorum, pro tempore existente, qui per præsentes judices
curiæ palatii regis Westmonasterii, ut præfertur, appunctuantur,
necnon prædictus Edmundus Verney, miles, marescallus hospitii
nostri, et marescallus hospitii nostri, heredum et successorum nostrorum, pro tempore existente, et dictus Edwardus Harbert, et quæcunque alia persona imposterum a nobis, aut heredibus aut successoribus nostris, pro judice in dicta curia palatii regis Westmonasterii, ut prædictum est nominanda et assignanda, atque etiam quilibet deputatus ejusdem Edwardi Harbert et cujuscunque aliæ personæ sic ut præfertur nominandæ et assignandæ, qui de tempore
in tempus nominabitur, eligetur, deputabitur, et assignabitur ut
prædictum est, respective, antequam ad officia sua respective exequendum admittantur, vel eorum aliquis respective admittatur,
coram cancellario Angliæ vel custode magni sigilli Angliæ, et coram marescallo Angliæ, camerario hospitii regis, thesaurario et
contrarotulatore hospitii nostri, heredum vel successorum nostrorum, vel coram eorum aliquo vel aliquibus, in loco publico, ubi
curia prædicta tunc respective tenebitur, sacramentum corporale
super sancta Dei evangelia, ad officium illud judicis curiæ palatii
regis Westmonasterii prædictæ rite, bene, juste, et fideliter exequendum, et ad plenam et celerem justitiam populo regis in
eadem curia, juxta eorum sanam discretionem et meliorem scientiam, intellectum, et judicium sua, administrandum et exhibendum,
et ad omnia alia ad officium judicis in dicta curia in aliquo spectanti
sive pertinentia observandum, præstabunt, et quilibet eorum respective præstabit

Quare volumus, ac per præsentes pro nobis, heredibus et successoribus nostris, damus et concedimus cancellario Angliæ, custodi magni sigilli Angliæ, marescallo Angliæ, camerario hospitii regis, thesaurario et contrarotulatori hospitii prædicti, tam præsentibus quam futuris, et quibuslibet et cuilibet eorum pro tempore
existente, vel temporibus existentibus, plenam potestatem et auctoritatem administrandi sacramentum corporale super sancta Dei
evangelia, tam modernis judicibus curiæ prædictæ in præsentibus
nominatis, quam omnibus aliis judicibus ejusdem curiæ deinceps in
perpetuum juxta tenorem præsentium literarum nostrarum patentium futuris, tam pro vera et fideli executione officii illius, in omnibus et per omnia officium illud tangentia, modo et forma prædictis,
quam sacramentum concernens primatiam regiam ecclesiasticam in
parliamento dominæ Elizabethæ nuper reginæ Angliæ, anno regni
sui primo tento, præstari ordinatum, et sacramentum de allegiantia
nobis, heredibus et successoribus nostris præstandum in parliamento domini Jacobi, nuper regis Angliæ, anno regni sui tertio tento,
ordinatum, et hoc absque aliqua commissione vel ulteriori warranto

Bert, Esq to be the first and present Prothonotary of the court of
the palace of the king at Westminster aforesaid, to do and execute
all things which belong to the office of prothonotary of the court of
the palace of the king at Westminster afore.. ud, To have, hold, exercise and execute the said office of Prothonotary of the court of the
palace of the King at Westminster aforesaid to the said John Bert,
by himself, or by his sufficient deputy or sufficient deputies, during the natural life of the said John Bert.

We will also, and we do by these presents, for us, our heirs and
successors, ordain and constitute, that the stewards of the household
of us, our heirs and successors, for the time being, who are by these
presents appointed judges of the court of the palace of the king at
Westminster, as is aforesaid, And also the aforesaid Sir Edmund
Verney, Knight, marshal of our household, and the marshal of the
household of us, our heirs and successors, for the time being, and
the said Edward Harbert, and whatsoever other person hereafter to
be nominated and appointed by us, or our heirs or successors, as judge
in the said court of the palace of the king at Westminster, as is aforesaid, and also every deputy of the said Edward Harbert, and of whatsoever other person so as is aforesaid to be nominated and appointed, who from time to time shall be nominated, elected, deputed and
appointed, as is aforesaid, respectively, before they are admitted, or
each of them respectively is admitted, to perform their offices respectively, they, and every one of them respectively shall take their corporal oath on the Holy Gospels of God, before the Chancellor of England, or the Keeper of the Great Seal of England, and before the Marshal of England, the Chamberlain of the king's household, the Treasurer and Comptroller of the household of us, our heirs or successors, or before any one or more of them, in a public place, where
the court aforesaid shall then be respectively holden, rightly, well,
justly, and faithfully to perform the said office of judge of the court
of the palace of the king at Westminster, aforesaid, and to administer and impart full and speedy justice to the king's people, in the
said court, according to their sound discretion and best skill, understanding and judgment, and to observe all other things in any wise
belonging or appertaining to the office of judge in the said court

Wherefore we will, and we do by these presents, for us, our
heirs and successors, give and grant to the Chancellor of England,
the Keeper of the Great Seal of England, the Marshal of England,
the Chamberlain of the king's household, the Treasurer and Comptroller of the household aforesaid, as well present as future, and to
every one and each of them for the time being, full power and
authority of administering a corporal oath, upon the holy gospels of God, as well to the present judges of the court aforesaid,
in these presents named, as to all other future judges of the said
court, from henceforth for ever, according to the tenor of our
present letters patent, as well for the true and faithful execution
of that office, in and by all things touching the said office, in
manner and form aforesaid, as the oath of supremacy ordained to
be taken in the parliament of the Lady Elizabeth, late Queen of
England, held in the first year of her reign, and the oath of allegiance to us, our heirs, and successors, ordained to be taken in the
parliament of the Lord James, late king, of England, held in the
third year of his reign And this, without any commission or fur-

a nobis, heredibus, vel successoribus nostris, in ea parte procurando aut obtinendo

Volumus tamen quod prædictus thesaurarius et contrarotulator hospitii pro tempore existente antequam ad executionem officii sive loci prædicti admittantur, seperaliter sacramentum prædictum coram cancellario Angliæ, sive custode magni sigilli Angliæ, marescallo Angliæ, et camerario hospitii, aut eorum aliquibus vel aliquo, præstabunt, quibus et eorum aliquibus vel aliquo, potestatem sacramentum prædictum administrandi pro nobis, heredibus et successoribus nostris, damus per præsentes

Volumus etiam, ac per præsentes pro nobis, heredibus et successoribus nostris, concedimus, quod de tempore in tempus, et ad omnia tempora post mortem prædicti Johannis Bert, aut postquam officium illud prothonotarii curiæ prædictæ per resignationem, amotionem, vel cessionem prædicti Johannis Bert, aut alio modo vacari contigerit, ac sic deinceps toties quoties casus sic acciderit, bene liceat et licebit marescallo hospitii nostri, heredum et successorum nostrorum, pro tempore existente, nominare et eligere unum alium virum discretum et idoneum fore et esse prothonotarium curiæ prædictæ. Quiquidem prothonotarius sic nominatus et electus per marescallum hospitii prædicti, ad officium illud exequendum de tempore in tempus admissus erit. Et quod ille qui sic in officium prothonotarii curiæ prædictæ de tempore in tempus nominatus, electus et admissus fuerit, officium illud habeat et exerceat durante vita sua naturali, per se vel per sufficientem deputatum suum, sive deputatos suos sufficientes, exequendum

Volumus insuper, et pro nobis, heredibus et successoribus nostris concedimus per præsentes, præfato senescallo et marescallo hospitii nostri, heredum et successorum nostrorum, pro tempore existente, et in tempore vacationis officii senescalli hospitii prædicti, marescallo ejusdem hospitii soli, plenam potestatem et authoritatem nominandi, ordinandi, constituendi, et admittendi quatuor personas consiliarios eruditos in lege, fore consiliarios, et sex alias idoneas personas fore attornatos in dicta curia palatii regis Westmonasterii prædicti, pro termino vitæ cujuslibet talis personæ, ad prosequendum et defendendum omnia et singula actiones, placita, et querelas in eadem curia mota sive movenda. Ac etiam damus, et pro nobis, heredibus et successoribus nostris concedimus marescallo hospitii nostri, heredum et successorum nostrorum, pro tempore existente, plenam potestatem et authoritatem nominandi, ordinandi, constituendi et admittendi, unam aliam personam fore submarescallum curiæ prædictæ, ac custodem prisonæ curiæ prædictæ, qui faciat et exequatur omnia quæ ad custodem prisonæ curiæ prædictæ pertinent facienda, et unam aliam idoneam personam fore janitorem ejusdem prisonæ, necnon unam aliam idoneam personam fore præconem vel proclamatorem dictæ curiæ, pro termino vitæ cujuslibet talis personæ, ad omnia et singula eisdem officiis respective, pro meliori servitio curiæ illius et expeditione causarum ibidem dependentium et dependendarum, in quo spectantia vel pertinentia, præstandum et exequendum. Quodque præfatus prothonotarius, quatuor consiliarii, sex attornati, submarescallus, janitor, et proclamator, antequam ad loca sive officia illa exequendum respective admittantur, seu eorum aliquis admittatur, sa-

ther warrant from us. our heirs or successors in that behalf to be procured or obtained   We will nevertheless that the aforesaid treasurer and controller of the household for the time being, before that they be admitted to the execution of the office or place aforesaid, shall separately take the oath aforesaid before the Chancellor of England, or the keeper of the great seal of England, the marshal of England, and the chamberlain of the household, or some or one of them, to whom and to some or one of them we by these presents, for us, our heirs and successors, give the power of administering the aforesaid oath

We also will, and do by these presents, for us, our heirs and successors, grant, that, from time to time, and at all times after the death of the aforesaid John Bert, or after that the said office of prothonotary of the court aforesaid shall happen to be vacant, by the resignation, removal, or cession of the aforesaid John Bert, or by any other means, and so hereafter as often as the case shall so happen, it may and shall be lawful for the marshal of the household of us, our heirs and successors, for the time being, to nominate and choose one other discreet and fit person to become and to be the Prothonotary of the court aforesaid, which prothonotary, so nominated and chosen by the marshal of the household aforesaid, shall be admitted from time to time to execute that office   And that he who shall be, from time to time, so nominated, chosen, and admitted into the office of prothonotary of the court aforesaid, may, during his natural life, have and exercise the said office, to be executed by himself, or by his sufficient deputy or deputies.

We also will, and do, by these presents, for us, our heirs and successors, grant to the aforesaid steward and marshal of the household of us, our heirs and successors, for the time being, and during the vacancy of the office of steward of the household aforesaid, to the marshal of the said household alone, the full power and authority of nominating, ordaining, constituting and admitting, four persons, counsellors learned in the law, to be counsel, and six other fit persons to be attornies in the said court of the palace of the king at Westminster aforesaid, for the term of the life of every such person, to prosecute and defend all and every actions, pleas, and plaints, commenced or to be commenced in the same court

And we also give, and for us, our heirs and successors, do grant to the marshal of the household of us, our heirs and successors, for the time being, the full power and authority of nominating, ordaining, constituting, and admitting one other person to be sub marshal of the court aforesaid and keeper of the prison of the court aforesaid, who may do and execute all the duties which belong to the keeper of the prison of the court aforesaid, and one other fit person to be turnkey of the said prison, and also one other fit person to be crier or proclamator of the said court, for the term of the life of every such person, to perform and execute all and singular the duties to the said offices respectively in any wise belonging or pertaining, for the better service of the said court, and the despatch of causes there pending and to be pending   And that the aforesaid prothonotary, the four counsellors, six attornies, submarshal, turnkey and crier, and every of them, before they or any one of them respectively be admitted to execute the said places or offices

cramentum corporale super sancta Dei evangelia, coram prædicto
senescallo hospitii, seu coram prædicto marescallo, pro tempore
existente, et coram prædicto senescallo curiæ palatii regis Westmonasterii, vel deputato ejus ut præfertur deputando, eorumve uno,
in curia prædicta, ad loca et officia illa respective bene et fideliter
exequendum, et in eisdem respective se bene gerendum, præstabunt, et eorum quilibet præstabit. Quibus quidem senescallo
et marescallo ac senescallo curiæ prædictæ, et deputato ejus, et
eorum cuilibet pro tempore existente, hujusmodi sacramentum de
tempore in tempus eisdem prothonotario, consiliariis, attornatis,
submarescallo, janitori, et proclamatori, et cuilibet et quibuslibet
eorum administrandi plenam potestatem et authoritatem, pro nobis, heredibus et successoribus nostris, damus et concedimus per
præsentes. Ac volumus quod in eadem curia, ad aliquod tempus,
sint tantum unus prothonotarius, quatuor consiliarii, sex attornati,
unus custos prisonæ, unus janitor prisonæ, et unus proclamator
curiæ prædictæ, quibus feoda in dicta curia allocata fuerint, pro
causis prosequendis et defendendis, seu aliis rebus agendis in eadem
curia et prisona prædictis.

Volumus insuper, ac per præsentes, pro nobis, heredibus et successoribus nostris, concedimus, ordinamus et constituimus quod
sint in perpetuum in curia palatii regis Westmonasterii prædicta
viginti portatores virgarum hospitii nostri ad minus, qui sint et
erunt officiarii curiæ palatii regis Westmonasterii prædictæ ad
exequendum mandata, brevia et processus e dicta curia palatii regis
Westmonasterii emanentia.

Damus ulterius, et per præsentes pro nobis, heredibus et successoribus nostris, concedimus marescallo hospitii nostri, heredum
et successorum nostrorum, et singulis marescallis ejusdem hospitii
pro tempore existente· Ac volumus tenore præsentium quod plenam potestatem et auctoritatem habeant successive nominandi,
constituendi et admittendi, de tempore in tempus, ad minus viginti
portatores virgarum nostrarum, fore officiarios curiæ nostræ prædictæ, heredum et successorum nostrorum, ad exequendum mandata, brevia et processus e dicta curia palatii regis Westmonasterii
emanantia Quodque quilibet eorundem portatorum virgarum,
antequam ad officium illud exequendum admittatur, sacramentum
corporale super sancta Dei evangelia, coram senescallo curiæ præ
dictæ vel deputato ejus pro tempore existente, ad seipsum in officio
illo bene gerendum præstabit, cui quidem senescallo curiæ prædictæ et deputato ejus hujusmodi sacramentum de tempore in tempus administrandi plenam potestatem et authoritatem, pro nobis,
heredibus et successoribus nostris, damus et concedimus per præsentes. Et quod iidem portatores virgarum prædictarum, sic de
tempore in tempus nominati, præfecti et jurati officia et loca illa
habeant et exerceant, et quilibet eorum habeat et exerceat, quamdiu se bene gesserit et gesserint in eodem vel eisdem, seu ad voluntatem dicti marescalli pro tempore existente prout ei placuerit.

Volumus etiam, ac per præsentes, pro nobis, heredibus et
successoribus nostris, firmiter injungendo præcipimus senescallo
hospitii nostri, heredum et successorum nostrorum, pro tempore
existente, et in tempore vacationis officii illius marescallo dicti
hospitii pro tempore existente, et senescallo curiæ palatii regis

shall take a corporal oath on the holy gospels of God, before the aforesaid steward of the household, or before the aforesaid marshal, for the time being, and before the aforesaid steward of the court of the palace of the king at Westminster, or his deputy, as is aforesaid, to be deputed, or one of them, in the aforesaid court, well and faithfully to execute the said places and offices respectively, and well to conduct themselves in the same respectively. To which said steward and marshal, and steward of the court aforesaid, and his deputy, and to each of them for the time being, we do by these presents, for us, our heirs and successors, give and grant full power and authority of administering such oath from time to time to the said prothonotary, counsellors, attornies, submarshal, turnkey and crier, and to each and every of them   And we will that, in the same court, at any time, there be only one prothonotary, four counsellors, six attornies, one keeper of the prison, one turnkey of the prison, and one crier of the court aforesaid, to whom the fees in the said court shall be allowed for causes prosecuted and defended, or other business done in the same court and prison aforesaid.

We will moreover, and by these presents, for us, our heirs and successors, do grant, ordain, and constitute, that there be for ever in the court of the palace of the king at Westminster aforesaid, at least twenty bearers of the rods of our household, who may and shall be the officers of the court of the palace of the king at Westminster aforesaid, to execute the orders, writs, and processes issuing out of the said court of the palace of the king at Westminster

We give moreover, and do by these presents, for us, our heirs and successors, grant to the marshal of the household of us, our heirs and successors, and to every marshal of the said household for the time being, and we will, by the tenor of these presents, that they may have full power and authority of successively nominating, constituting, and admitting, from time to time, at least twenty bearers of our rods, to become the officers of the aforesaid court of us, our heirs and successors, to execute the orders, writs, and processes issuing out of the said court of the palace of the king at Westminster.   And that every one of the same bearers of the rods, before he be admitted to execute that office, shall take a corporal oath on the holy gospels of God, before the steward of the court aforesaid or his deputy for the time being, to behave himself well in the said office, to which steward of the court aforesaid, and to his deputy, we give and grant, by these presents, for us, our heirs and successors, full power and authority of administering such oath from time to time   And that the same bearers of the rods aforesaid, so from time to time nominated, made, and sworn, and each of them may have and exercise the said offices and places, as long as they and each of them shall well behave themselves in the same, or at the will of the said marshal for the time being, as it shall seem right to him

We also will, and do by these presents, for us, our heirs and successors, firmly enjoin and command the steward of the household of us, our heirs and successors, for the time being, and, in the time of the vacancy of that office, the marshal of the said household for the time being, and the steward of the court of the palace

Westmonasterii, quod non omittant respective, nec ullus eorum respective omittat attendere in curia prædicta de die in diem, ut prædictum est, ad causas ibidem dependentes vel dependendas secundum leges et consuetudines regni nostri Angliæ audiendum et terminandum; et quod circa præmissa diligenter sint intendentes. Et quod iidem judices respective in omnibus hujusmodi causis, actionibus, placitis et querelis, coram eis vel eorum aliquo dependentibus, in quibus parti defendenti vel partibus defendentibus per legem regni nostri Angliæ, misæ, custagia et expensæ, quæ occasione sectarum versus ipsos vel eorum aliquem in curia prædicta sustinebunt, allocari vel adjudicari debeant, pro misis, custagiis et expensis suis ad plenas denariorum summas circa sectas illas respective per ipsos vel eorum aliquem expensas, taxent et assidant, et eorum quilibet taxet et assidat.

Ac ulterius, de uberiori gratia nostra speciali, ac ex certa scientia, et mero motu [nostris], concessimus et allocavimus, ac per præsentes pro nobis, heredibus et successoribus nostris, concedimus et allocamus præfatis judicibus, prothonotario, consiliariis, attornatis, submarescallo, janitori, proclamatori, et portatoribus virgarum prædictarum, et aliis officiariis et ministris curiæ prædictæ, pro tempore existente, ac volumus quod bene liceat et licebit eis et eorum cuilibet, de tempore in tempus, capere, percipere, et habere de omnibus et singulis personis in curia prædicta negotiantibus seu intromittentibus, talia et consimilia feoda et vada qualia in schedula his præsentibus annexa continentur et specificantur, secundum veram intentionem nostram in eadem schedula declaratam, et non alia neque plura feoda vel regarda.

Mandavimus etiam, ac pro nobis, heredibus et successoribus nostris, firmiter injungendo præcipimus omnibus et singulis justiciariis, vicecomitibus, custodibus gaolarum et prisonarum, ballivis, constabulariis, ac officiariis, et subditis nostris quibuscunque, infra duodecim leucas prædictas, tam infra libertates quam extra, quod sint prædictis judicibus curiæ prædictæ, et mandatis cujuslibet eorum, juxta tenorem et veram intentionem harum literarum nostrarum patentium in omnibus obedientes, et eorum cujuslibet præcepta et mandata diligenter et firmiter perimpleri et custodiri causare, ac omnibus officiariis et ministris curiæ prædictæ in executione officiorum suorum fore intendentes et auxiliantes, sub violatoris mandati nostri regii periculo incurrendi.

Et pro meliori et rectiori levatione exituum juratorum in eadem curia, volumus, statuimus, et ordinamus, quod licebit portatoribus virgarum, officiariis ejusdem curiæ, et eorum cuilibet de tempore in tempus, per mandatum judicum prædictorum, sub sigillo curiæ prædictæ sigillatum, exitus et fines juratorum in eadem curia contingentes per districtiones seu alio modo legitimo levare et recipere, et denarios sic levatos et receptos solvere in manus senescalli hospitii nostri, heredum et successorum nostrorum pro tempore existente, et hujusmodi senescallo non existente in manus marescalli ejusdem hospitii nostri pro tempore existente, ad usum nostrum, heredum et successorum nostrorum, priusquam extractus inde in scaccarium nostrum, heredum et successorum nostrorum, mittantur, ac licet non mittantur; de quibus quidem exitibus non

of the king at Westminster, that neither they respectively, nor any of them respectively, do omit to attend in the court aforesaid, from day to day, as is aforesaid, to hear and determine the causes there pending or to be pending, according to the laws and customs of our realm of England; and that they be diligently attentive with regard to the premises. And that the said judges respectively, and each of them, in all such causes, actions, pleas, and plaints, depending before them or any one of them, in which, by the law of our kingdom of England, to the party defendant or parties defendants the charges, costs, and expenses (which they shall sustain by occasion of the suits in the aforesaid court against them or any of them), ought to be allowed or adjudged, may tax and assess for their charges, costs, and expenses, to the full sums expended by them or any of them in their suits respectively.

And further, of our more abundant special grace, and of our certain knowledge, and mere motion, we have granted and allowed, and by these presents, for us, our heirs and successors, do grant and allow to the aforesaid judges, prothonotary, counsellors, attornies, sub-marshal, turnkey, crier, and bearers of the rods aforesaid, and to the other officers and ministers of the court aforesaid for the time being, and we will that it may and shall be lawful for them and every one of them, from time to time to take, receive, and have, of all and singular the persons having business or suits in the court aforesaid, such and the like fees and wages, as in the schedule to these presents annexed are contained and specified, according to our true intent in the said schedule declared, and no other or greater fees or rewards.

We have also commanded, and for us, our heirs and successors, do strictly enjoin and order all and singular our justices, sheriffs, keepers of gaols and prisons, bailiffs, constables, and officers and subjects whatsoever, within the aforesaid twelve miles, as well within liberties as without, that they be obedient in all things to the aforesaid judges of the court aforesaid, and to the commands of each of them, according to the tenor and true intent of these our letters patent, and cause the precepts and commands of each of them, to be diligently and firmly fulfilled and kept, and be aiding and assisting to all the officers and ministers of the court aforesaid in the execution of their offices, under the peril of incurring [the punishment] of a violator of our royal command.

And for the better and more ready levying of the issues of the jurors in the same court, we will, appoint, and ordain, that it shall be lawful for the bearers of the rods, (the officers of the same court), and any one of them, from time to time, by order of the judges aforesaid, sealed with the seal of the court aforesaid, by distress or any other lawful means, to levy and receive the issues and fines of the jurors arising in the same court; and to pay the sums so levied and received into the hands of the steward of the household of us, our heirs and successors for the time being, and there being no such steward, into the hands of the marshal of our same household for the time being, to the use of us, our heirs and successors, before the estreats thereof are sent into the exchequer of us, our heirs and successors, and although they are not sent. And of the

receptis prædictum senescallum hospitii nostri, heredum et successorum nostrorum, pro tempore existente, et in vacatione officii senescalli hospitii prædictum marescallum ejusdem hospitii pro tempore existente, in quolibet anno inter festum Omnium Sanctorum, et festum Purificationis beatæ Mariæ Virginis, extractus mitti facere in scaccarium nostrum, heredum et successorum nostrorum; et de denariis inde receptis prædictum senescallum hospitii nostri, heredum et successorum nostrorum pro tempore existente, et in vacatione officii senescalli hospitii nostri prædictum marescallum dicti hospitii pro tempore existente, computum reddere coram baronibus de scaccario nostro, heredum vel successorum nostrorum, singulis annis inter festa prædicta, volumus per præsentes: quibus baronibus tenore præsentium mandamus, quatenus denarios non levatos ad opus nostrum, heredum et successorum nostrorum levari faciant; et de denariis prædictis solutis solvent inde erga nos heredes et successores nostros acquietare absque feodo aliquo proinde solvendo. Quibus quidem virgarum portatoribus denarios prædictos levare, et prædictis judicibus eosdem levari mandare, potestatem damus et concedimus per præsentes, statuto seu ordinatione de forma mittendi extractus ad scaccarium aut aliquo alio statuto, actu seu ordinatione non obstante.

Volumus etiam, et per præsentes pro nobis, heredibus et successoribus nostris concedimus, quod hæ literæ nostræ patentes, et omnia in eisdem contenta et specificata, sunt et erunt in omnibus et per omnia firmæ, validæ et effectuales in lege, non obstante non nominando aliquam concessionem de præmissis seu de aliqua inde parcella, per nos vel aliquem progenitorum sive prædecessorum nostrorum antehac factam, ac non obstante male nominando, male recitando, vel non nominando vel non recitando, vel non recte nominando præmissa vel aliquam inde parcellam; ac non obstante statuto in parliamento domini Edwardi nuper regis Angliæ primi, progenitoris nostri, [anno regni sui tertio] tento, edito; ac non obstante statuto in parliamento domini Henrici nuper regis Angliæ quarti, anno regni sui primo [tento, edito]; et non obstante statuto in parliamento dicti domini Henrici nuper regis Angliæ quarti, anno regni sui secundo tento, edito; et non obstante statuto in parliamento domini Henrici nuper regis Angliæ sexti, anno regni sui vicesimo tertio tento, edito; aut aliquo alio statuto, actu, ordinatione, provisione, constitutione, vel restrictione, aut aliqua alia causa vel materia quacunque in contrarium inde non obstante. IN cujus rei, &c. teste rege apud Canbury, duodecimo die Julii, &c.

Per breve de Privato Sigillo.

*** *The schedule of costs attached to the Letters Patents of 22 Jac. I & 6 Car. I. are precisely the same as that of 9 Jac I., excepting that in these the words* Senescallo et Marescallo Hospitii Domini Regis *are substituted in all the items where the word* Judicibus *occurs in the former; and the words* et in vacatione officii Senescalli, prædicto Marescallo tantum, *are added after the word* dividendum.

issues not recovered, we will, by these presents, that the aforesaid steward of the household of us, our heirs and successors for the time being, and in the vacancy of the office of steward of the household, that the aforesaid marshal of the same household for the time being, every year, between the feast of All Saints and the feast of the Purification of the blessed Virgin Mary, do cause the estreats to be sent into the Exchequer of us, our heirs and successors; and of the money thence received, that the aforesaid steward of the household of us, our heirs and successors, for the time being, and in the vacancy of the office of steward of our household, that the aforesaid marshal of the said household for the time being, do render an account before the barons of the exchequer of us, our heirs or successors, every year, between the aforesaid feasts. Which barons, by the tenor of these presents, we command, that they cause the monies not levied to be levied to the use of us, our heirs and successors; and to give a quietus of the monies paid as aforesaid, against us, our heirs and successors, without any fee to be paid for the same: to which said bearers of the rods we give and grant by these presents, power to levy the monies aforesaid, and to the judges aforesaid to command the same to be levied, notwithstanding the statute or ordinance respecting the manner of transmitting estreats to the Exchequer, or any other statute, act, or ordinance.

We also will, and do by these presents, for us, our heirs and successors, grant, that these our letters patent, and all things contained and specified therein, may and shall be firm, valid, and effectual in law, in and by all things, notwithstanding the not naming any grant touching the premises, or any parcel thereof, by us, or any of our ancestors or predecessors heretofore made, and notwithstanding the mis-naming, mis-reciting, or not naming or not reciting, or not correctly naming the premises, or any parcel thereof: And notwithstanding the statute enacted in the Parliament of Lord Edward the First, our progenitor, late King of England, held in the third year of his reign; and notwithstanding the act of parliament of Lord Henry the Fourth, late King of England, in the first year of his reign; and notwithstanding the statute enacted in the Parliament of the said Lord Henry the Fourth, late King of England, held in the second year of his reign; and notwithstanding the statute enacted in the Parliament of Lord Henry the Sixth, late King of England, held in the twenty-third year of his reign, or any other statute, act, ordinance, provision, constitution or restriction, or any other cause or matter whatsoever to the contrary hereof notwithstanding.

In witness whereof, &c   Witness the King at Canbury, the 12th day of July, &c.

By writ of Privy Seal.

16 *CAR. II*[*].

RëX omnibus ad quos, &c. salutem. CUM nobis expediens et necessarium visum fuerit, ut omnes et singuli subditi nostri et personæ
quæcunque infra duodecim milliaria circumquaque a palatio nostro
de Westmonasterio, situato in comitatu nostro Middlesexiæ, ubi vel
juxta quod nos plerumque et concilium nostrum sæpius et magis
quam in aliis palatiis nostris alibi sitis residere consuevimus, ac magis quam aliqui progenitores nostri reges Angliæ et concilia sua olim
residere consueverunt, residentes, inhabitantes, confluentes, commorantes, contrahentes, negotiantes, seu existentes, in omnibus et
omnimodis actionibus, placitis, et querelis suis personalibus celeriorem haberent justitiam, eo quod ipsi tam in negotiis et servitiis nostris quam in occasionibus charissimæ consortis nostræ et concilii nostri necnon officiariorum et famulorum nostrorum, multo magis et
sæpius quam alii subditi nostri in remotioribus partibus Angliæ
commorantes, occupantur et implicantur Quod ideo imprimis
evenit, quia quoties et quandocunque ad alias ædes seu palatia nos-

* In the following extract from Rushworth, we may discover the reasons
which induced Charles II. to revise the preceding letters. The petition presented to both houses of parliament, in 1663, praying redress of the great
abuses which existed in the practice of the court; and the opinion expressed
by Keeling, in Hilary Term, 1664, (Sid. 186) that the letters of Charles I.
" were void, and every defendant taken might bring trespass and false imprisonment," were perhaps the immediate causes of the present grant.

A New Court for them which were not of the King's Household.

" It pleased the king's majesty to write unto the judges of the King's
Bench, letters in some manner expostulatory, as if they took exceptions at
the erection of the new court of the marshal of the household, to hold plea
de non existentibus de hospitio regis, which court was first erected by the
grant of King James, *February* 15th, 22 *Jac.*, and again renewed with more
perfection, as was conceived, in *November,* 6 *Caroli.* And a writ of error
being brought into the King's Bench, upon a judgment given in this court,
the knight marshal fearing this new grant would not be held good in law,
caused the king to write to the said judges, as aforesaid.

" To which letter an answer was sent to the king penned by me (Mr. J.
Whitelock) per mandatum curiæ
" Dread Sovereign,
" We make bold to inform your majesty, in answer to your gracious letter unto us, of the 24th of *June* last, that about two years since, we were consulted
with, by your attorney general, about the validity of letters patent of the
twenty-second year of your late dear father, for the erection of a new court
within the verge, for those not of the household; and the said letters patent
were once read over before us, being assembled privately about that business, and copies were appointed to be brought unto us to take the better
consideration thereof; but no copies were delivered unto us, neither did we
hear any more of the business.
" We find it also to be true, that some against whom judgments had been

16 *CHARLES II.*—1664.

CHARLES, &c , to all to whom, &c. greeting —Whereas, it hath appeared unto us expedient and necessary, that all and singular our subjects and persons whatsoever residing, inhabiting, resorting, tarrying, contracting, trafficking or being within twelve miles, every way, from our palace of Westminster, situate in our county of Middlesex, (where or near which we most commonly, and our council oftener and more than in our other palaces elsewhere situate have been accustomed to reside, and more than any of our progenitors, the kings of England, and their councils have formerly been accustomed to reside), should have more speedy justice in all and all manner of their personal actions, pleas, and plaints, because they are much more and more frequently occupied and engaged, as well in our affairs and service as in the business of our most dear consort and of our council, and also of our officers and domestics, than other our subjects residing in more remote parts of England which happens on this account especially, because as often and whensoever at our pleasure we are accustomed to retire to our other houses or palaces situated elsewhere, we sooner return to Westmin-

given in the said court, did bring them before us by writ of error, but did not proceed so far as to argument or judgment, and as to the new patent sithence granted, we knew not of it until after it was passed, nor were ever acquainted with the penning or passing thereof.

"We understand also, that a writ of error is brought before us by *Fisher* v *Wagstaff*, upon a judgment given in the last erected court, which cause hath proceeded no further than to the reading of the record. And the error assigned is only this, that neither of the parties were of your majesty's household, but the day to hear counsel not being yet come, we cannot understand, till we hear them, upon what points they will stand.

"And your majesty may be pleased to be informed that the cause cometh before us by an ordinary course of proceeding, which we cannot stop, neither did we know of the cause, nor take notice of it, until the record was read in court, but when it shall be spoken unto, and we know what the question will be, we will be exceeding careful and circumspect according to our oaths, that your majesty shall not suffer any prejudice or diminution in your power, royal and prerogative, neither do we make doubt, but that your majesty hath as full and as great power, and high prerogative, as any of your noble progenitors ever had, and we will ever maintain it to be so. And whereas your majesty's pleasure is to be informed by us of the defects in the said last patent, we have not yet heard the counsel open them what they are, that they mean to stand upon. However, if it be your majesty's pleasure, that we should, by way of consultation, take this patent into our consideration, we humbly desire your majesty, that forasmuch as it is a matter of so great importance, that your majesty will be pleased for your better satisfaction to give order, that herein we may have the assistance of your judges of the Common Pleas, and barons of your Exchequer. And we shall all endeavour to do your majesty true and faithful service herein, and so we recommend your majesty by our prayers to the protection of the Almighty, and rest

    Your majesty's faithful servants and subjects."

2 Rush Coll p. 104 *Ed.* 1680. *Trin 7 Car.* 2 *B. R*

tra alibi sita ad libitum nostrum secedere nobis contingere solet, reditus noster ad Westmonasterium citius contingit; unde etiam residentes, inhabitantes, confluentes, et commorantes, infra dicta duodecim milliaria, eam ob causam maxime, tam durante præsentia nostra ad dictum palatium nostrum quam dum absumus, contractibus atque aliis negotiis ad provisionem in reditum nostrum et servitia nostra alia spectantibus perpetuo involvuntur, et præ cæteris subditis nostris onerantur: AC licet Curia Marescaltiæ Hospitii Regum Angliæ sit antiqua curia, ordinata pro bona conservatione ac custodia pacis infra hospitium regum Angliæ, ubicunque pro tempore fuerit, ac ad placita tenendum in diversis actionibus et querelis inter diversas personas infra hospitium et virgam hospitii prædicti emergentibus, prout per leges et statuta hujus regni nostri Angliæ liquet et apparet. Ac nihilominus subditi nostri infra præcincta virgæ prædictæ inhabitantes, confluentes aut commorantes, non autem de hospitio nostro existentes, in eadem curia marescaltiæ hospitii nostri, in diversis legitimis causis [et] actionibus nulla remedia habere potuerunt: Ac præterea placita et querelæ in eadem curia inchoatæ, et antequam nos ex limitibus virgæ ejusdem hospitii discesserimus non finitæ et determinatæ, secundum leges et statuta hujus regni nostri Angliæ per discessionem nostram ex dictis limitibus cessare solent, adeo etiam ut sæpenumero infra dicta duodecim milliaria contingit, quod justitia in placitis et querelis ibi ut præfertur inchoatis, et per nostram ut præfertur discessionem cessituris, non sine gravi et multa dilatione exhibeatur*

Sciatis igitur, quod nos, de cura nostra regia festinum in hac parte remedium adhibere cupientes, ut omnes et omnimodæ actiones, placita et querelæ personales omnium et singulorum subditorum nostrorum et personarum quarumcunque residentium, inhabitantium, confluentium, contrahentium, negotiantium, seu existentium, infra prædicta duodecim milliaria a dicto palatio nostro de Westmonasterio circumquaque extensa, et infra præcincta illa surgentes et emergentes, celerius tractentur et expediantur, de gratia nostra speciali, ac ex certa scientia et mero motu nostris, fecimus, creavimus, ereximus, ordinavimus, et constituimus, ac per præsentes, pro nobis, heredibus et successoribus nostris, facimus, creamus, erigimus, ordinamus, et constituimus unam curiam de recordo infra palatium nostrum Westmonasterii, et duodecim milliaria a dicto palatio circumquaque extendentia, coram judicibus infra scriptis duobus vel uno eorum, infra prædictum palatium nostrum Westmonasterii vel in aliquo alio loco publico et idoneo infra dicta duodecim milliaria ab eodem palatio nostro Westmonasterii ut præfertur extendentia, magna aula nostra placitorum Wesmonasterii et locis in quibus curia cameræ stellatæ, curia scaccarii, curia ducatus Lancastriensis, ac curia vocata Whitehall, teneri solebant, exceptis, tenendam; quæ per nomen Curiæ Domini Regis Palatii Regis Westmonasterii vocabitur et nuncupabitur, pro administratione et exhibitione justitiæ in actionibus, placitis et querelis personalibus, omnibus et singulis personis ibidem placitare volentibus, de omnibus et omnimodis transgressionibus vi et armis, transgressionibus super casum, debitis, com-

---

* Before the Palace Court was instituted, where a suit was discontinued in the Marshalsea, the plaintiff had no other resource than to commence a fresh suit at common law, for, in inferior courts, if the suit is once discontinued, it cannot be renewed

ster; whence also the persons residing, inhabiting, resorting, and tarrying within the said twelve miles, on that account especially, as well during our presence at our said palace as while we are absent, are constantly engaged in contracts and other businesses relating to the providing for our return and our other services, and are more burthened than the rest of our subjects:

And although the Court of the Marshalsea of the Household of the kings of England is an ancient Court, constituted for the good preservation and keeping of the peace within the household of the kings of England, wheresoever for the time it shall be, and for holding pleas in divers actions and plaints arising between divers persons within the household and the virge of the household aforesaid, as by the laws and statutes of this our realm of England is clear and evident: And, nevertheless, our subjects inhabiting, resorting, or tarrying within the precincts of the virge aforesaid, but not being of our household, could have no remedy in divers lawful causes [and] actions in the said court of the Marshalsea of our household: And besides, the pleas and plaints commenced in the same court, and not finished and determined before we shall have departed from the limits of the virge of the same household, according to the laws and statutes of this our kingdom of England are accustomed to abate on account of our departure out of the said limits; so that it oftentimes happens within the said twelve miles, that justice cannot be administered without grievous and great delay in the pleas and plaints there (as above mentioned) commenced, and abating (as above mentioned) by our departure: KNOW ye, therefore, that we, of our royal care, being desirous to apply a speedy remedy in this behalf, that all and all manner of personal actions, pleas, and plaints of all and singular our subjects and persons whatsoever residing, inhabiting, resorting, contracting, trafficking, or being within the aforesaid twelve miles, extending every way from our said palace of Westminster, and arising and happening within those precincts, may be more quickly proceeded in and facilitated;—We of our special grace, and of our certain knowledge and mere motion, have made, created, erected, ordained, and constituted, and by these presents, for us, our heirs and successors, do make, create, erect, ordain, and constitute one court of record within our palace of Westminster, and twelve miles extending every way from the said palace, to be holden before the two judges under-mentioned, or one of them, within our aforesaid palace of Westminster, or in some other public and proper place within the said twelve miles extending as aforesaid from our said palace of Westminster, except our Great Hall of Pleas at Westminster, and the places in which the court of Star Chamber, the court of Exchequer, the court of the Duchy of Lancaster, and the court called Whitehall, are accustomed to be holden; which shall be called and named by the name of The Court of the Lord the King of the Palace of the King at Westminster, for the administration and exhibition of justice in personal actions, pleas, and plaints, to all and every the persons willing to plead there concerning all and all manner of trespasses *vi et armis*, trespasses upon the case, debts, accounts, detinues of goods and

putis, detentionibus bonorum et catallorum, deceptionibus et contractibus, et aliis causis, loquelis, et placitis personalibus quibuscunque, de quacunque summa*, infra palatium prædictum, seu in aliquibus locis sive aliquo loco infra dicta duodecim milliaria, a dicto palatio nostro Westmonasterii sic ut præfertur extendentia, surgentibus, perpetratis, habitis, motis, vel emergentibus, cujuscunque comitatus fuerint loca illa, infra dicta duodecim milliaria, (excepta civitate nostra Londini), et exceptis omnibus hujusmodi actionibus placitis, et querelis personalibus, in quibus tam querens vel querentes quam defendens vel defendentes sint vel fuerint, sit vel fuerit de hospitio nostro, heredum vel successorum nostrorum, tempore quo dictum palatium infra virgam hospitii nostri, heredum et successorum nostrorum, pro tempore existente, fore contigerit, et omnibus aliis actionibus de transgressionibus vi et armis, in quibus vel querens vel defendens sit vel fuerit de hospitio prædicto tempore quo dictum palatium infra virgam hospitii nostri, heredum et successorum nostrorum, pro tempore existente, fore contigerit†: Et curiam illam de novo erigi et constitui volumus, ac erigimus et constituimus per præsentes. VOLUMUS etiam, ac per præsentes pro nobis, heredibus et successoribus nostris, concedimus, ordinamus et constituimus, quod curia illa sit curia de recordo de die in diem qualibet septimana per annum, exceptis diebus Dominicis et diebus festis Natalis Domini, Circumcisionis Domini, Epiphaniæ, Purificationis et Annunciationis Beatæ Mariæ Virginis, Parasceves, Ascensionis Domini, Nativitatis Sancti Johannis Baptistæ, Sancti Michaelis Archangeli, Omnium Sanctorum, et Omnium Animarum, coram senescallo hospitii nostri, heredum et successorum nostrorum, pro tempore existente, ac marescallo hospitii nostri, heredum et successorum nostrorum, pro tempore existente, et senescallo dictæ Curiæ Domini Regis Palatii Regis Westmonasterii, pro tempore existente; ac in absentia prædicti marescalli pro tempore existente, seu hujusmodi marescallo non existente, coram senescal-

---

* Although by these general words the jurisdiction is limited to no sum, yet when the alleged damages exceed 5l., the cause may be removed into the superior courts by *habeas corpus* (21 Jac. 1, c 23); provided the writ is delivered to the judges before the jury are sworn, or before issue or demurrer is joined, if it has happened that the joining of such issue or demurrer has been delayed six weeks after the defendant's appearance. This writ of *habeas corpus* would very generally be resorted to by defendants, to avoid the quick proceedings of the court, were it not restrained by the stat. 19 Geo. 3, cap. 70, sec 6, which enacts, that no cause, where the cause of action shall not amount to the sum of 15l., shall be removed into a superior court, unless the defendant shall enter into a recognizance to the plaintiff with two sufficient sureties in double the sum due for payment of the debt and costs, in case judgment shall pass against him.

In actions above 15l there is no restriction whatever, and although some defendants are found willing to try their actions for this amount in the Palace Court, at one fourth of the expense of a trial in the superior Courts, yet it is the result of practical observation that almost all actions of this class (not immediately settled on the execution of the process) are removed by the defendants into either the courts of King's Bench or Common Pleas. This obviously proceeds from the facility which the writ of *habeas corpus* gives a defendant of throwing delay and expense in the way of his plaintiff, joined also

rhattels, frauds and contracts, and other personal causes, plaints, and pleas whatsoever, of whatsoever amount, arising, done, had, moved, or happening, within the aforesaid palace, or in any places or place within the said twelve miles, so extending as aforesaid from our said palace of Westminster, of whatsoever county those places within the said twelve miles shall be, (except our city of London), and except all such personal actions, pleas, and plaints in which as well the plaintiff   plaintiffs as the defendant or defendants may or   . of the   household of us, our heirs or successors at the time when the said   palace shall happen to be within the virge of the household of us, our heirs and successors for the time being, and all other actions of trespass *vi et armis*, in which either the plaintiff or defendant may or shall be of the household aforesaid, at the time when the said palace shall happen to be within the virge of the household of us, our heirs and successors for the time being; and we will that the same court be new erected and constituted, and by these presents we do erect and constitute it.

We also will, and do by these presents, for us, our heirs, and successors, grant, ordain, and constitute, that the said court be a court of record, to be holden from day to day, every week throughout the year, except the Lord's-day and the feast days of Christmas, Circumcision of our Lord, Epiphany, Purification and Annunciation of the blessed Virgin Mary, Good Friday, Ascension of our Lord, Nativity of St John the Baptist, St. Michael the Archangel, All Saints, and All Souls, before the steward of the household of us, our heirs, and successors for the time being, and the marshal of the household of us, our heirs and successors for the time being, and the steward of the said Court of the lord the King of the Palace of the King at Westminster for the time being; and in the absence of the aforesaid marshal for the time being, or there being no such marshal, before the steward of the household

to the advice he receives from his solicitor, who rarely happens to be an attorney practising in the Palace Court.

A writ of error lies from the Palace Court into the King's Bench, but is restrained by the stat. 19 Geo 3, c 70, from reversing any judgment given therein, provided the damages laid in the declaration are under 15*l.*, unless the defendant and two sufficient sureties shall first become bound in a recognizance to prosecute the said writ of error, and to pay the debt and costs in case judgment shall be affirmed.

See as to what constitutes error in plea to jurisdiction, 2 Inst. 229. 3 Lev. 25 1 Lev 105 1 Ro. Abr 797, 8, 9. 1 Keb. 846. 1 Vent. 369. 2 Mod 58. 271 *Lucking* v *Denning*, Salk. 201, and 9 B Moore, 413.

† The exception in favour of the household was made to prevent the jurisdiction of this court interfering with that of the Marshalsea, and therefore renders the common averment necessary, that neither the plaintiff nor the defendant, nor either of them at the time of levying the plaint, were, or now are, of the King's household, yet, notwithstanding, a prohibition was prayed (*Mich.* 10 *Wil.* 3, *Salk.* 430) to the Marshalsea, [Palace Court], because they refused to admit a plea that neither of the parties were *de hospitio regis* which was refused.

Although no business is now done in the Marshalsea, the Court is regularly opened and adjourned with the Palace Court.

lo hospitii prædicti pro tempore existente, ac senescallo dictæ curiæ domini regis palatii regis Westmonasterii, pro tempore existente; et in absentia hujusmodi senescalli hospitii prædicti, seu hujusmodi senescallo hospitii prædicti non existente, coram marescallo hospitii prædicti pro tempore existente, ac senescallo dictæ curiæ domini regis palatii regis Westmonasterii, pro tempore existente; ac in absentia hujusmodi senescalli hospitii prædicti ac marescalli, seu neutro eorum existente, coram prædicto senescallo dictæ curiæ domini regis palatii regis Westmonasterii, pro tempore existente, tenenda*.

Volumus etiam, pro nobis, heredibus et successoribus nostris, quod de cætero in perpetuum erit quoddam officium, quod officium senescalli curiæ domini regis palatii regis Westmonasterii vocabitur et nuncupabitur, ac officium senescalli curiæ domini regis palatii regis Westmonasterii facimus, creamus, et constituimus pro nobis, heredibus et successoribus nostris per præsentes. VOLUMUS etiam, pro nobis, heredibus et successoribus nostris quod de cætero in perpetuum erit quidam officiarius, per nos, heredes et successores nostros de tempore in tempus nominandus et constituendus, qui in legibus hujus regni nostri Angliæ eruditus erit, et qui senescallus curiæ domini regis palatii regis Westmonasterii vocabitur et nuncupabitur, et de tempore in tempus quamdiu se bene gesserit in officio illo, officium illud senescalli curiæ domini regis palatii regis Westmonasterii exequetur et fungetur. Quodque erunt in perpetuum judices quidam in eadem curia, qui judices curiæ domini regis palatii regis Westmonasterii vocabuntur et nuncupabuntur, ad cognoscendum et cognitionem habendum de omnibus et singulis placitis, actionibus, et querelis in his literis patentibus, secundum formam earum, specificatis, et ad omnia et singula placita de omnibus et singulis dictis actionibus, placitis, et querelis tenendum; qui, de tempore in tempus, respective cognoscent, cognitionem habebunt, et placita tenebunt in dicta curia per querelas in eadem curia levandas, de omnibus et omnimodis transgressionibus vi et armis, transgressionibus super casum, debitis, computis, detentionibus bonorum et catallorum, deceptionibus, contractibus, et aliis causis, loquelis, et placitis personalibus quibuscunque, de quacunque summa, infra dictum palatium nostrum Westmonasterii, seu in aliquo loco sive aliquibus locis infra dicta duodecim milliaria a prædicto palatio circumquaque extendentia, surgentibus et emergentibus, (excepta civitate Londini prædicta), ac exceptis omnibus hujusmodi actionibus, placitis, et querelis personalibus, in quibus tam querens vel querentes, quam defendens vel defendentes sint vel fuerint, sit vel fuerit de hospitio nostro, heredum vel successorum nostrorum, tempore quo dictum palatium infra virgam hospitii nostri, heredum vel successorum nostrorum pro tempore existente, fore contigerit, et omnibus aliis actionibus de transgressionibus vi et armis, in quibus vel querens vel defendens sit vel fuerit de hospitio prædicto, tempore quo dictum palatium infra virgam hospitii nostri, heredum et successorum nostrorum, pro tempore existente, fore contigerit. VOLUMUS insuper, et concedimus pro nobis, heredibus et successoribus nostris quod senescallus hospitii nostri, heredum et successorum nostrorum, qui pro tempo-

---

* The Steward of the court is now in fact the only Judge.

aforesaid for the time being, and the steward of the said court of
the lord the king of the palace of the king at Westminster for the
time being ; and in the absence of such steward of the household
aforesaid, or there being no such steward of the household aforesaid, before the marshal of the household aforesaid for the time being, and the steward of the said court of the lord the king of the
palace of the king at Westminster, for the time being; and in the
absence of such steward and marshal of the household aforesaid,
or there being neither of them, before the aforesaid steward of the
said court of the lord the king of the palace of the king at Westminster, for the time being.

We also will, for us, our heirs and successors, that from henceforth for ever there shall be a certain office, which shall be called
and named The Office of the Steward of the Court of the lord the
King of the Palace of the King at Westminster; and we by these
presents, for us, our heirs and successors, do make, create, and
constitute The Office of Steward of the Court of the lord the King
of the Palace of the King at Westminster.

We also will for us, our heirs and successors, that from henceforth
for ever there shall be a certain officer, by us, our heirs, and successors from time to time to be nominated and appointed, who
shall be learned in the laws of this our kingdom of England, and
who shall be called and named The Steward of the Court of the
lord the King of the Palace of the King at Westminster; and from
time to time, as long as he shall behave himself well in that office,
he shall execute and enjoy the said office of steward of the court
of the lord the king of the palace of the king at Westminster. And
that there shall be for ever certain judges in the same court, who
shall be called and named The Judges of the Court of the Lord
the King of the Palace of the King at Westminster, to hear and
take cognizance of all and singular the pleas, actions, and plaints
in these letters patent specified, according to the form thereof,
and to hold all and singular the pleas of all and singular the said
actions, pleas, and plaints; who from time to time respectively
shall hear and take cognizance, and hold pleas in the said court,
by plaints to be levied in the same court, of all and all manner of
trespasses *vi et armis*, trespasses on the case, debts, accounts, detinues of goods and chattels, frauds, contracts, and all other personal
causes, plaints, and pleas whatsoever, of whatsoever sum, arising or
happening within our said palace of Westminster, or in any place or
places within the said twelve miles every way extending from the
aforesaid palace, except the aforesaid city of London, and except all
such personal actions, pleas and plaints, in which as well the plaintiff
or plaintiffs, as the defendant or defendants, may or shall be of
the household of us, our heirs or successors, at the time when the
said palace shall happen to be within the virge of the household of
us, our heirs or successors for the time being, and all other.ac-
tions of trespasses *vi et armis*, in which either the plaintiff or defendant may or shall be of the household aforesaid, at the time
when the said palace shall happen to be within the virge of the
household of us, our heirs and successors for the time being.

We will moreover, and for us, our heirs and successors, do grant,
that the steward of the household of us, our heirs and successors for

ro fuerit, et marescallus hospitii nostri, heredum et successorum nostrorum pro tempore existente, et senescallus dictæ curiæ domini regis palatii regis Westmonasterii pro tempore existente in perpetuum, erunt et sint judices conjunctim, et quilibet eorum sit et erit judex divisim et separatim in dicta curia, ad cognoscendum et cognitionem habendam de querelis, actionibus, et placitis prædictis in curia prædicta, ut præfertur, cognoscendis et tenendis seu tractandis, et ad placita inde tenendum ; et quod quandocunque, quotiescunque, et quamdiu contigerit nullum senescallum hospitii nostri, heredum vel successorum nostrorum —— existere, tunc et tamdiu marescallus hospitii nostri, heredum et successorum nostrorum, qui pro tempore fuerit, et senescallus dictæ curiæ domini regis palatii regis Westmonasterii, pro tempore existente, sint et erunt judices conjunctim, et uterque et alteruter eorum sit et erit judex divisim et separatim in eadem curia, ad cognoscendum et cognitionem habendum de actionibus, querelis, et placitis prædictis in curia prædicta, ut præfertur, cognoscendis et tenendis seu tractandis, et ad placita inde tenendum   Et quod eodem modo quandocunque, quotiescunque et quamdiu contigerit nullum marescallum hospitii nostri, heredum et successorum nostrorum, existere, tunc et tamdiu senescallus hospitii nostri, heredum et successorum nostrorum, qui pro tempore fuerit, et senescallus dictæ curiæ domini regis palatii regis Westmonasterii pro tempore existente, sint et erunt judices conjunctim, et uterque et alteruter eorum sit et erit judex divisim et separatim in eadem curia, ad cognoscendum et cognitionem habendum de actionibus, querelis et placitis prædictis in curia prædicta, ut præfertur, cognoscendis et tenendis seu tractandis, ac ad placita inde tenendum.   Et quod dicti senescallus et marescallus hospitii prædicti, et senescallus curiæ domini regis palatii regis Westmonasterii, qui pro tempore respective fuerit, et eorum quilibet, ut prædictum est, habeant et habebunt, habeat et habebit potestatem et authoritatem personas defendentes, versus quas hujusmodi querelæ, placita, sive actiones in prædicta curia levari vel moveri contigerint, in placita deducere per summonitiones, attachiamenta et districtiones, et alios processus, secundum leges et consuetudines regni nostri Angliæ, portatoribus virgarum hospitii prædicti, officiariis et ministris curiæ prædictæ, per marescallum hospitii prædicti, qui pro tempore fuerit, nominandis et constituendis, vel eorum alicui vel aliquibus, dirigenda, et pro defectu catallorum et terrarum hujusmodi defendentium infra jurisdictionem curiæ illius, ubi sive per quæ summoniri, attachiari, vel distringi possint, per attachiamenta aut captionem corporum suorum, ubivis infra jurisdictionem curiæ illius ; Et de actionibus, querelis et placitis superdictis omnibus et singulis (exceptis in casibus præexceptis), cognitionem habere, et placita inde cognoscere et tenere respective, in tam amplis modo et forma prout aliqua alia curia nostra de recordo*, per leges et

---

* Notwithstanding these words it was made a question, Siderf. 248, *Rogers* v *Marshall*, whether a *capias* in mesne process, in any action on the case, would lie in the Palace Court, because 19 H 7, which gives a *capias* upon mesne process in an action on the case, mentions only the Courts of Westminster Hall, but the practice of awarding such process doth now, and hath long since prevailed

the time being, and the marshal of the household of us, our heirs and successors for the time being, and the steward of the said court of the lord the king of the palace of the king at Westminster, for the time being for ever, shall and may be judges conjointly, and any one of them may and shall be a judge severally and separately in the said court, to hear and take cognizance of the aforesaid plaints, actions, and pleas in the court aforesaid, as is aforesaid, to be heard and held or proceeded on, and to hold pleas thereon, and that whensoever and as often soever and as long as it shall happen that there be no steward of the household of us, our heirs or successors, then and so long the marshal of the household of us, our heirs and successors, for the time being, and the steward of the said court of the lord the king of the palace of the king at Westminster, for the time being, may and shall be judges conjointly, and both and either of them may and shall be judge severally and separately in the same court, to hear and take cognizance of the aforesaid actions, plaints, and pleas in the aforesaid court, as is aforesaid, to be heard and held, or proceeded on, and to hold pleas thereon. And that in the same manner, whensoever and as often soever, and as long as it shall happen that there be no marshal of the household of us, our heirs and successors, then and so long the steward of the household of us, our heirs and successors, for the time being, and the steward of the said court of the lord the king of the palace of the king at Westminster for the time being, may and shall be judges conjointly, and both and either of them may and shall be judge severally and separately in the same court, to hear and take cognizance of the aforesaid actions, plaints, and pleas in the court aforesaid, as is aforesaid, to be heard and held, or proceeded on, and to hold pleas thereon. And that the said steward and marshal of the household aforesaid, and the steward of the court of the lord the king of the palace of the king at Westminster respectively, for the time being, and any one of them, as is aforesaid, may and shall have power and authority to bring into plea, by summonses, attachments, and distresses, and other processes, (to be directed to the bearers of the rods of the household aforesaid, the officers and ministers of the aforesaid court, to be named and appointed by the marshal of the aforesaid household, for the time being, or to any one or some of them), the persons of the defendants, against whom such plaints, pleas, or actions shall happen to be levied or moved in the aforesaid court, according to the laws and customs of our realm of England, and for deficiency of chattels and lands of such defendants within the jurisdiction of that court, where or by which they may be summoned, attached, or distrained by attachments or *capias*, any where within the jurisdiction of the same court, and of all and singular the actions, plaints and pleas aforesaid, (except in the cases before excepted), to have cognizance, and to hear and hold pleas thereon respectively, in as ample manner and form as any other of our courts of record, by the laws and customs of our realm of England does, may, or ought to have cognizance, hear or hold pleas of such and the like pleas, plaints, or actions; and that the executions of the

o

consuetudines regni nostri Angliæ, de talibus et consimilibus placitis, querelis, seu actionibus cognitionem habet, cognoscit, vel placita tenet, seu cognitionem habere, cognoscere vel placita tenere
possit aut debet. Executionesque processuum et judiciorum ejusdem curiæ per prædictos portatores virgarum hospitii prædicti, officiarios et ministros curiæ prædictæ, fiant et serviantur : Salvis nobis, heredibus et successoribus nostris, finibus et amerciamentis inde provenientibus.

Volumus præterea, et pro nobis, heredibus et successoribus nostris, concedimus, ordinamus, et constituimus, quod de tempore in
tempus senescallus curiæ domini regis palatii regis Westmonasterii,
per nos, heredes et successores nostros, ut prædictum est, nominandus et assignandus, plenam potestatem habeat et auctoritatem nominandi, eligendi, deputandi, et assignandi unum probum et discretum virum, in legibus hujus regni nostri Angliæ etiam eruditum, qui loco et vice ejusdem senescalli curiæ domini regis palatii
regis Westmonasterii, ac ut deputatus ejus, de tempore in tempus,
omnia quæ ad officium senescalli curiæ domini regis palatii regis
Westmonasterii pertinent, in absentia senescalli curiæ prædictæ, de
tempore in tempus præstabit et exequetur. Et quod quicquid in
dicta curia factum aut præstitum fuerit per ejusmodi deputatum senescalli curiæ prædictæ pro tempore existente, vice seu loco ejusdem senescalli curiæ prædictæ, et in ejus absentia, in omnibus ratum habebitur, et vim et effectum sortietur, ac si factum fuerit et
præstitum per ipsum senescallum curiæ prædictæ. VOLUMUS
tamen et firmiter inhibemus, ne aliquis deputatus senescalli curiæ
domini regis palatii regis Westmonasterii prædictæ, aliquo tempore, per se sive simul cum aliquo alio judice dictæ curiæ cognoscet
aut tenebit placita de aliqua actione seu querela in dicta curia per
has literas patentes erecta et creata, in qua actione seu querela ipse
deputatus tunc vel antea fuerit vel fuisset e consiliis seu consiliariis.

Volumus etiam, ac per præsentes pro nobis, heredibus et successoribus nostris concedimus, ordinamus, et constituimus, quod sit in
perpetuum in curia domini regis palatii regis Westmonasterii prædicta quoddam officium, quod officium prothonotarii curiæ domini
regis palatii regis Westmonasterii prædictæ vocabitur et nuncupabitur; ac officium prothonotarii curiæ domini regis palatii regis Westmonasterii facimus, creamus, et constituimus pro nobis, heredibus et
successoribus nostris, per præsentes. Volumus etiam, ac per præsentes pro nobis, heredibus et successoribus nostris, concedimus, quod
sit in perpetuum in eadem curia quidam officiarius, qui prothonotarius curiæ domini regis palatii regis Westmonasterii vocabitur et
nuncupabitur, ad scribendum, faciendum et irrotulandum omnia et
singula brevia, processus, manucaptiones sive ballia, billas, narrationes, barras, responsiones, replicationes, rejunctiones, surrejunctiones, exitus, warranta attornati, veredicta, judicia, et alia processus et recorda quæcunque in eadem curia domini regis palatii regis
Westmonasterii prædicta; et ad custodiendum brevia, rotulos, et
recorda quæcunque ejusdem curiæ.

Volumus etiam, ac per præsentes pro nobis, heredibus et successoribus nostris, concedimus, ordinamus et constituimus, quod
sit in perpetuum in curia domini regis palatii regis Westmonaster-
rii prædicta commune sigillum, ab aliis sigillis curiarum nostrarum

processes and judgments of the same court be made and served by the aforesaid bearers of the rods of the household aforesaid, the officers and ministers of the court aforesaid. Saving to us, our heirs and successors, the fines and amerciaments thereon arising.

We also will, and for us, our heirs and successors, do grant, ordain, and constitute, that from time to time the steward of the court of the lord the king of the palace of the king at Westminster, to be nominated and appointed as is aforesaid by us, our heirs and successors, may have full power and authority of nominating, choosing, deputing, and appointing one honest and discreet man, also learned in the laws of this our kingdom of England, who in the place and stead of the same steward of the court of the lord the king of the palace of the king at Westminster, and as his deputy, from time to time shall perform and execute, in the absence of the steward of the court aforesaid, from time to time, all things relating to the office of steward of the court of the lord the king of the palace of the king at Westminster. And that whatever shall be done or performed in the said court by such deputy of the steward of the court aforesaid, for the time being, in the stead or place of the same steward of the court aforesaid, and in his absence, shall be ratified in all things, and have force and effect, as if it shall have been done and performed by the steward himself of the court aforesaid. We will, nevertheless, and firmly injoin, that no deputy of the steward of the court of the lord the king of the palace of the king at Westminster aforesaid, at any time, by himself, or together with any other judge of the said court, shall have cognizance or hold pleas of any action or plaint in the said court, erected and created by these letters patent, in which action or plaint the same deputy then or before shall or may have been of counsel.

We also will, and by these presents for us, our heirs, and successors, do grant, ordain, and appoint, that there be for ever, in the court of the lord the king of the palace of the king at Westminster aforesaid, a certain office, which shall be called and named The Office of the Prothonotary of the court of the lord the king of the palace of the king at Westminster; and by these presents we make, create, and constitute, for us, our heirs and successors, The Office of the Prothonotary of the Court of the Lord the King of the Palace of the King at Westminster: We will also, and by these presents, for us, our heirs and successors, do grant that there be for ever in the same court a certain officer, who shall be called and named the Prothonotary of the Court of the Lord the King of the Palace of the King at Westminster, to write, draw, and enrol all and singular the writs, processes, mainprizes or bails, bills, declarations, bars, answers, replications, rejoinders, surrejoinders, issues, warrants of attorney, verdicts, judgments, and other processes and records whatsoever in the same court of the lord the king of the palace of the king at Westminster aforesaid, and to keep all writs, rolls, and records whatsoever of the same court.

We also will, and by these presents, for us, our heirs, and successors, do grant, ordain, and constitute, that there be for ever in the court of the lord the king of the palace of the king at Westminster aforesaid, a common seal, different from other seals of our other courts, to serve for sealing writs, attachments, and other pro-

aliarum diversum, pro brevibus, attachiamentis, et aliis processibus curiæ illius sigillandis, et pro causis et negotiis ejusdem curiæ quibuscunque peragendis et expediendis, deserviturum Et quod dictum commune sigillum fabricabitur et formabitur ad arbitrium marescalli hospitii prædicti pro tempore existente *.

Et quod sit de cætero in aliquo convenienti loco infra duodecim milliaria a dicto palatio nostro Westmonasterii, et infra jurisdictionem curiæ prædictæ, una prisona sive gaola pro conservatione, detentione, et salva custodia omnium et singulorum prisonariorum, infra præcincta sive jurisdictionem curiæ prædictæ attachiatorum seu attachiandorum pro quacunque causa, quæ in curia prædicta cognosci et tereri vel ibidem inchoari contigerit, ibidem moraturi donec et quousque legitimo modo deliberentur Volumus etiam, ac pro nobis, heredibus et successoribus nostris, concedimus, ordinamus et constituimus per præsentes, quod sit in perpetuum in curia domini regis palatii regis Westmonasterii prædicta, quidam submarescallus curiæ prædictæ, qui habeat custodiam prisonæ sive gaolæ prædictæ, et prisonariorum in eadem existentium.

Assignavimus etiam, ac per præsentes, pro nobis, heredibus et successoribus nostris, assignamus, nominamus, et constituimus Henricum Wynne, de Interiori Templo, Londini, armigerum, fore et esse primum et modernum senescallum dictæ curiæ domini regis palatii regis Westmonasterii ad omnia quæ ad senescallum curiæ domini regis palatii [regis] Westmonasterii pertinent faciendum et exequendum; Et eidem Henrico Wynne per præsentes pro nobis, heredibus et successoribus nostris, damus et concedimus prædictum officium senescalli dictæ curiæ domini regis palatii regis Westmonasterii—Habendum, tenendum, exercendum, et exequendum dictum officium senescalli curiæ domini regis palatii regis Westmonasterii, eidem Henrico Wynne, quamdiu se bene gesserit.

Assignavimus etiam, ac per præsentes, pro nobis, heredibus et successoribus nostris, assignamus, ordinamus, et constituimus Gulielmum Bluck, armigerum, fore primum et modernum prothonotarium curiæ domini regis palatii regis Westmonasterii prædictæ, ad omnia quæ ad officium prothonotarii curiæ domini regis palatii regis Westmonasterii prædictæ pertinent faciendum et exequendum, Et eidem Gulielmo Bluck, per præsentes, pro nobis, heredibus et successoribus nostris, damus et concedimus officium prædictum prothonotarii dictæ curiæ domini regis palatii regis Westmonasterii,—Habendum, tenendum, exercendum, et exequendum dictum officium prothonotarii curiæ domini regis palatii regis Westmonasterii prædictæ, eidem Gulielmo Bluck, per se, vel per sufficientem deputatum suum sive deputatos suos sufficientes, durante vita naturali ejusdem Gulielmi Bluck. VOLUMUS etiam, ac per præsentes, pro nobis, heredibus et successoribus nostris, ordinamus et constituimus, quod senescalli hospitii nostri, heredum et successorum nostrorum, pro tempore existente, qui per præsentes judices curiæ domini regis palatii regis Westmonasterii, ut præfertur, appunctuantur; necnon marescallus hospitii nostri, heredum et successorum nostrorum, pro tempore existente, et dictus Henricus Wynne, et quæcunque alia persona imposterum a nobis, aut heredibus aut successoribus nostris, quæ in officium senescalli curiæ domini regis

* The present seal of the Court is a port cullis.

cesses of the same court, and for performing and dispatching all affairs and business whatsoever of the same court: And that the device and form of the said common seal shall be at the discretion of the marshal of the household aforesaid for the time being.

And that there be from henceforth, in some convenient place within the twelve miles from our said palace of Westminster, and within the jurisdiction of the court aforesaid, one prison or gaol, for the keeping, retaining, and safe custody of all and singular the prisoners within the precincts or jurisdiction of the court aforesaid, attached or to be attached for any cause whatsoever, which shall happen to be heard and determined in the court aforesaid, or there to be commenced, there to be detained until they be lawfully discharged. We also will, and for us, our heirs and successors, by these presents do grant, ordain, and constitute, that there be for ever in the court of the lord the king of the palace of the king at Westminster aforesaid, a sub-marshal of the court aforesaid, who may have the custody of the prison or gaol aforesaid, and of the prisoners therein

We have also assigned, and by these presents, for us, our heirs and successors, do assign, nominate, and constitute Henry Wynne, of the Inner Temple, London, esquire, to become and be the first and present steward of the said court of the lord the king of the palace of the king at Westminster, to do and execute all things which belong to the steward of the court of the lord the king of the palace of the king at Westminster, and by these presents for us, our heirs and successors, we give and grant to the same Henry Wynne the aforesaid office of steward of the said court of the lord the king of the palace of the king at Westminster,—To have, hold, exercise, and execute the said office of steward of the court of the lord the king of the palace of the king at Westminster, to the said Henry Wynne, as long as he behaves himself well.

We have also assigned, and by these presents, for us, our heirs and successors, do assign, ordain, and constitute William Bluck, Esq. to be the first and present Prothonotary of the court of the lord the king of the palace of the king at Westminster aforesaid, to do and execute all things which belong to the office of prothonotary of the court of the lord the king of the palace of the king at Westminster· And by these presents, for us, our heirs and successors, we give and grant to the said William Bluck the aforesaid office of Prothonotary of the said court of the lord the king of the palace of the king at Westminster,—To have, hold, exercise and execute the said office of Prothonotary of the court of the lord the king of the palace of the king at Westminster aforesaid, to the said William Bluck, by himself, or by his sufficient deputy or sufficient deputies, during the natural life of the same William Bluck.

We will also, and by these presents, for us, our heirs and successors, do ordain and constitute, that the stewards of the household of us, our heirs and successors, for the time being, who are by these presents appointed judges of the court of the lord the king of the palace of the king at Westminster, as is aforesaid. And also the marshal of the household of us, our heirs and successors, for the time being; and the said Henry Wynne, and every other person hereafter who by us, or our heirs and successors, shall be no-

palatii regis Westmonasterii, ut prædictum est, nominabitur et assignabitur, atque etiam quilibet deputatus ejusdem Henrici Wynne, et cujuscunque alius senescalli dictæ curiæ domini regis palatii regis Westmonasterii respective; antequam ad officia sua judicum curiæ prædictæ respective exequendum admittantur, vel eorum aliquis respective admittatur, coram cancellario Angliæ vel custode magni sigilli Angliæ pro tempore existente, marescallo Angliæ pro tempore existente, camerario hospitii nostri, heredum et successorum nostrorum pro tempore existente, thesaurario hospitii nostri, heredum et successorum nostrorum pro tempore existente, et contrarotulatore hospitii nostri, heredum vel successorum nostrorum pro tempore existente, vel coram eorum aliquo vel aliquibus, sacramentum corporale super sancta Dei evangelia, ad officium illud judicis curiæ domini regis palatii regis Westmonasterii rite, bene, juste, et fideliter exequendum; et ad plenam et celerem justitiam populo regis in eadem curia, juxta eorum sanam discretionem et meliorem scientiam, intellectum, et judicium suum, administrandum et exhibendum, et ad omnia alia ad officium judicis in dicta curia in aliquo spectantia sive pertinentia observandum, præstabunt, et quilibet eorum respective præstabit.

Quare volumus, ac per præsentes pro nobis, heredibus et successoribus nostris, damus et concedimus cancellario Angliæ, custodi magni sigilli Angliæ, marescallo Angliæ, camerario hospitii nostri, heredum et successorum nostrorum, thesaurario hospitii nostri, heredum et successorum nostrorum, et contrarotulatori hospitii prædicti, tam præsentibus quam futuris, et quibuslibet et cuilibet eorum pro tempore existente, vel [temporibus] existentibus, plenam auctoritatem et potestatem administrandi sacramentum corporale super sancta Dei evangelia, tam personis in præsentibus assignatis esse judices curiæ prædictæ, et eorum cuilibet, quam omnibus aliis judicibus ejusdem curiæ deinceps in perpetuum juxta tenorem præsentium literarum nostrarum patentium futuris, tam pro vera et fideli executione officii prædicti judicis curiæ illius, in omnibus et per omnia officium illud tangentia, modo et forma prædictis, quam sacramentum concernens primatiam regiam ecclesiasticam per statutum in parliamento dominæ Elizabethæ nuper reginæ Angliæ, anno regni sui primo tento, editum, præstari ordinatum, et sacramentum de allegiantia nobis, heredibus et successoribus nostris præstandum per statutum in parliamento domini Jacobi, nuper regis Angliæ, anno regni sui tertio tento, editum, ordinatum; et hoc absque aliqua commissione seu ulteriori warranto a nobis, heredibus et successoribus nostris, in ea parte procurando seu obtinendo.

Volumus etiam, ac per præsentes pro nobis, heredibus et successoribus nostris, concedimus, quod de tempore in tempus, et ad omnia tempora post mortem prædicti Gulielmi Bluck, aut postquam officium illud prothonotarii curiæ prædictæ per resignationem, amotionem, vel cessionem prædicti Gulielmi Bluck, aut alio modo vacari contigerit, et sic deinceps toties quoties casus sic acciderit, bene liceat et licebit marescallo hospitii nostri, heredum et successorum nostrorum, pro tempore existente, nominare et eligere unum alium virum discretum et idoneum fore

minated and appointed to the office of steward of the court of the lord the king of the palace of the king at Westminster, as is aforesaid, and also every deputy of the same Henry Wynne and of every other steward of the said court of the lord the king of the palace of the king at Westminster, respectively; before they are admitted, or any of them respectively is admitted, to perform their offices of judges of the court aforesaid respectively, they, and every one of them respectively shall take a corporal oath on the Holy Gospels of God, before the Chancellor of England, or the Keeper of the Great Seal of England for the time being, the Marshal of England for the time being, the Chamberlain of the household of us, our heirs and successors for the time being, the Treasurer of the household of us, our heirs and successors for the time being, and the Comptroller of the household of us, our heirs or successors for the time being, or before any one or some of them, rightfully, well, justly, and faithfully to perform the said office of judge of the court of the lord the king of the palace of the king at Westminster, and to administer and impart full and speedy justice to the king's people, in the same court, according to their sound discretion and best skill, understanding and judgment, and to observe all other things in any wise belonging or appertaining to the office of judge in the said court.

Wherefore we will, and by these presents, for us, our heirs and successors, do give and grant to the Chancellor of England, the Keeper of the Great Seal of England, the Marshal of England, the Chamberlain of the household of us, our heirs and successors, the Treasurer of the household of us, our heirs and successors, and the Comptroller of the household aforesaid, as well the present as future, and to every one and each of them for the time being, full authority and power of administering a corporal oath, upon the Holy Gospels of God, as well to the persons in these presents assigned to be judges of the court aforesaid, and to any one of them, as to all other future judges of the same court, from henceforth for ever, according to the tenor of our present letters patent, as well for the true and faithful execution of the aforesaid office of judge of that court, in and by all things touching the said office in manner and form aforesaid, as the oath of supremacy ordained to be taken by the statute made in the parliament of the Lady Elizabeth, late Queen of England, held in the first year of her reign, and the oath of allegiance to us, our heirs, and successors, ordained to be taken by the statute made in the parliament of the lord James, late king of England, held in the third year of his reign. and this, without any commission or further warrant from us, our heirs and successors in that behalf to be procured or obtained.

We also will, and by these presents, for us, our heirs and successors, do grant, that, from time to time, and at all times after the death of the aforesaid William Bluck, or after the said office of prothonotary of the court aforesaid shall happen to be vacant, by the resignation, removal, or cession of the aforesaid William Bluck, or by any other means, and so hereafter as often as the case shall so happen, it may and shall be lawful for the marshal of the household of us, our heirs and successors, for the time being, to nominate and choose one other discreet and fit person to become and

et esse prothonotarium curiæ prædictæ. Quiquidem prothonotarius, sic nominatus et electus per marescallum hospitii prædicti, pro tempore existente, ad officium illud prothonotarii curiæ prædictæ exequendum de tempore in tempus admissus erit. Et quod ille qui sic in officium prothonotarii curiæ prædictæ de tempore in tempus nominatus, electus et admissus fuerit, officium illud habeat et exerceat durante vita sua naturali, per se vel per sufficientem deputatum suum, sive deputatos suos sufficientes, exequendum.

Volumus insuper, et pro nobis, heredibus et successoribus nostris concedimus per præsentes, senescallo hospitii nostri, heredum et successorum nostrorum, pro tempore existente, et marescallo hospitii nostri, heredum et successorum nostrorum, pro tempore existente, et in tempore vacationis officii senescalli hospitii prædicti, marescallo ejusdem hospitii soli, plenam potestatem et authoritatem nominandi, ordinandi, constituendi, et admittendi quatuor personas consiliarios eruditos in lege, fore consiliarios in eadem curia domini regis palatii regis Westmonasterii, pro termino vitæ cujuslibet talis personæ; et sex alias idoneas personas fore attornatos in dicta curia domini regis palatii regis Westmonasterii prædicta, pro termino vitæ cujuslibet talis personæ, ad prosequendum et defendendum omnia et singula actiones, placita, et querelas in eadem curia mota sive movenda. AC etiam damus, et pro nobis, heredibus et successoribus nostris concedimus marescallo hospitii nostri, heredum et successorum nostrorum, pro tempore existente, plenam potestatem et auctoritatem nominandi, ordinandi, constituendi et admittendi, unam aliam personam fore submarescallum curiæ prædictæ, et custodem prisonæ curiæ prædictæ, et prisonariorum in eadem existentium, qui faciat et exequatur omnia quæ ad officium custodis prisonæ curiæ prædictæ pertinent facienda, et unam aliam idoneam personam fore janitorem ejusdem prisonæ; necnon unam aliam idoneam personam fore præconem vel proclamatorem prædictæ curiæ, ad omnia et singula eisdem officiis respective, pro meliori servitio curiæ illius et expeditione causarum ibidem dependentium vel dependendarum, in aliquo spectantia vel pertinentia, pro respectivo termino vitæ cujuslibet talis personæ, respective præstandum et exequendum. Quodque præfatus prothonotarius, quatuor consiliarii, sex attornati, submarescallus, janitor, et proclamator, antequam ad loca sive officia illa exequendum respective admittantur, seu eorum aliquis respective admittatur, sacramentum corporale super sancta Dei evangelia, coram prædicto senescallo hospitii nostri, heredum et successorum nostrorum pro tempore existente, marescallo hospitii prædicti pro tempore existente, et senescallo curiæ domini regis palatii regis Westmonasterii, vel ejus deputato, eorumve aliquo sive aliquibus in curia prædicta, ad loca et officia illa respective bene et fideliter exequendum, et in eisdem respective se bene gerendum, præstabunt, et eorum quilibet præstabit. Quibus quidem senescallo hospitii prædicti, marescallo ac senescallo curiæ prædictæ, et deputato ejus, et eorum cuilibet, pro tempore existente, hujusmodi sacramentum de tempore in tempus eisdem prothonotario, consiliariis, attornatis, submarescallo, janitori, et proclamatori, ac cuilibet eorum, administrandi plenam potestatem et auctoritatem, pro nobis, heredibus et successoribus nostris, damus et concedimus per præsentes. Ac

be the Prothonotary of the court aforesaid; which prothonotary, so nominated and chosen by the marshal of the household aforesaid for the time being, shall be admitted from time to time to execute the said office of prothonotary of the court aforesaid. And that he who shall be, from time to time, so nominated, chosen, and admitted into the office of prothonotary of the court aforesaid, may, during his natural life, have and exercise the said office, to be executed by himself, or by his sufficient deputy or deputies.

We further will, and by these presents, for us, our heirs and successors, do grant to the steward of the household of us, our heirs and successors for the time being, and to the marshal of the household of us, our heirs and successors, for the time being, and during the vacancy of the office of steward of the household aforesaid, to the marshal of the same household alone, the full power and authority of nominating, ordaining, constituting and admitting, four persons, counsellors learned in the law, to be counsel in the same court of the lord the king of the palace of the king at Westminster, for the term of the life of every such person, and six other fit persons to be attornies in the said court of the lord the king of the palace of the king at Westminster aforesaid, for the term of the life of every such person, to prosecute and defend all and singular the actions, pleas, and plaints, commenced or to be commenced in the same court.

And we also give, and for us, our heirs and successors, do grant to the marshal of the household of us, our heirs and successors, for the time being, full power and authority of nominating, ordaining, constituting, and admitting one other person to be sub-marshal of the court aforesaid and keeper of the prison of the court aforesaid, and of the prisoners in the same, who may do and execute all the duties which belong to the office of keeper of the prison of the court aforesaid; and one other fit person to be turnkey of the same prison; and also one other fit person to be crier or proclamator of the aforesaid court, for the respective term of the life of every such person, to perform and execute all and every thing to the said offices respectively in any wise belonging or pertaining, for the better service of the said court, and expediting causes there pending or to be pending. And that the aforesaid prothonotary, the four counsellors, six attornies, submarshal, turnkey and crier, and every of them, before they or any one of them respectively be admitted to execute the said places or offices, shall take a corporal oath on the holy gospels of God, before the aforesaid steward of the household of us, our heirs and successors for the time being, the marshal of the household aforesaid for the time being, and the steward of the court of the lord the king of the palace of the king at Westminster, or his deputy, or any one or some of them, in the aforesaid court, well and faithfully to execute those places and offices respectively, and well to conduct themselves in the same respectively. To which steward of the household aforesaid, the marshal, and steward of the court aforesaid, and his deputy, and to any of them for the time being, we do by these presents, for us, our heirs and successors, give and grant full power and authority of administering such oath from time to time to the same prothonotary, counsellors, attornies, submarshal, turnkey and crier, and to every of them. And we

volumus quod in eadem curia, ad aliquod tempus, sint tantum unus prothonotarius, quatuor consiliarii, sex attornati, unus custos prisonæ, unus janitor prisonæ, et unus proclamator curiæ prædictæ, quibus feoda in dicta curia allocata fuerint, pro causis prosequendis et defendendis, seu aliis rebus agendis in eadem curia et prisona prædicta.

Volumus insuper, ac per præsentes, pro nobis, heredibus et successoribus nostris, concedimus, ordinamus et constituimus quod sint in perpetuum in dicta curia domini regis palatii regis Westmonasterii quidam officiarii et ministri ad exequendum mandata, brevia et processus e dicta curia domini regis palatii regis Westmonasterii emanantia, qui sint et nuncupentur portatores virgarum hospitii domini regis.

Damus ulterius, et per præsentes pro nobis, heredibus et successoribus nostris, concedimus marescallo hospitii nostri, heredum et successorum nostrorum, et singulis marescallis ejusdem hospitii pro tempore existente; Ac volumus tenore præsentium, quod ipsi respective plenam potestatem et auctoritatem habeant successive nominandi, constituendi et admittendi, de tempore in tempus, quosdam portatores virgarum hospitii prædicti, fore officiarios et ministros dictæ curiæ domini regis palatii regis Westmonasterii ad exequendum mandata, brevia, et processus e prædicta curia domini regis palatii regis Westmonasterii emanantia. Volumus etiam quod omnibus temporibus futuris sint viginti tales ministri curiæ prædictæ ad exequendum mandata, brevia, et processus e curia prædicta emanantia, vel plures, ad discretionem marescalli hospitii prædicti pro tempore existente. Quodque quilibet eorundem portatorum virgarum, antequam ad officium illud exequendum admittatur, sacramentum corporale super sancta Dei evangelia, coram senescallo curiæ prædictæ pro tempore existente, vel deputato ejus, ad seipsum in officio illo bene gerendum præstabit; cui quidem senescallo curiæ prædictæ et deputato ejus, respective et divisim, hujusmodi sacramentum de tempore in tempus administrandi plenam potestatem et auctoritatem, pro nobis, heredibus et successoribus nostris, damus et concedimus per præsentes. Et quod iidem portatores virgarum prædictarum, sic de tempore in tempus nominati, admissi et jurati in officia illa officiariorum et ministrorum curiæ prædictæ, officia et loca illa habeant et exerceant, et quilibet eorum habeat et exerceat, ad voluntatem dicti marescalli pro tempore existente.

Volumus etiam, ac per præsentes, pro nobis, heredibus et successoribus nostris, firmiter injungendo præcipimus senescallo hospitii nostri, heredum et successorum nostrorum, pro tempore existente, marescallo dicti hospitii pro tempore existente, et senescallo curiæ domini regis palatii regis Westmonasterii pro tempore existente, quod sine causa rationabili non omittant respective, nec ullus eorum respective omittat attendere in curia prædicta de die in diem, ut prædictum est, ad placita ibidem dependentia vel dependenda, secundum leges et consuetudines regni nostri Angliæ, tenendum et deducendum, et quod circa præmissa diligenter sint respective intendentes. Et quod iidem judices vel aliqui seu aliquis eorum in omnibus hujusmodi causis, actionibus, placitis et querelis, coram eis vel eorum aliquo in curia prædicta dependentibus vel depen-

will that, in the same court, at any time, there be only one prothonotary, four counsellors, six attornies, one keeper of the prison,
one turnkey of the prison, and one crier of the court aforesaid, to
whom the fees in the said court shall be allowed for causes prosecuted and defended, or other business done in the same court and
prison aforesaid.

We will moreover, and by these presents, for us, our heirs and
successors, do grant, ordain, and constitute, that there be for ever
in the said court of the lord the king of the palace of the king at
Westminster, certain officers and ministers to execute the orders,
writs, and processes issuing out of the said court of the lord the
king of the palace of the king at Westminster, who shall be and be
called the bearers of the rods of the household of the lord the king.

We give moreover, and by these presents, for us, our heirs, and
successors, do grant to the marshal of the household of us, our
heirs and successors, and to every marshal of the same household
for the time being; and we will, by the tenor of these presents,
that they respectively may have full power and authority of successively nominating, constituting, and admitting, from time to time,
certain bearers of the rods of the household aforesaid, to become
the officers and ministers of the said court of the lord the king of
the palace of the king at Westminster, to execute the orders, writs,
and processes issuing out of the aforesaid court of the lord the king
of the palace of the king at Westminster. We will also that at
all times hereafter there be twenty such ministers of the court aforesaid to execute the orders, writs, and processes issuing out of the
aforesaid court, or more, at the discretion of the marshal of the
household aforesaid for the time being.   And that every one of the
same bearers of the rods, before he be admitted to execute that
office, shall take a corporal oath on the holy gospels of God, before
the steward of the court aforesaid for the time being, or his deputy,
to behave himself well in that office; to which steward of the court
aforesaid, and to his deputy, respectively and severally, we give and
grant, by these presents, for us, our heirs and successors, full power
and authority of administering such oath from time to time: And
that the same bearers of the rods aforesaid, so from time to time
nominated, admitted, and sworn into the said offices of officers and
ministers of the court aforesaid, and every of them, may have and
exercise the said offices and places, at the will of the said marshal
for the time being.

We also will, and by these presents, for us, our heirs and successors, firmly injoining, do command the steward of the household of us, our heirs and successors, for the time being, the marshal of the said household for the time being, and the steward of
the court of the lord the king of the palace of the king at Westminster for the time being, that neither they respectively, nor any
of them respectively, without reasonable cause, do omit to attend
in the court aforesaid, from day to day, as is aforesaid, to hold and
determine the pleas there pending or to be pending, according to
the laws and customs of our realm of England, and that they respectively be diligently attentive with regard to the premises. And
that the same judges or some or any of them, in all such causes, actions, pleas, and plaints, pending or to be pending in the court afore-

dendis in quibus parti defendenti vel partibus defendentibus per legem regni nostri Angliæ, misæ, custagia et expensæ litis allocari et adjudicari debeant, pro misis, custagiis et expensis suis tantas denariorum summas quantas ipsi respective circa sectas illas respectivas expendiderunt taxent et assidant, seu taxet et assidat.

Mandamus etiam, ac pro nobis, heredibus et successoribus nostris, firmiter injungendo præcipimus omnibus et singulis justiciariis, vicecomitibus, custodibus gaolarum et prisonarum, ballivis, constabulariis, ac officiariis, et subditis nostris quibuscunque, infra duodecim milliaria a dicto palatio nostro Westmonasterii, tam infra libertates quam extra, quod sint prædictis judicibus curiæ prædictæ, et eorum cuilibet, et mandatis eorum et cujuslibet eorum, juxta tenorem et veram intentionem harum literarum nostrarum patentium in omnibus obedientes, et eorum et cujuslibet eorum præcepta et mandata diligenter et firmiter perimpleri et custodiri causare, ac omnibus officiariis et ministris curiæ prædictæ in executione officiorum suorum fore intendentes et auxiliantes, sub violationem mandati nostri regii periculo incurrendi.

Et pro meliori et rectiori levatione exituum juratorum in eadem curia forisfaciendorum volumus, statuimus, et ordinamus, quod licebit portatoribus virgarum prædictarum officiariis et ministris ejusdem curiæ, et eorum cuilibet, de tempore in tempus, per mandatum judicum prædictorum, sub sigillo curiæ prædictæ sigillatum, exitus et fines juratorum in eadem curia contingentes et forisfaciendas, per districtiones seu alio modo legitimo infra prædictam jurisdictionem ejusdem curiæ, levare et recipere, et denarios sic levatos et receptos solvere in manus senescalli hospitii nostri, heredum et successorum nostrorum pro tempore existente; et hujusmodi senescallo non existente in manus marescalli ejusdem hospitii pro tempore existente, ad usum nostrum, heredum et successorum nostrorum, priusquam extractus inde in scaccarium nostrum, heredum et successorum nostrorum, mittantur, ac licet non mittantur; et de hujusmodi exitibus non receptis volumus quod senescallus hospitii nostri, heredum et successorum nostrorum, pro tempore existente, et in vacatione officii senescalli hospitii prædicti marescallus ejusdem hospitii pro tempore existente, in quolibet anno, inter festum Omnium Sanctorum et festum Purificationis beatæ Mariæ Virginis, extractus mitti faciat in scaccarium nostrum, heredum et successorum nostrorum, et de hujusmodi exitibus per ipsos respective receptis [quod] prædictus senescallus hospitii nostri, heredum et successorum nostrorum pro tempore existente, et in vacatione [officii] senescalli hospitii prædicti marescallus hospitii prædicti pro tempore existente, computum reddat coram baronibus de scaccario nostro, heredum et successorum nostrorum, singulis annis, inter festa prædicta· quibus baronibus tenore præsentium mandamus, quatenus exitus illis non levatos ad opus nostrum, heredum et successorum nostrorum, levari faciant; et de ejusmodi exitibus levatis et solutis solvent inde erga nos heredes et successores nostros acquietare absque aliquo feodo proinde solvendo. Nosque tenore præsentium portatoribus virgarum prædictarum, officiariis et ministris curiæ prædictæ, et eorum cuilibet, exitus ejusmodi levandi, et prædictis judicibus et eorum cuilibet eosdem levari mandandi potestatem damus et concedimus, statuto seu ordinatione de forma mittendi

said before them or any of them, in which, by the law of our kingdom of England, the charges, costs, and expenses of suit ought to be allowed and adjudged to the defendant or defendants, may tax and assess for their charges, costs, and expenses, such sums as they respectively shall have expended in their respective suits

We also command, and for us, our heirs and successors, firmly injoining do order all and singular our justices, sheriffs, keepers of gaols and prisons, bailiffs, constables, and officers and subjects whatsoever, within twelve miles from our said palace of Westminster, as well within liberties as without, that they be obedient in all things to the aforesaid judges of the court aforesaid, and to every of them, and to the commands of them and of every of them, according to the tenor and true intent of these our letters patent, and cause the precepts and orders of them and of every of them, to be diligently and firmly fulfilled and kept, and be aiding and assisting to all the officers and ministers of the court aforesaid in the execution of their offices, under the peril of incurring the violation of our royal command.

And for the better and more ready levying of the issues of the jurors in the same court to be forfeited, we will, appoint, and ordain, that it shall be lawful for the bearers of the rods aforesaid, the officers and ministers of the same court, and every of them, from time to time, by the order of the judges aforesaid, sealed with the seal of the court aforesaid, by distress or any other lawful means within the aforesaid jurisdiction of the same court, to levy and receive the issues and fines of the jurors arising in the same court and forfeited; and to pay the sums so levied and received into the hands of the steward of the household of us, our heirs and successors for the time being, and there being no such steward, into the hands of the marshal of the same household for the time being, to the use of us, our heirs and successors, before the estreats thereon are sent into the exchequer of us, our heirs and successors, and although they are not sent. And of such issues not received, we will, that the steward of the household of us, our heirs and successors for the time being, and in the vacancy of the office of steward of the household aforesaid, that the marshal of the same household for the time being, every year, between the feast of All Saints and the feast of the Purification of the blessed Virgin Mary, do cause the estreats to be sent into the Exchequer of us, our heirs and successors; and of such issues by them respectively received, that the aforesaid steward of the household of us, our heirs and successors, for the time being, and in the vacancy of the office of steward of the household aforesaid, that the marshal of the household aforesaid for the time being, do render an account before the barons of the exchequer of us, our heirs and successors, every year, between the aforesaid feasts. Which barons, by the tenor of these presents, we command, that they cause to be levied the issues not levied to the use of us, our heirs and successors; and that they give a quietus of such issues levied and paid as aforesaid, against us, our heirs and successors, without any fee to be paid for the same And we by the tenor of these presents do give and grant to the bearers of the rods aforesaid, the officers and ministers of the court aforesaid, and to every of them, power to levy such issues, and to the judges aforesaid and every of them, to command the same to be levied, notwithstanding the statute or ordinance respecting the manner of

extractus ad scaccarium, aut aliquo alio statuto, actu seu ordinatione non obstante

Volumus etiam quod thesaurarius hospitii nostri, heredum et successorum nostrorum, pro tempore existente, et contrarotulator ejusdem hospitii pro tempore existente ut et quoties ... que ... vel ... eorum interesse voluerint vel voluerit, habeant vel alteru ter eorum habeat locum et sedem inter judices ejusdem curie, et inter judices curie prædictæ sedeant et locum habeant, sedeat et locum habeat

Volumus etiam, ac per præsentes pro nobis, heredibus et successoribus nostris concedimus, quod hæ literæ nostræ patentes, et omnia in eisdem contenta et specificata, sint et erant in omnibus et per omnia firmæ, validæ et effectuales in lege, non obstante non nominando aliquam concessionem de præmissis seu de aliqua inde parcella, per nos vel per aliquem progenitorum sive prædecessorum nostrorum antehac factam, ac non obstante male nominando, male recitando, vel non nominando vel non recitando, vel non recte nominando præmissa vel aliquam inde parcellam ac non obstante statuto in parliamento domini Edwardi nuper regis Angliæ primi, progenitoris nostri, [anno regni sui tertio] tento, edito, et non obstante statuto in parliamento domini Henrici nuper regis Angliæ quarti, anno regni sui primo tento, edito, ac non obstante statuto in parliamento dicti domini Henrici nuper regis Angliæ quarti, anno regni sui secundo tento, edito, ac non obstante statuto in parliamento domini Henrici nuper regis Angliæ sexti, anno regni sui vicesimo tertio tento, edito, aut aliquo alio statuto, actu, ordinatione, provisione, constitutione, vel restrictione, vel aliqua alia re, causa vel materia quacunque in contrarium inde non obstante IN cujus rei, &c teste rege apud Westmonasterium, quarto die Octobris, &c

Per ipsum Regem

transmitting estreats to the Exchequer, or any other statute, act, or ordinance

We also will, that the treasurer of the household of us, our heirs and successors for the time being, and the comptroller of the same household for the time being, (if, and as often as, they or either of them shall be willing to be present), and either of them, may have a place and seat amongst the judges of the same court, and that they and either of them may sit and have place among the judges of the court aforesaid

We also will, and by these presents, for us, our heirs and successors, do grant, that these our letters patent, and all things contained and specified therein, may and shall be firm, valid, and effectual in law, in and by all things, notwithstanding the not naming any grant touching the premises, or any parcel thereof, by us, or any of our ancestors or predecessors heretofore made, and notwithstanding the mis-naming, mis-reciting, or not naming or not reciting, or not correctly naming the premises, or any parcel thereof. And notwithstanding the statute made in the Parliament of Lord Edward the First, our progenitor, late King of England, held [in the third year of his reign,] and notwithstanding the statute made in the parliament of Lord Henry the Fourth, late King of England, held in the first year of his reign, and notwithstanding the statute made in the Parliament of the said Lord Henry the Fourth, late King of England, held in the second year of his reign, and notwithstanding the statute made in the Parliament of Lord Henry the Sixth, late King of England, held in the twenty-third year of his reign, or any other statute, act, ordinance, provision, constitution or restriction, or any other thing, cause or matter whatsoever to the contrary hereof notwithstanding.

In witness whereof, &c. Witness the King at Westminster, the fourth day of October, &c.

By the King himself.

ORDERS AND RULES OF THE COURT.

Orders and Rules made and established by the Judges of the Court of the King's Palace at Westminster, A. D. 1675, to be from thenceforth kept and observed by the same Court, as followeth, viz.

RULES OF PRACTICE.

1. That every defendant put in good bail in Court on the day of appearance, of two sufficient housekeepers, within the jurisdiction of the Court, or take a rule so to do within three days next following, if the plaintiff also appear; but if the plaintiff do not appear, then such defendant may take out a rule so to do within a week.

2. That no bond be assigned that is not duly pyed upon the return, and that every attorney that shall be retained for the plaintiff (the defendant not appearing) shall assign over the defendant's bond upon the account of his retaining fee, and not take any new or other fee for the assignment thereof, though assigned after the day of the return.

3. That the practice now used of presenting only the names of bails, and not acknowledging them, be no longer used, and that nothing shall be filed, entered, or reputed bail, but where the parties are acknowledged in court, before the steward or his deputy, or the steward or his deputy's name subscribed to the bail-piece.

4. That bails being matter of record be plainly and fairly written, and the parish and place where the bail do inhabit be particularly set forth, that they may be easily found out.

5. That no bail-piece, declaration, plea, replication, or other proceeding whatsoever be delivered to the attorney of the adverse party, before the same be duly entered in the court-book, by the secondary, and the same marked by him, that the king's duty and fees of the court be duly accounted for, upon pain of 5*l.* for every such default.

6. That if the plaintiff appear not at the day of appearance, and the defendant put in bail in court, the defendant may give a rule to the plaintiff to declare within three days next after, or a nonsuit to be entered; and after such rule the plaintiff shall not be admitted to except against the bail.

7. That in future all bail-pieces shall be made for the defendant *ad sectam querentis in querelâ*, and the bail so acknowledged, and that in the same bail-piece the plaintiff's christian and surnames be likewise inserted, (though not mentioned in the caption), that it may be known to what action the defendant intends his bail, and where the plaintiff's name is not inserted, the same not to be reputed bail but refused.

8. That every bail taken in court be joint or several, according to the nature of the action; and that care be taken before it be acknowledged that it be agreeable to the plaint, and that the bail-

piece be made *ad sectam querentis in querelâ,* and so taken as is ordered before

9. That all bails put in, against which exceptions have been taken, shall be justified upon oath in court, the next court-day after exceptions taken, or others then put in, that shall be made good the same court-day.

10. That if the defendant shall not justify his bail the next court-day after exceptions taken thereto, yet upon payment of costs to the plaintiff's attorney, the bail-bond may stand assigned, but no proceedings to be had thereupon, in case the defendant justify his bail and plead to the plaintiff's declaration, the court next follow ing, so that no delay may come to the plaintiff thereby

11. That every plaintiff, next court-day after an arrest, appear in Court by his attorney, to the end that the bond of appearance may be then assigned

12. That when any person is brought into prison by arrest upon a mesne process, or committed in discharge of his bail, the plaintiff to declare upon the same court-day of the return of the writ upon which such person is arrested, or of the commitment of such person as aforesaid, or within three days peremptorily next after such return or commitment, and the next court-day to call the prisoner to plead, (if actually in custody, and not having pleaded the first court), and to perfect his declaration, and to reply to the prisoner's plea the same court. And in default in any of the cases aforesaid, a nonsuit to be entered of course upon filing a common bail, and the prisoner immediately discharged without a rule to declare or perfect.

13. That every plaintiff, the same court in which the bail is acknowledged, or the next court after, take his exceptions against the bail upon oath, or the bail to stand.

14. That the plaintiff may declare the first court day if he please, or else he shall be compelled to declare the next court-day after the bail settled.

15. That the plaintiff's attorney deliver a true copy of every incipitur to the defendant's attorney the same day it is filed, wherein he shall fully express the true cause of action, otherwise the defendant is not bound to plead the next court.

16. That upon a declaration or bill entered against a privileged person, he shall appear the next court after due notice of the rule in that behalf given either to himself in person, or left at his house. But upon oath that such officer is no housekeeper, or cannot be found, such notice to be set up in the prothonotary's office and at the return place be sufficient.

17 That every plaintiff declaring upon a rule within three days shall bring in his declaration perfect, the next court-day, or take a rule to perfect and reply the court then next following, and that when any declaration is brought in as perfect, the same to be plainly and fairly written, without any blank, or otherwise not to be accepted, but a nonsuit entered for want of a perfect declaration.

18 That no plaintiff, after a declaration by incipitur, or otherwise, shall change the nature of his action, without paying costs

19. That any plaintiff or defendant paying costs may amend his

P

declaration, or any other pleading being on paper, and not entered upon record, the defendant having liberty to plead *de novo* upon such amendment.

20 That the next court-day after a declaration, where the defendant comes into court by bail, the plaintiff shall bring in his declaration, or take a rule to perfect, and reply, the court then next following.

21. That where the plaintiff, by his declaration, replication, or otherwise, doth mention to be produced in court any deed or other writing to maintain his action, upon oyer thereof craved, the same to be presently produced and shewn to the attorney of the adverse party, or in default thereof a rule given to the plaintiff to produce the same the next court day, or otherwise to be nonsuited

22. That where the plaintiff enters his plaint jointly, and it appears to the court upon motion that he cannot otherwise, he shall not be compelled to declare upon the appearance of any one defendant, unless the rest appear also

23. That in case the plaintiff's action be joint against several defendants, though one of the defendants appear and plead, if the other defendant in the same writ comes in before issue joined, the plaintiff may have liberty to put him into the declaration.

24 That where any nonsuit is entered (except against prisoner), the plaintiff may vacate the same upon payment of costs the same court the nonsuit is entered, but at no time afterwards

25. That where any variance shall happen between the plaint and declaration, or other pleadings, in either party's name only, the same not being entered upon record, to be amended and made agreeable to the plaint, without payment of costs, and no plea of variance in such cases to be received, but the defendant may in such cases compel the plaintiff, at any time whilst the proceedings are on paper, to take a rule to declare or perfect his declaration according to his plaint.

26 That where the plaintiff is mistaken only as to the nature of the action, so as the plaintiff cannot conform his declaration thereunto, there the defendant to take no advantage of such variance by pleading or otherwise

27 That all incipiturs of declarations, and all other declarations, be duly brought into the office and there filed, every day's *incipiturs* together by themselves, and the other declarations weekly by themselves, and so kept in order, one court-day after another, and that the attorneys or their clerks may have a sight thereof when required.

28. That every defendant shall imparl to the plaintiff's declaration the first court day, if he hath received the fee thereof of his client, otherwise to pay the same when he pleads.

29 That no defendant shall have any longer time than a week to plead, demur, rejoin, rebut, or join in demurrer, unless the court upon motion give longer time, and that all special pleadings, when brought, be plainly and fairly written, without blanks and under counsel's hand

30. That if the plaintiff make default the first court day after issue joined, the defendant may summon the cause by proviso the court following, or at any other time

31. That when any defendant shall make a tender of any money in court after the action brought, the plaintiff not to be obliged to stay proceedings, but to proceed if he please, losing his costs from the time of the tender, if the jury give no greater damages than the sum tendered; and if the plaintiff be contented to take the money tendered, and give notice thereof to the defendant or his attorney, in such case, the defendant to have three days time after such notice given, and no longer, if he lives within the lines of communication, to bring in his money and charges to the time of the tender but if he live at a greater distance, he to have a week's time to do the same; during which times respectively neither party proceeds and for default of payment within the respective times, the rule of tender to be set aside, and the plaintiff to proceed as if no such tender had been made, and no tender whatsoever to be made in any actions grounded upon specialty, or any action of trover, trespass, or other action whatsoever, other than actions upon the case brought in the nature of debt upon simple contracts

32 That the plaintiff shall reply, surrejoin, surrebut, demur, or join in demurrer, or any the like act on his part to be done, the next court after the defendant's plea, rejoinder, demurrer, or any such other proceedings on his part, and also that the defendant shall in like manner answer to all such special pleadings and proceedings on the plaintiff's behalf, by the time before limited, and that neither plaintiff nor defendant shall have any longer time for the doing thereof than before specified, except the Court upon motion shall think fit to give it them

33. That where the defendant pleads the general issue, the plaintiff must join issue the same court day.

34. That in case any special pleadings be in any action, the same be annexed and filed to their proper declaration

35. That all special pleadings, and all demurrers, and joinders in demurrer, be drawn up perfect under counsel's hand, without the least blank in them

36 That when there is any demurrer upon evidence or special verdict found, the secondary to draw it up, and deliver copies thereof and of the original notes to the attorney of each party, within a week after the said demurrer or special verdict found as aforesaid, each paying for the draft and copies as hath been usually done, viz 4d drawing, 4d copy, and that they advise with their respective counsel thereupon, and return the said copies within a week after the delivery, to be entered on record, and if any material variance be made in the copy by the counsel, so that they cannot agree upon the draft, such variance to be decided by the steward of the court, but if either party fail either in taking copies or returning them within the time prefixed, the entry to be made *ex parte* of him that does his duty.

37. That all special pleadings be drawn out at length, as they are to be entered upon record, and the same to be subscribed by counsel, otherwise to be refused

38. That the precise time for doing business upon rules for three days, be ten of the clock every Wednesday morning, and when any court is holden in the weeks of Easter or Whitsuntide, no rule of

the preceding court to be given for three days, unless in cases where a prisoner is concerned; but all other rules of those courts to be made for a week.

39. That no time be given to plaintiff, upon his motion in Court for time to declare perfect before he hath brought in his *incipitur* or other declaration, nor to the defendant praying time to plead specially to the plaintiff's declaration, before he hath pleaded *nisi aliter*, &c and both accountable for the respective fee thereof in the court books, that when any issue is joined, the attorney to whom the declaration or other pleadings therein are delivered, to return the same to the attorney that is to summons the cause by Wednesday ten of the clock, next after the court of which the same issue is joined, or in default thereof, shall pay such costs as shall be sustained by the other attorney, by reason of his not doing the same

40 That all declarations or other pleadings brought in for trial, be plainly and fairly written, and perfected, without blanks, and that the same be all brought in with the special pleadings (if any be) affixed to the declaration, by seven of the clock every Monday night, that the secondary may have convenient time to enter the same upon record, and not hindered in his other business relating to the court; and where any default shall happen contrary to this rule, the party that summons the cause not to be permitted to go on that court day, but to lose the charge of his summons.

41. That no trial be put off upon pretence that witnesses are absent, unless subpœna be first taken out in the cause, or good cause be shewn to the court, upon oath, why such subpœna hath not been taken out, and that no tickets or notes be delivered or sent to any person whatsoever, requiring them to appear at any trial, before a subpœna be first taken out to warrant those notes, upon pain of 5*l.* for every such offence

42 That the attorney that calls upon a prisoner to plead to a declaration, and afterwards makes an alteration or addition to it, must recal him up again to plead, and when he summons on the Saturday to try any cause against a prisoner, to give notice thereof the same day to the clerk of the prison in writing, otherwise the plaintiff not to go on

43. That when a *procedendo* is allowed, the plaintiff shall not proceed till the next court-day after the court wherein the same is allowed, and if the plaintiff in any case whatsoever forbear proceeding for a month's space inclusive, the plaintiff not to proceed without a week's notice thereof first given.

44 That no discovery of writs be made to any person whatsoever by him that keeps the book before the return thereof be past, without order from the steward or one of the judges of the court, upon pain of 5*l*

45 That no attorney of the court advise his client to bring a *habeas corpus* to remove any cause out of this court, nor procure any writs to be taken out above value, on purpose to remove any cause under value, or advise his client so to do, or any ways promote the same, upon pain of 5*l.* for every such offence.

46 That after the time appointed for meeting of attornies to dispatch business on Saturday mornings, it shall be lawful for any attorney calling for a declaration, plea, replication, or other pleading,

(though the attorney for the adverse party be not there present, or being present is not ready, or doth delay to give answer thereunto), to enter judgment by *non-pros, nil dicit,* or otherwise, as the case shall require, the same not to be vacated without special order of the court.

47 That at such meetings of the attornies or other clerks of the court, they do wholly intend the business of the court, until it be dispatched, not trifling away the time nor delaying of business.

48. That what business is done on such meetings on Saturday mornings shall have relation to the next precedent court, as effectual to all intents as if the same had been done in the same court, but whatsoever is done after the said meeting is broke up, to be accounted as business of the court following, except nonsuits entered upon rules given to declare or perfect *sedente curia,* which may be entered afterwards, and have their commencement from the precedent court, and execution made accordingly.

49 That when any court is holden on a Thursday, the attornies or the clerks to meet by eight of the clock precisely the next morning, for the dispatch of the business of that court, unless the court shall appoint another day for the doing thereof, and that all things be done and observed at such meetings in all respects as is appointed for the Saturday meetings

50 That when any cause is summoned for trial, or inquiry of damages, before issue joined or judgment given, in such case the cause not to be tried that court-day, but the plaintiff to lose his summons.

51 That according to the ancient custom of the attornies, and former orders of this court, the attornies of the same do every Thursday, at ten of the clock in the forenoon next after every court-day, pay in at the office of the said court, such monies as shall from time to time be respectively due from them, for the profits of the precedent court-day, to the prothonotary of the said court, or to such person or persons as he appoints to receive the same, that he or they may be able to make up their accounts and pay away the same money to the judges and other persons to whom the same shall be respectively due and payable, or else such attorney or attornies making default [shall pay] for each default 3s. 6d. to the poor prisoners, and shall stand suspended until the same be paid.

THE PROTHONOTARY'S DUTY.

52. That the prothonotary's office be attended with sufficient help to dispatch all business, daily, from seven of the clock in the morning until twelve at noon, and from two of the clock in the afternoon until seven in the evening in the summer time; and from eight of the clock in the morning until twelve at noon, and from two of the clock in the afternoon until seven at night in the winter season, and that the same be always kept in a convenient place, provided and furnished with convenient seats and places for the attornies and all persons concerned on the behalf of the judges and officers of this court, that they may the better and with more ease dispatch the business thereof.

53. That a bail-book be kept without any interlining or amend-

ments; and that the bails, as they are taken in court or before the steward at his chamber, be fairly transcribed into the said book, within two days next after the court of which they are taken.

54. That alphabets and pie-books be kept relating to all bail-bonds and other returns, as also to bails taken in court, and declarations, the alphabets of returns to be made up every Saturday morning by nine of the clock after the return day, and the other by Wednesday following the court-day.

55 That there be a general and a special rule-book duly kept, and the rules, both special and general, entered before the Wednesday next after they are given, and the bonds assigned entered in the said general rule book, by the secondary himself, or his clerk, at the time of assignment.

56. That all issues, whether general or special, and all demurrers and special verdicts, be entered upon record before trial or argument

57. That all writs of *scire facias* be fairly written and duly issued for summoning of juries, and the juries duly summoned, and panels thereof returned by the officer of the court appointed for the same; and at the trial, the verdict or nonsuit to be recorded by the secondary.

58 That in case the cause be not tried upon the first *venire facias*, there duly issue out writs of *alias* and *pluries venire facias*, if occasion serve, which shall be returned, and juries thereupon impanelled, and the verdicts or nonsuits recorded thereupon as before.

59 That all verdicts and nonsuits upon evidence, and the judgments thereupon, and all judgments upon demurrers, and other issues tried by record, be entered upon the roll with as much expedition as may be, and if any damage shall happen to the court or suitors thereof for default of such entries, the secondary to be responsible for it

60. That all judgments by *nil dicit* and *non sum informatus in debt*, and all nonsuits *pro defectu replicationis*, and other like judgments, after declarations, be likewise duly entered upon the roll with all expedition.

61. That all nonsuits for want of a declaration, be duly entered in the bail-book, together with the day of the entry of such nonsuit.

62 That a docket be kept of all causes entered upon the roll, to be seen by the attornies or their clerks when required.

63. That all judgments upon *scire facias* to revive judgments, and all judgments against the bail, be likewise duly entered and recorded.

64. That all writs of execution returned in court, be duly filed and kept in order.

65. That all writs of *Habeas Corpus* to remove causes, be duly returned when they are called for, a certificate of the causes, if the defendant is in custody, being first brought to the secondary or his clerk.

66. That writs of *capias*, *alias*, and *pluries*, be duly and orderly filed.

67. That order be given for transcribing records upon writs of error, before the beginning of the term wherein such writs are re-

turnable, if not returnable the same term they are brought , and if they be to give order at the delivery of the writs; and the secondary having such order, and being paid for the doing of them, to carry them in by the return of the writ, or by the end of the term wherein they are returnable, at the farthest

68. That the presses of parchment of all transcripts upon writs of error, do contain in them as much as presses of that kind do usually contain in the superior courts at Westminster.

69 That all rules, general or special, to plead or to appear, all bonds assigned, judgments or nonsuits, be marked and entered by the secondary or his clerk, and none other, so that he may answer for any irregularity committed therein , and that no bond may be delivered out of court but by his hand, and none to be delivered to any attorney or his clerk, without the attorney's receipt for it under his hand.

70 That the secondary take care that the judge's fees be justly and honestly paid to the profit book.

THE DEPUTY MARSHAL'S DUTY.

71. That the Deputy Marshal, if the court think fit to assign his bond, shall appear to a declaration filed against him for an escape, or an extortion, or otherwise, as the case shall require, to try the matter of fact; and that he shall bring no *habeas corpus* in such case, or writ of error, and that upon his putting in good bail to such action, his bond not to be assigned or he suspended; but if the court think fit not to proceed that way, then the profits of such Deputy Marshal, upon any such escape or other misdemeanor, may be stopped and detained in the hands of the court, and applied to the payment of what shall be judged due of him, or payable by him, until satisfaction shall be given to the party injured.

72. That a table of fees be set up in the prison, and another in the court, containing all fees due to the Deputy Marshal and any under him.

73. That if a man and his wife be arrested upon mesne process made jointly against them both, and both of them thereupon be carried to prison, in such case the woman to be discharged without fees, and if the woman only be brought to prison upon such writ, she to be discharged in like manner as aforesaid.

74 That the Deputy Marshal shall provide an honest learned man to be his clerk, who shall attend at the court-day to execute the commands of the court, to receive prisoners there committed, and to bring up others to plead, to trial, or to be charged in execution, and to have by him the book of all the prisoners charged in custody, and he to give security and be sworn duly to pay and dispose all monies by him received for the benefit of poor prisoners, and all other monies by him received for the judges and officers of this court, and also to be sworn as an officer to arrest, so that he may be forced to return all bail-bonds by him taken, take up the securities, or make the plaintiff's debt good.

75 That the Deputy Marshal shall permit none to go out at large, but such as are bailed in court, upon pain of

76. That the clerk of the prison take care that every action against a prisoner proceed to issue and trial.

77. That the Deputy Marshal of this court, and his clerk, shall, twice every year, viz. on the 10th day of December, and on the Monday next before Whitsunday, give an account upon oath of all fines, and charity money by them received or disposed to or for the relief of the poor prisoners, charged by process of this court, the same account first to be audited and examined by the Secondary of this court; that the Deputy Marshal of this court, and his clerk, or one of them, do always, in their own persons, receive such fees from all persons as shall be due, for the commitment of all persons, and they be both sworn to take no more than the due fees allowed by this court, and that they shall make true payment of all fees by them received, which are due to the Knight Marshal or any officer of this court.

THE APPOINTMENT OF OFFICERS AND THEIR DUTY

78 That such a competent number of officers be admitted and continued as to the Knight Marshal of the court shall from time to time in his discretion seem necessary, and that all of them be housekeepers of good repute, that they give good security of two housekeepers at the least, for their honest behaviour in their offices; and all the officers be dispersed in convenient places, and that the person appointed to take the officers' security do, from time to time, enter the day of admission, suspension, and discharge of such officers, together with the names of the securities, as shall from time to time be taken, and the places of their abode, in a book fairly written, and always ready to be produced in court.

79 That none of the officers of the court be put out of their places, suspended, or their writs stopped, or their bonds assigned, without special rule and motion in court upon oath, and the affidavit filed, that he may know his charge, and have a copy thereof if he will, and no counsel or attorney be admitted to speak for him after the court is fully possessed of the matter of the complaint, nor to aggravate or speak against the said officer, but the matter of the complaint left wholly to the examination of the court. (*See Order, May* 19, 1738, *post.*)

80. That no officer which shall be suspended or put out of his place, shall be readmitted without rule made in open court for that purpose.

81. That none of the officers of this court become bail, or solicit in any cause, upon pain of suspension or other punishment, as the court shall think fit

82. That every officer of the court do from time to time give an account in writing to the Secondary or his clerk, of what followers he employs to assist him in his business.

83. That the Secondary or his clerk do, every Saturday morning, set up in the office the names of six officers living within the lines of communication, who shall attend in court all the court day then next following, and this to be done equally in their turns; and that such officer as shall be appointed to keep the juries be sworn according to usual form in that case.

84. That no officer do meddle with the disposing of clients to any of the attornies of the court, but leave them to themselves, to

retain whom they please, and that no attorney shall give to any officer or solicitor any reward for clients' causes brought by them, or lend any money, upon pain of 10*l*.

85. That no officer keep any prisoner in his custody above twelve hours, and in case the prisoner be bailable by law, that he take two good housekeepers with reference to the damage or matter in demand in the writ for bail if offered, which are to be inhabitants within the jurisdiction of the court; but where no such bail is tendered, or the prisoner not bailable by law, the officer safely to convey such prisoner to the prison of the court, within the time above limited. (*See Order, Dec* 10, 1736, *post*.)

86. That no officer demand or take of any person arrested, or of any other on that behalf, any more than 2*s* 8*d*. for the Knight Marshal's fee and bond of appearance.

87. That every officer shall take out all writs within six hours after money received by him for that purpose, at his peril.

88 That the officer, after the first bond assigned, bring in the defendant and both his securities for a shilling by the return of the *alias capias*, unless the court give him longer time, and that the officers in any case take no more of the plaintiff for any arrest to be made than ordinary court fees, or what the plaintiff shall voluntarily give him without his demanding of it; that upon the issuing forth of every writ of *scire facias*, the officer that first made the arrest in that cause, shall be obliged to execute and return the said writ without any fee or reward for doing the same.

89 That if any officer be found to promote, stir up, or solicit actions, or dispose of any fees, or take upon him to arbitrate or make any agreement in any cause, the same officer to be turned out of his place, or fined, at the discretion of the judge of the court.

90. That every officer do every court day return all his writs by twelve of the clock, but shall attend precisely by ten to meet the clerks appointed to take those returns, and that such clerks do not depart from the place where the returns are made, util four of the clock every court day.

91. That no officer that is prejudged or otherwise discharged of his place, shall be entertained as a follower to any other officer of this court, upon pain of suspension of such officer as shall employ him.

92. That no officer fail to make his returns in person, once in two court days, upon pain of 5*s*. to the use of the poor prisoners.

93 That no officer be admitted without warrant from the Knight Marshal or steward, and the name of such officer be set up publicly in the office by the space of a week before admittance.

94. That no officer give any person employed by the Knight Marshal to enquire after his security, above the sum of 20*s*. for his admittance, and 2*s*. 6*d*. for his bond given for his good behaviour.

95 That if a feme covert be arrested by a writ against baron and feme, and the husband not arrested, the officer shall forthwith discharge such feme covert without bond for appearance or fee, and moreover shall pay such costs as the feme shall be at, if complaint be thereof made.

96. That no officer of the court shall commence a suit as a privileged person, without order in court or one of the judge's hands to that purpose, and that when such officer hath recovered, he shall pay all the court fees before he take out execution, and that all persons admitted, or which shall hereafter be admitted *ex credito* or *in forma pauperis* after recovery had, shall likewise pay all the court fees before execution made out, or otherwise the execution to be delivered to such officer as the court shall appoint, who shall be responsible for these fees when the execution is served; and that all bails, pleadings, and proceedings whatsoever, for prisoners in custody, be paid by their respective attornies, and the same accounted for in the profit book, unless such prisoner be admitted *in forma pauperis.*

97. That when any rescue is made of any prisoner arrested, to return the rescue and make affidavit of it, together with the names of the rescuers, within a week after the arrest made, and shall also within the same time procure a warrant from the Knight Marshal or steward of the court to take up the said rescuers upon pain of

98. That upon the impanelling of juries in Middlesex or elsewhere, the officer not to take any directions nor receive any names from either plaintiff or defendant, or any of their attornies or agents, but shall impartially and indifferently return able and substantial juries, upon pain of dismission.

99. That no discoveries be made by the said officers, or any other, of the names of any of the said juries, or any other juries, to either of the said parties, or any that deals for them, before trial be had in the said causes.

100. That all such fines as are or shall be imposed upon any officers of this court, shall be duly paid, according to the direction and order of the judges of this court, for the relief and discharge of such poor debtors as are charged or detained in the prison of this court.

101. That a book be constantly kept by the steward's clerk who now is, or such person who hereafter shall be employed to collect and receive the said fines, wherein shall be fairly set down and kept a true account of all fines received and paid by him, for which the receiver of the said fines shall be allowed so much as the Knight Marshal and Steward of the court shall by writing under their hands appoint.

102 That the receiver of the said fines shall once every year viz. within one week next after the birth of our Lord Christ, give an account upon oath of all fines by him received and paid, by order of the said court, the same account first to be audited and examined by the secondary of this court.

ORDERS TO BE OBSERVED IN COURT

103. That the counsel and attornies every court-day do attend with their gowns on

104. That the counsel do keep an orderly course of evidence in the trial of every cause, without interrupting, or breaking in one upon the other's evidence, and not to ask leading questions, but leaving the Court to direct the jury.

105. That the counsel and attornies of the court, do not shew any dislike, either in speeches or behaviour, of the opinion or judgment of the steward or his deputies sitting as judges, but behave themselves civilly, respectfully and discreetly, and shew good manners, as becomes men of reason and learning, in the presence of a court of justice, to preserve the honour and authority and majesty of the court.

106. That neither counsel nor attornies shall shew any dislike publicly to a jury's verdict, but acquiesce therein, they being judges of fact, and discharging their consciences.

107. That six officers at the least do attend every court-day during the sitting of the court, with verges in their hands, to keep order and silence, and to execute the commands of the court.

108. That when the jury is gone from the bar to consider their verdict, an officer to be appointed to keep the door, that none may have access to them.

109. That no jurors be summoned out of the counties of Middlesex, Essex, Kent, or Hertford, without motion, and special rule of court, but that the juries of Southwark, who give constant attendance, may serve the court, wherein special care is to be taken that no victuallers or alehouse keepers do serve in them; and in case any juries shall be summoned from the counties aforesaid, care be taken that they be indifferent persons, and not packed; and that no juryman be solicitor or bail in any cause in this court.

110 That no attorney of the court, whilst any cause is trying in the same court, shall speak publicly, give his opinion, or ask any question of any witnesses or any other person whatsoever, whereby any disorder may arise, but shall, during all trials, sit down quietly in court; and if he speak at all, it be softly, only to inform counsel, to whom he shall leave the whole management of the trial.

111. That every attorney of the court sit duly and orderly in court during the trial of the causes in their respective places, and every one to move according to seniority, and that none interpose or make answer, unless he or they be retained on the other side, or be required thereto by the court.

112. That no attorney be admitted to make a motion in court, in any matter where a rule hath been formerly made, without producing the rule, and causing the same to be read, and then to move upon it.

113. That all motions in court be plainly and distinctly made, and none to interrupt or make any new motion before the first be determined, and the rules pronounced by the court, which being done, the counsel or attorney that moves to acquiesce and rest satisfied with the rules given by the court, and not to trouble the court with further importunity.

114. That no attorney in his practice at court, or in the office whilst he is doing the business of the court, shall, at any time, utter or speak any uncivil or unseemly words, or speech, or use any uncomely or indecent behaviour or gestures to any other of the attornies or any other member of the said court

115. That no attorney of the court do practise fraudulently, or endeavour to surprise another.

116. That no attorney of the court shall intermeddle with, or interlope in any cause wherein another attorney of the said court hath been retained, the said attorney still enjoying his place, unless it be by the consent of the attorney so forsaken, or by special direction of the court, and then the attorney newly retained shall pay the attorney forsaken all his fees that are due to him.

EDMUND WYNDHAM
JAMES BULLER.

Sep 19, 1712.—Ordinatum est quod nullus attornatus hujus curiæ sub aliquo pretensu quocunque solvet juratoribus pro aliquo veredicto pro cliente suo reddito, sive pro nonpros. super evident. plus quam sex solid. vel conscius fuerit solutioni pluris sine notitiâ inde hunc curiæ per eundem attornatum indilate dandâ sub periculo incumbente.

Mar. 6.—Ordinatum est quod regula generalis decimo nono die Septembris ultimi facta evacuatur, quodque nullus attornatus hujus curiæ sub aliquo pretensu quocunque solvet juratoribus pro aliquo veredicto pro cliente suo reddito, vel pro aliquo judicio de nonpros. super evident. plus quam octo solid. vel conscius fuerit solutioni pluris sine notitiâ inde hunc curiæ per eundem attornatum indilate dandâ sub periculo incumbente.

June 19, 1713.—Ordinatum est quod nullum breve de capias in aliqua originali actione e curia hic imposterum emanandum supersessam fuerit per aliquem attornatum hujus curiæ sub pœna forisfacturæ quinque librarum ad usum pauperum prisonariorum hujus curiæ per quemcunque dictorum attornatorum qui contra hanc regulam aget solvendarum.

Jan. 29.—Ordinatum est quod nullus attornatus hujus curiæ scienter retentus fuerit tam pro querente quam pro defendente in eadem causa, quodque si aliquis attornatus hujus curiæ ignoranter sic retentus fuerit, idem attornatus indilate postquam inde conscius fuerit, et antequam procedet pro alterutra parte, deliberabit alii attornato hujus curiæ feod' unius partium.

Ordinatum est quod nullus attornatus hujus curiæ dabit clienti suo aut attornato alterius partis, vel recipiet, aliquam manucaptionem, aliquam narrationem vel aliquod placitum, vel aliquam copinam inde, vel informationem de nominibus manucaptorum in aliqua prima manucaptione (defendente prisonario existente), vel de materia alicujus narrationis aut placiti in aliqua causa in curia hic pendente, antequam tale manucaptio, narratio, vel placitum affilatum et intratum fuerit in officina prothonotarii hujus curiæ, ita quod debitum reginæ et feoda curiæ proinde debito modo respondeantur

Ordinatum est etiam quod nullus attornatus hujus curiæ vel solvet vel recipiet custagia pro aliquo actu in curia hic non constante in libris hujus curiæ, quodque nullus attornatus defendentis in aliqua causa in curia hic pendente dabit attornato querentis notitiam de

aliquo brevi de habendo corpus cum causa &c. antequam dictum
breve allocatum fuerit

Ordinatum est etiam quod per Hac. Ter. ^1 ^1 quis eunus de narios a
cliente suo recipiens vel ad comparendum pro eodem cliente vel
pro aliquo alio act in curia hic agendo voluntarie omittet talem
actum agere vel talem comparentiam in piena obligationum notare,
ita quod magis secrete denarios a cliente suo pro aliquo actu in
curia hic agendo receptos ad usum suum proprium convertat.

Cumque antehac ordinatum fuit quod consiliarii hujus curiæ non
placitarent alicui narrationi vel placito, antequam signata forent per
secundarium hujus curiæ, quodque nomina sua subscribent narra-
tionibus et placitis per ipsos advisatis. Ulterius ordinatum est quod
idem consiliarii notabunt diem et annum talium subscriptionum
suarum; quodque nulla narratio nec aliquod placitum per dictos consiliarios subscriptum sine tali notatione per dictum secundarium
recipietur.

Dec. 31, 1725.—Ordinatum est per curiam quod nullus in futuro
admittatur officiarius hujus curiæ antequam habitabit in loco pro
quo appunctuabitur, et certificationem inde sub manibus gardia-
norum ecclesiæ istius parochiæ curiæ producat

July 1, 1726—Cum antiquum feodum debitum marescallo hospitii
domini regis super arrestationem cujuslibet defendentis, virtute alicujus brevis de capias e curia hic emanantis, per officiarios dictos defendentes arrestantes ab eisdem defendentibus recipi solebat, et per eosdem officiarios ad retornas brevium sic executorum dicto marescallo
solvi; cumque per statutum intitulatum *"An act to prevent frivolous
and vexatious arrests,"* enactitatum est, quod in diversis casibus in dicto statuto specificatis defendentes non fuerint arrestati sed personaliter serviti cum copiis processuum, ordinatum est ergo per curiam,
quod in omnibus talibus casibus in quibus personale servitium in
loco arrestationis per dictum statutum requiritur, dictum antiquum
feodum solutum fuerit dicto marescallo per attornatum comparen-
tem vel affilantem communia ballia pro defendentibus sic personaliter servitis secundum exigentiam statuti prædicti

July 15—Ordinatum est per curiam quod copiæ processuum hujus curiæ per statutum nuper directæ personaliter serviri servientur
per portatores virgarum hospitii, officiarii omnia brevia per ipsos ser-
vita returnabunt curiæ hic ad diem returnæ eorundem, et indorsa-
bunt super dicta brevia nomina diei et loci talis servitii.

Aug. 5.—Ordinatum est per curiam, quod in qualibet actione in
qua defendens servitus fuit copia processus hujus curiæ, et per defal-
tum defendentis querens affilabit commune ballium pro defendente,
idem querens dabit defendenti notitiam per quatuor dies inclusive de
regula ad placitandum narrationi ipsius querentis, et si querens
inde pro defectu placiti obtinebit judicium interlocutorium, similis
notitia dabitur defendenti de tempore exequendi brevis ad inquir-
endum, si tamen nec defendens nec locus habitationis suæ inventi
fuerint, tunc dictæ notitiæ affixæ fuerint in officina prothonotarii
hujus curiæ

Mar. 15, 1727—Ordinatum est quod nulla breve de capias ema-
nabit e curia super sacramentum de causa actionis querentis priusquam
dictum sacramentum signatum fuerit per attornatum hujus curiæ.

Ordinatum est quod nullus officiarius hujus curiæ exonerabit ali-

quem defendentem e custodia sua ex assensu querentis nisi talis assensus ei significatus fuerit per notam sub manu ejusdem querentis vel attornati hujus curiæ.

April 18, 1728.—Ordinatum est quod in qualibet actione versus prisonarium, nisi querens infra tres menses post imprisonationem defendentis procedat ad triationem, defendens exoneretur e prisona super commune ballium

May 31.—Ordinatum est quod quilibet officiarius hujus curiæ, qui sacramentum de servitio alicujus processus hujus curiæ per ipsum serviti non dabit intra biduum post requisitionem adinde per attornatum querentis, ab officio suo in curia hic exercendo suspendetur.

Oct. 4 —Ordinatum est quod in futuro nullum placitum oblationis per secundarium hujus curiæ recipietur antequam denarii oblati eidem secundario solventur.

Oct. 17, 1729.—Ordinatum est quod quicunque juratorum attendentium servitio hujus curiæ sine causa per seneschallum hujus curiæ allocanda se absentabit a dicto servitio, non abinde penitus exonerabitur.

April 25, 1735.—Ordered that the first of the two general rules made the 15th day of March, 1727, be discharged.

June 20 —Ordered that all bail-bonds taken upon arrest made by process issuing out of this court be for the future taken by the officer who makes such arrest in his own name, and by the name of his office, and that the execution of the bail-bonds be witnessed by one credible witness at the least, so known to such officer, that he may be ready to produce such witnesses to attest the due execution of such bail-bond, when such officer shall be thereto required And it is also hereby further ordered, that no officer of this court shall, directly or indirectly, at any time or times whatsoever, do or suffer to be done, any act, matter, or thing whatever, whereby or by reason whereof any such bail-bond taken by him as aforesaid shall or may be impeached, weakened, defeated, or destroyed, or whereby the plaintiff or plaintiffs to whom such bail-bond shall be assigned, shall be let, hindered, obstructed, or barred from putting the same in suit, or from recovering thereupon against any person or persons who shall have executed such bail-bond by such officer as aforesaid.

Dec 10, 1736.—Ordered that no officer keep any prisoner in his custody above twenty-four hours. That upon every arrest the officer take bail or carry the party arrested to the prison of this court, unless the party arrested pay the debt and costs of such arrest, or otherwise satisfy the plaintiff. And that if any officer shall let any prisoner go without complying with the terms aforesaid, it is declared by the court to be a misbehaviour in such officer.

July 8, 1737 —Ordered by the court that in all cases where the plaintiff or plaintiffs in any action shall except against the defendant's bail, such plaintiff or plaintiffs shall be at liberty to deliver a declaration by incipitur conditionally at the time of excepting against such bails, and also that in all cases where the defendant or defendants in any action shall obtain a rule for proceeding on the bail-bond, assigned for a week, pursuant to a former rule of this court, that he, she, or they, may be indulged with a week's further time to jus

tify his, her, or their bail, the plaintiff or plaintiffs in every such action shall be at liberty to deliver a perfect declaration conditionally at the time of such defendant or defendants obtaining such rule, and enter a rule to plead thereon; to which declaration such defendant or defendants shall plead of the same court that he, she, or they, shall justify bail, or in default thereof, judgment may be entered against such defendant or defendants by default.

Ordered by the court, that at the time of taxing costs in all causes, either before or after a verdict, respect shall be had by the proper officer appointed to tax such costs between the parties, to all the rules the plaintiff or defendant shall be charged with, either in the necessary prosecuting or defending his, her, or their suit, and that all such rules shall be allowed in costs to such plaintiff or defendant.

May 19, 1738.—Ordered by this court, that upon all complaints hereafter made against any of the officers thereof, for any misdemeanor in their offices, the facts complained of be supported by affidavits in writing, and that such officer's defence be likewise supported by affidavit or affidavits in writing, and that no counsel or attornies be admitted to speak for them after the court is fully possessed of the matter of the complaint, nor to aggravate or speak against such officers, but the matter of the complaint is to be left wholly to the examination and decision of the court

Dec. 1, 1738.—It is ordered by the court that no special jury be granted but on motion in open court, and that when any special jury is ordered, the same be summoned and returned by one of the bearers of the virges of this court, whom this court declareth to be the only proper officers for that purpose, and that twenty four persons inhabiting within the jurisdiction of this court, with their proper additions, as well of their trade or mystery, as of their place of abode, be inserted in the panel, and that such panel be placed in the public office two days before the day of their appearance, that the plaintiff or defendant may be enabled to make their proper and legal challenges to the said jurors

Dec 8.—To prevent the inconveniences which may and are likely to arise from persons unskilful in the business, acting in the names of or as agents to the six attornies of this court, it is ordered by this court that from henceforth no person whosoever shall be permitted and sworn according to the letters patent of King Charles II. bearing date the 4th day of October, in the sixteenth year of his reign, nor shall any person be permitted to act in the name of, or as agent to any of the said six attornies, (except Mr. Wm Monk, Mr. Geo. Wilson, Mr Hubert Harvey, and Mr J. R Lewis, persons who have been examined and approved of by the court,) unless such person shall have served a clerkship of five years, at least, to some of the said six attornies, or shall have first been admitted an attorney of one of his Majesty's courts at Westminster, and also to be examined and approved of by one of the judges of this court

May 11, 1739.—Ordered, that from henceforth no prisoner in custody of the keeper of the prison of this court, either by commitment in execution by the court, or by *capias ad satisfaciendum*, shall be admitted to petition, or move the court by attorney, for the benefit of the act of parliament, intituled "An Act for the Relief of Debtors with respect to the Imprisonment of their Persons" until

the next court subsequent to such commitment or return of such *capias ad satisfaciendum*

April 11, 1740 —Whereas, by a rule made by the court on the 8th day of July, in the year of our Lord, 1787, it is ordered, that at the time of taxing costs in all causes, either before or after a verdict, respect should be had by the officer appointed to tax such costs between the parties, to all rules the plaintiff or defendant should be charged with, either in the necessary prosecuting or defending his, her, or their suit, and that all such rules should be allowed in costs to such plaintiff or defendant, and some doubts having arisen about the sense of the said rule, and the judgment of the court being thereupon prayed, the court is of opinion that the said rule does extend to the allowance of such rules, with the necessary motions made in court thereupon, where the party whose bill to be taxed has on such motions the judgment of the court with him

March 6.—Ordered, that the rule relating to the time allowed for officers of this court to detain prisoners in their custody, and other parts of their duty in discharging them, which was made on the 10th day of Dec 1786, be publicly notified by affixing a copy thereof in the prothonotary's office, for the information of all whom it may concern

Dec 17, 1742.—Ordered, that no officer of this court discharge any defendant or defendants out of his custody from and after Friday, the 17th day of this instant December, by consent and order of the plaintiff, unless such consent and order be first given to the officer in waiting, under the hand of the plaintiff, his or her attorney or agent.

April 11, 1723 —Cum secundum praxim hujus curiæ non tantum executores et administratores qui arrestati sunt per process' hujus curiæ allocantur affilare commune ballium, quinetiam omnes defendentes in prisonam hujus curiæ ducti super breve de capias in actionibus pro verbis vel pro exiguis insultibus sive transgressionibus, super applicationem huic curiæ, indilate exonerantur super affilationem communis ballii Cumque etiam in ulteriori favore defendentium in aliis exiguis actionibus nullus querens allocatur per hanc curiam excipere versus manucapt' alicujus defendentis in aliqua actione pro aliquo debito sive demand' non attingente ad quadraginta solidos, modo aliqua persona residens infra et subjectus juris diction' hujus curiæ devenit manucaptor pro tali defendente, etiamsi talis manucaptor non sit domum tenens, Anglice *a housekeeper* Ad extendendum ergo beneficentiam ejusdem praxeos proveniend' in futurum imprisonament' defendentium in actionibus supramentionalibus, ordinatum est quod in quacunque actione in qua defendens nominatur executor vel administrator in brevi de capias, offi ciarius hujus curiæ qui defendentem arrestabit, postulabit tantum obligationem defendentis propriam pro comparentia sua, una cum warranto subinde per talem defendentem signando ad authorizandum aliquem attornatum hujus curiæ comparere et affilare commune ballium pro tali defendente Quodque in qualibet actione in curia hic prolata in qua per breve de capias, vel aliter, constabit officiario hujus curiæ qui defendentem arrestabit, quod debitum vel demand' querentis non attingit ad quadraginta solidos, necnon in quacunque actione in curia hic pro verbis, insult' vel transgress', in qua seues-

callus hujus curiæ extraordinariam manucaptionem non direxerit,
officiarius hujus curiæ qui defendentem arrestabit in aliqua tali actione postulabit unam tantum personam subjectam arrestari per processum hujus curiæ, obligari una cum defendente pro comparentia
dicti defendentis, etiamsi talis persona non sit domum tenens,
Anglice, *a housekeeper,* modo sit residens infra jurisdictionem hujus
curiæ, et apparet aliquo honesto modo victum suum quæritare Ordinatum est etiam ulterius quod cuilibet defendenti dehinc arrestato
per breve de capias hic emanans allocetur spatium viginti et quatuor
horarum ad procurandum securitatem pro comparentia sua Quodque post expirationem dicti spatii temporis si nulla talis securitas
interim data fuerit, officiarii hujus curiæ in prisonam curiæ ducent
prisonarios, prisonariis solum exceptis quos sub custodia sua ulterius
detinere senescallus hujus curiæ licentiam dabit. Quodque officiarii hujus curiæ per hanc regulam requiruntur diligenter exami-
nare processum suum eorundem, et si aliquem errorem in aliquibus
eorum invenerint, quod tales erroneos processus indilate intulerint
in officium prothonotarii hujus curiæ, ita quod ibidem emendentur.
Talesque officiarii hujus curiæ qui ipsi non satis callent obligationes
pro comparentia defendentium per ipsos arrestatorum conscribere,
per hanc curiam injuncti sunt procurare aliquem notarium, sive
aliam peritam personam ad conscribendum obligationes pro comparentia defendentium per ipsos in futurum arrestendorum Quodque
non permittent tales obligationes conscribi per aliquem attornatum,
solicitatorem vel agentem alicujus talis defendentis.

Oct. 16, 1747.—It is ordered that in all cases in this court where
the plaintiff shall be entitled to and require good bail, an indorsement shall be made on the writ of capias by the attorney of this
court, who shall sign the same for what sum the officer shall take
bail of every defendant named in such writ, and that bail shall
be taken for no more than the sum so indorsed. And in default
of the writ being so indorsed, the officer executing the same shall
demand no other or better bail than is appointed by a former rule
of this court, in case of arrest for small debts or trespasses.

Oct. 30, 1747.—It is ordered that in all cases in this court
where the plaintiff shall be entitled to and require good bail, an
indorsement shall be made on the writ of capias by the attorney
of this court, who shall sign the same for what sum the officer shall
take bail of every defendant named in such writ, and that bail shall
be taken for no more than the sum so indorsed. And in default
of the writ being so indorsed, the officer executing the same shall
demand only the defendant's own bond for his appearance in double the sum of the damages contained in the writ, provided such
double damages do not exceed the sum of 5*l* , and if such double
damages shall exceed the sum of 5*l.* then he shall take such bond for
5*l* only.

TABLE OF FEES.

To be taken by the gaoler or keeper of the Marshalsea prison in Southwark, in the county of Surry, for any prisoner or prisoners committed, on coming into gaol, for chamber rent there, or discharged from thence, on any civil action, settled and established the 17th day of May, in the fifth year of the reign of his late Majesty, King George the Third, 1765, pursuant to an Act of Parliament, intituled, " An Act for the Relief of Debtors with respect to the Imprisonment of their persons."

To the Knight Marshal, upon the discharge of every prisoner charged with one or more actions · · · ·	0	1	8
To the Keeper, for his care and safe custody of every prisoner, upon the discharge of such prisoner on the first action* · · · · · · · · · · · ·	0	4	8
To the Keeper, upon the discharge of such persons charged with one or more actions · ·	0	3	8
To the Surgeon or Apothecary, on the discharge of every person charged with one or more actions · · ·	0	1	0
To the Chaplain, on the like discharge · · ·	0	1	0
To the Turnkey, on the discharge of every prisoner, on the first action · · · · · · · ·	0	1	6
To the Turnkey, on the discharge of such prisoner charged with one or more actions after the first ·	0	1	0
To the clerk, for entering the discharge of a prisoner on one or more actions · · · · · · · · · ·	0	1	0
To the keeper, for the use of a bed, bedding, and sheets for every prisoner, if found by the gaoler, at the prisoner's request, for the first night · · · ·	0	0	6
Every night after the first · · · · · · · · · · · · · · · ·	0	0	3
If two lie in a bed, each · · · · · · · · · ·	0	0	2

No other fees for the use of chambers, bed, bedding or upon commitment or discharge of any prisoner, in any civil action.

W. Richardson,	Mansfield,
A. Bishop,	C. Pratt,
T. Hervard,	P. Barker.

* The Knight Marshal is, in fact, the *keeper of the prison,* and is responsible for all escapes When the late Sir James Bland Lamb, Bart., was knight marshal, an action was brought against him for an escape, and he paid the debt and costs

ORDER OF SESSION

AT the General Quarter Session of the Peace of our Lord the King, holden in and for the county of Middlesex, at the Sessions house for the said county, (by adjournment), on Thursday, the 20th day of February, in the 23rd year of the reign of our Sovereign Lord George the Third, King of Great Britain, before William Mainwaring Esq., the Rev Sir George Booth, Bart., Charles Shepherd, John Bamfather, Esqs, and others their fellow Justices, &c. &c

The standing order respecting the charges at lock-up houses, &c within this county being called for and read, a motion was made, That the said order be rescinded, and the same being agreed to, the said order was rescinded accordingly

And this court doth hereby order and ascertain that the bailiff or officer of the sheriff of this county for the time being, and also the bailiff of the Duchy of Lancaster, at the Strand, in this county, for the time being, and his under bailiffs or officers, and also the bailiff of the liberty of the manor of Stepney in the same county, for the time being, and his under-bailiffs or officers, and also the bailiffs, officers, or ministers of his Majesty's Palace Court, at Westminster, and of the court commonly called Whitechapel Court in this county, legally arresting or detaining any person or persons in their respective custodies, may take and receive of such person or persons so legally arrested or detained, as follows —

For breakfast (tea or coffee) ...	0	0	10
For dinner, including bread, beer, vegetables, &c	0	1	6
For supper, including ditto	0	1	0
For house-room per day · ... · · ·	0	1	0
Fire per day (if any) · · ... ·· ... ·	0	0	6
Lodging, with good bed and clean sheets, (first night)	0	1	0
Every night after the first .. · · · · ..	0	0	6

And that no greater rate and expenses be demanded, taken, or received by such bailiffs, officers, or ministers, or any of them, of any prisoner or prisoners in their respective custodies, for their lodging, diet, or other expenses, than what is allowed and ascertained as aforesaid, until further order of the court to the contrary And it is further ordered by this court that copies of this order be left with the sheriff of this county, and the prothonotaries of his Majesty's Palace Court, and Whitechapel Court, or their respective deputies, to the intent that they may respectively give notice of the said order to all bailiffs, officers, and ministers acting within this county, by virtue of any warrant or warrants granted or to be granted, by the sheriff of the same county, or of any writ or writs, or legal process, issuing out of the said respective courts

(By the Court,) SELBY

FORMS.

LORD STEWARD'S OATH

I —— do sincerely promise and swear that I will be faithful and bear true allegiance to his Majesty, King George the fourth.—So help me God.

I —— do swear, That I do from my heart abhor, detest, and abjure, as impious and heretical, that damnable doctrine and position, that princes excommunicated, or deprived by the pope, or any authority of the see of Rome, may be deposed or murthered by their subjects, or any other whatsoever. And I do declare, that no foreign prince, prelate, state, or potentate, have or ought to have any jurisdiction, power, superiority, pre-eminence, or authority, ecclesiastical or spiritual, within this realm.— So help me God.

May it please your grace—You as steward of the honourable household of our sovereign lord the king, shall well, truly, justly, and faithfully execute the office of judge of the Court of our sovereign lord the king of the King's Palace of Westminster, and shall administer and exhibit full and speedy justice to the king's people in the said court, according to your sound discretion, better knowledge, understanding, and judgment, and shall observe all things to the office of judge, in the court aforesaid, belonging or appertaining —So help you God

Sworn, &c

OATH TAKEN BY OFFICERS UPON ADMISSION

You shall well and truly behave yourself in the office which you now undertake, of one of the bearers of the virges of the household of our Sovereign Lord King George, and one of the officers and ministers of the Court of our said sovereign lord, of his Majesty's Palace of Westminster.

You shall well and truly execute all such writs of this court, (which shall come to your hands, and may be by you executed), with as much expedition as possibly you can.

You shall execute no writ or process but such as shall issue out of this court, during the time you shall continue in your said office.

You shall make a true and just return of all such writs of this court as shall be by you executed.

You shall take no bribe, reward, or gratuity for the executing of any process of this court, other than the court will allow of, or the parties themselves *(without exaction)* shall willingly afford you

You shall not disclose any writ or process of this court to the defendant or any other, whereby he may have intelligence thereof.

You shall not conceal any wrong or injury done or offered to this court, but shall forthwith discover the same to some or one of the judges thereof, and shall be ready, with all diligence, to perform the utmost you shall be commanded by the judges of the court aforesaid.—So help you God, &c.

Sworn in Court.

OFFICER'S SECURITY BOND

KNOW all men by these presents, that we, A. B. of ———— C D. of ————, E F. of ————, G. H of————, and I. K. of ————, are held and firmly bound unto Sir C. M. Lamb, Bart. Knight Marshal of the King's Household, in five hundred pounds of good and lawful money of Great Britain, to be paid to the said Sir C. M. Lamb, Bart., or his certain attorney, his executors or administrators, to which said payment well and truly to be made, we bind ourselves, each and every one of us, by himself, our heirs, executors, and administrators, firmly by these presents, sealed with our seals, dated this ———— day of ———— in the year of our Lord ————.

THE condition of this obligation is such, that whereas the above bounden A. B is admitted by the said Sir C M. Lamb, Bart. Knight Marshal, and one of the judges of the said court of the King's Palace at Westminster, to be one of the bearers of the virges of the household of our sovereign lord the king, and one of the officers and ministers of the Court of our sovereign lord the king of the king's palace of Westminster, during the will and pleasure of the said Sir C. M. Lamb, Bart. If, therefore, the said A B. and his followers for the time being do and shall from time to time, and at all times hereafter, during the continuance of the said A.B in the said place or office, well, faithfully, and honestly behave themselves in the same place or office, in all things according to the duty of the same place, or office, and therein the said A. B. do and shall faithfully and honestly serve and execute all such writs, process, or warrants issued out of the said court, as shall be delivered unto him to be executed by him, according to his utmost power, and shall make a due and true return thereof, in all cases, when a return thereof is required by law, and do and shall upon every arrest by the said A B. to be made, take sufficient bail of all persons within the jurisdiction of the said court, where the party arrested is by law bailable, for the appearance of the party so arrested, at the next court of the said palace of Westminster, after such arrest made, and do and shall duly and truly return, and deliver unto the said court the said bail-bond, thereupon so taken, at the next court-day after such arrest made as aforesaid; And further, if the said A. B., after any arrest by him to be made by force or virtue of any writ, process, or execution, issuing out of the said court, do not detain the party so arrested in his custody above the space of *twenty-four hours* from the time of such arrest made, but as well in case of mesne process where no sufficient bail can be given as aforesaid, as in case of execution, do presently, after the said *twenty-four hours*, carry or convey the party so arrested to the prison of the said court, according to law, and not any way directly or indirectly give or cause to be given any notice to the party against whom such process or execution is awarded, whereby the arrest may be avoided or retarded, and that the said A. B. shall not at any time hereafter deliver or suffer any goods or chattels to be taken out of his possession, which shall be seized or taken in execution by him alone, or together with any other of the officers or bearers of the virges of the said court, or which shall be de-

livered or left in the hands or custody of him the said A. B , by the said Sir C. M. Lamb, Bart , or the steward or prothonotary of the said court, or his or their deputies, without a lawful and sufficient warrant for the delivery of the same, *but shall make a just, true, and perfect inventory of all such goods by him so seized, or which shall come to his hands within the space of twenty-four hours after the same shall be seized or come to his hands as aforesaid, and shall cause the same to be appraised by two appraisers, one of them to be appointed by the said Sir C. M Lamb, Bart.,* and shall, so soon as conveniently may be, after such appraisement made, deliver a copy thereof, signed by the said A. B , to the said Sir C M Lamb, Bart., or return the same into the public office of the prothonotary of the said court, and likewise shall and will, when and so often as any goods or chattels by him so seized, or taken, or sold, (if the money for which such goods or chattels shall be sold shall come to the hands, custody, or possession, of the said A. B) forthwith pay or cause to be paid unto the said Sir C M Lamb, Bart., or the steward or prothonotary of the said court, or his or their deputies, some or one of them, at the public office of the said court, all such sum and sums of money for which the same shall be sold. *That the said A B shall not remove any goods or chattels, (which, at any time or times hereafter, during his continuance in the office aforesaid, he may seize or take in execution within the jurisdiction of the said court), from the place where such goods and chattels shall be so seized or taken in execution, before the rent (if any due) shall be paid to the landlord or landlords of the premises whereon any such goods or chattels shall have been seized or taken in execution, pursuant to the statute in that case made and provided* And shall from time to time make a just account and due payment at the next court day after the arrest made, of all such fees as belong to the said Sir C M Lamb, Bart , and shall from time to time do and execute all other things, writs, warrants, and processes, as shall be delivered to him, and which to his place or office belong to be done and executed; and shall not at any time hereafter employ as his follower any person or persons, which have been or shall be an officer of the said court, have left or been put out of his said office in the said court *Nor shall at any time hereafter serve and execute any other process or warrant except the process of the said court.* And do and shall also save and keep harmless the said Sir C M. Lamb, Bart., and the Steward and all and every other judge and judges of the said court; and their and every of their heirs, executors, and administrators, of and from all matters and things by the said A. B. to be done, omitted, committed, or suffered for or by reason of the not executing, or not due executing of any writ, process, or warrant, to him delivered, and also do and shall from time to time save and keep harmless the said Sir C M. Lamb, Bart., and the keeper of the prison of the said court, and his and their heirs, executors, and administrators, from all damage, loss, and danger which may happen or grow to him or them by reason of such not executing, or not due executing of any writ, process, or warrant as aforesaid· And also, if the said A B. do and shall from time to time, and at all times hereafter, observe, perform, and obey all the lawful order and orders, rule and rules, of the said Sir C M Lamb, Bart., or any other judge or judges of the said court, touching and

concerning himself or his duty and behaviour, in his place aforesaid, and do and shall shew and deliver a copy of the first clause
mentioned and enacted in and by an act of parliament made in the
thirty-second year of the reign of king George the Second, intituled,
*An Act for the relief of Debtors with respect to the imprisonment
of their Persons,* to every person whom he shall arrest or take into his custody by virtue of any writ, warrant or process, and carry or cause to be carried to any public or other house, and permit him or her, or any friend of theirs to read the same before any
liquor or meat shall be there called for, and do and shall well, faithfully, and honestly observe, perform, and execute the several directions prescribed in the said act of parliament, and all other matters and things, which, according to his duty or office, he ought to
observe, perform, and execute, *without fraud, oppression, or wrong,
to any person or persons whatsoever* Then this present obligation
to be void and of none effect, *or else to remain in full force and
virtue*

A. B. (L S.)
C D. (L. S.)
E. F. (L. S.)
G H. (L S)
I K (L S)

Received, (on the day of these presents,) of the clerk
of the security bonds, a printed copy of the clause of the act
of parliament within mentioned

(Witness) A. B.

* "That no sheriff, under-sheriff, bailiff, serjeant at mace, or other officer
or minister whatsoever, shall at any time or times hereafter convey or carry,
or cause to be conveyed or carried any person or persons by him or them
arrested, or being in his or their custody by virtue or colour of any action,
writ, process or attachment, to any tavern, alehouse, or other public victual-
ing or drinking house, or to the private house of any such officer or minister, or of any tenant or relation of his, without the free and voluntary consent of the person or persons so arrested or in custody, nor charge any
such person or persons with any sum of money for any wine, beer, ale, vic-
tuals, tobacco, or any other liquor or things whatsoever, save what he, she
or they shall call for of his, her or their own free accord, nor shall cause
or procure him, her or them, to call or pay for any such liquor or things,
except what he, she, or they shall particularly and freely ask for, nor shall
demand take or receive, or cause to be demanded, taken or received, directly or indirectly, any other greater sum or sums of money than is or
shall be by law allowed to be taken or demanded for any arrest or taking,
or for detaining, or waiting till the person or persons so arrested or in custody shall have given an appearance or bail, as the case shall require, or
agreed with the person or persons at whose suit or prosecution he, she or
they shall be taken or arrested, or until he, she or they shall be sent to the
proper gaol belonging to the county, riding, division, city, town or place
where such arrest or taking shall be, nor shall exact or take any reward,
gratuity or money for keeping the person or persons so arrested or in custody out of gaol or prison, nor shall carry any such person to any gaol or
prison within 'four-and-twenty hours from the time of such arrest, unless
such person or persons so arrested shall refuse to be carried to some safe
and convenient dwelling-house of his, her or their own nomination or appointment, within a city, borough, corporation, or market town, in case
such person or persons shall be there arrested, or within three miles from

AFFIDAVIT OF SERVICE OF PROCESS.

Doe v. Roe

In the Palace Court.

A. B of ——, being one of the officers of this court, maketh oath and saith, that he this deponent did personally serve the above-named defendant with a true copy of a writ of capias issued out of this court in this cause, on or before the return thereof, *and within the jurisdiction of this court.*

Sworn at the Palace Court Office.   A. B.

FORM OF SPECIAL BAIL.

Note.—This should be put in for the defendant on the Tuesday or Wednesday morning, at latest, after the appearance of the defendant, by an attorney of the Palace Court (but he must not be the attorney concerned for the plaintiff,) otherwise the plaintiff's attorney, for want of such bail, will, on the Thursday morning following, assign defendant's bail bond, and sue out writs immediately against the defendant and his bail

In the Palace Court,   The defendant is bailed by John Jones,
Alexander James, of the Borough High Street, in the parish of Saint George, Southwark, in the county of Surry, hop-merchant, and William Toms of the same street, parish, borough, and county, salter.

at the suit of the plaintiff
in the plaint,
John Jackson
W.

Taken conditionally, and acknowledged before

(Steward's signature)

Form of Acknowledgment to be repeated before the Steward of the Court

You and each of you (addressing the bail before the judge) undertake to become bail for Alexander James, at the suit of the plaintiff in the plaint, John Jackson, that should he the said Alexander James be cast in this action, that you and each of you undertake to pay the condemnation money, or render his body to the custody of the keeper of the prison of this court, (if he fail so to do) you undertake to do the same for him.

The bail are then asked if they are satisfied The answer to which must be in the affirmative.

The judge then signs the bail-piece.

the place where such arrest shall be made, if the same shall be made out of any city, borough, corporation, or market town, so as such dwelling-house be not the house of the person arrested, and be within the county, riding, division or liberty, in which the person under arrest was arrested, and then and in any such case it shall be lawful to and for any such sheriff, or other officer or minister, to convey or carry the person or persons so arrested, and refusing to be carried to such safe and convenient dwelling-house as aforesaid, to such gaol or prison as he, she or they may be sent to, by virtue of the action, writ or process against him, her or them."

⁎ ⁎⁎ For a great number of years the printed copy of the above clause was not delivered to the officers.

FORM OF COMMON BAIL.

In the Palace Court, *James Johnson,* at the suit of the plaintiff in the plaint, *Thomas Jones.* } The defendant is bailed by John Doe and Richard Roe. Taken, &c.

The like bail is filed in the same form as where a defendant does not appear.

FORM OF AFFIDAVIT,

SHEWING CAUSE TO BE EXCUSED FINE FOR NON-ATTENDANCE UPON JURY.

Palace Court.

Henry Pigeon, of the Borough High-street, in the county of Surry, distiller, maketh oath and saith, That he was summoned to serve on the jury in this court, on the first day of July instant, and that he this deponent was engaged on particular business on that day. And this deponent, living in the manor of Suffolk-place, which this deponent conceived to be out of the jurisdiction of the said court, and being also a deputy-lieutenant of the said county of Surry, and having served on grand juries of the county, conceived he was therefore exempt from serving on the said jury And this deponent further saith, that it was not out of any disrespect to this court, or for any other cause than as above mentioned, that he did not attend this court.

Sworn at Southwark, the 22d July, 1796 Before me, Wm. Cruchley. } Henry Pigeon.

FORM OF PLEA TO THE JURISDICTION OF THE PALACE COURT.

AND the defendant comes in his proper person and says that the court of our lord the king here ought not to have cognizance of this plaint, because he says that the plaintiff's cause of action arose in the city of London, out of the jurisdiction of this court, without this that his cause of action arose at Southwark aforesaid, in the county of Surry, or elsewhere within the jurisdiction of this court, as the plaintiff supposes in his said declaration, and this he the said defendant is ready to verify, wherefore he demands judgment if the said court here ought or will any further hold cognizance of the said plaint*.

* This plea is to be put in *in propria persona*, and not by attorney; and the defendant ought not to add the words " when, and so forth;" for that will amount to an admission of the jurisdiction of the court, for those words mean the same as if he had said, " when, where, and as the court shall think fit to order." Also the defendant is usually obliged to swear to the truth of this plea

FORM OF DEFENDANT'S PLEA,

WHERE AN ACTION OF TRESPASS AND FALSE IMPRISONMENT IS BROUGHT AGAINST HIM FOR EXECUTING THE PROCESS OF THIS COURT.

AND the said defendant, by Sir Charles Montolieu Lamb, his attorney, comes and defends the force and injury, when, &c. And as to the coming with force and arms, or whatever is against the peace of our lord the king, and also as to all the rest and residue of the trespass aforesaid, except assaulting, taking, and imprisoning the said plaintiff for the space of twenty-four hours, he the said defendant saith that he is not guilty, and therefore he puts himself upon the country, and the said plaintiff doth the same. And as to the said assault, taking and imprisoning of the said plaintiff for the space of twenty-four hours as aforesaid, he the said defendant saith, that the said plaintiff ought not to have or maintain his said action against him for the same, because he saith that before the time in which the said trespass is supposed to be committed, that is to say, at the court of our said lord the king of the palace of the king at Westminster, holden at Southwark in the county of Surry, and within the jurisdiction of the said court, on the fifteenth day of January, in the seventh year of the reign of our lord the king that now is, before Henry Burton, Marquess Conyngham, steward of the household of our said lord the king, Sir Charles Montolieu Lamb, Bart. knight marshal of the household, and Burton Morice, Esq. barrister at law, being judges of the said court by virtue of the letters patents of his Majesty King Charles the Second, made and bearing date at Westminster on the fourth day of October, in the sixteenth year of his reign, one J. T. in the said court levied his plaint before the said judges of the said court against the said plaintiff in a plea of trespass on the case to the damage of him the said J. T. of ninety shillings, the said court being a court of record, and having proper cognizance of the pleas specified in the said plaint, and the said J. T. did then and there in the said court find pledges to prosecute his said plaint, viz John Doe and Richard Roe, and did then and there in the said court demand that process should issue out of the said court against the said plaintiff on that behalf, and thereupon it was then and there ordered by the said court that process in due form of law should issue out of the court against the said plaintiff, and thereupon and before the time in which, &c. that is to say, at the court of our said lord the king of the palace of the king at Westminster, holden at Southwark aforesaid in the said county of Surry, and within the jurisdiction of the said court, on the twenty-ninth day of January, in the year aforesaid, before the judges of the court by virtue of the said letters patents, at the petition of the said J. T. it was by the said court then and there commanded the bearers of the virge of the household of our said lord the king, the officers and ministers of the said court, and every of them, that they, some, or one of them should take by his body the said plaintiff if to be found within the jurisdiction of the said court, and him safely keep, so that they, or some or one of them should have his body before the judges of the said court at the next court of our said lord the king of the palace of our said lord the king at Westminster aforesaid, on Friday, the fifth day of February, in the said seventh year, to be holden at Southwark in

the county of Surry aforesaid, to answer the said J. T. according to his said plaint, and that he should then and there have the said precept, which precept afterwards, and before the said fifth day of February, viz. on the third day of the said February, at Southwark aforesaid, was delivered to the said defendant, being at that time, and now, one of the bearers of the virge, and an officer and minister of the said court, to be executed by him in due form of law, by virtue of which precept, the said defendant, being then one of the bearers of the virges, and an officer and minister of the said court, afterwards, and before the return of the said precept, viz. on the day and year last mentioned, in the parish of St Andrew, Holborn, in the county of Middlesex, and within the jurisdiction of the said court, gently laid his hands upon the said plaintiff in order to arrest him by virtue of the said precept, and did then and there take and arrest the said plaintiff, and detained the said plaintiff in his custody during the said space of twenty-four hours, and at the next court of our said lord the king of the palace of the king at Westminster, holden at Southwark aforesaid, in the county of Surry, and within the jurisdiction of the said court, on the said fifth day of February, in the year aforesaid, before the said judges of the said court, made a return of the said precept duly served and executed in all things according to the commands thereof. And this the said defendant saith is the assault, taking, and false imprisonment whereof the said plaintiff above complains, and which he the said defendant is ready to verify when, &c. without this, that he the said defendant is guilty of any trespass, assault, or false imprisonment at, &c aforesaid, or elsewhere, or at any time before the issuing of the said precept, or after the return of the same; wherefore the said defendant demands judgment if the said plaintiff ought to have or maintain his said action against him *.

FORM OF HABEAS CORPUS CUM CAUSA

ISSUING OUT OF THE COURT OF KING'S BENCH, DIRECTED TO THE JUDGES OF THE PALACE COURT.

George the Fourth, by the grace of God, of the united kingdom of Great Britain and Ireland, king, defender of the faith, to the Judges of our Court of our Palace at Westminster, and to every of you, greeting: We command you that you have the body of A. B detained in our prison under your custody, as it is said, under safe and secure conduct, together with the day and cause of the taking and detaining the said A. B. howsoever he be denominated in the same, before our right trusty and well beloved Sir Charles Abbott, Chief Justice of our Common Bench, at his chambers, situate in Serjeant's-inn, Chancery-lane, London, immediately after the receiving this writ, to do and receive all and singular such things as our said Chief Justice shall then and there consider of him in this behalf, and have you there then this writ.

* It has been decided in *Rogers* v *Marseal*, Sid. 259, and *Chute* v. *Alport*, Sid. 311, that where a defendant justifies under the process of an inferior court, he ought to entitle that court to a jurisdiction of the cause, either by prescription or by charter, and if by charter, he ought to make a *profert in cur.* of the letters patents, especially if such defendant was an officer of the court. therefore this plea ought to conclude with a profert.

A LIST OF LEGACIES

To the Prison of the Marshalsea and Palace Court

	£	s.	d.
1 Of Henry Alnut, Esq., for the release of debtors, whose respective plaintiffs will accept of a small sum in full satisfaction for the debt and costs ··	100	0	0
2 Every city and county in England formerly paid one guinea annually to this prison, which was called "exhibition money;" but an act of parliament having abolished such, a certain sum is now paid in lieu thereof by the counties within the jurisdiction of the court· · · · · · · · · · · · · · · · · ·			
3 The legacy of Frederick Ashfield, to provide 2lbs. of meat per week for from fourteen to twenty prisoners· ·	50	0	0
N B. Paid by Mr. W. Railton of Clifford's Inn.			
4 Ditto of Mrs. Frances Ashton, for the release of prisoners, who are proper objects.			
N.B. Paid by Robert Long, Esq, in such proportions as the trustees think proper.			
5 Ditto of John Pelling, for the like purpose · · · · · ·	9	0	0
N. B Paid by Messrs. Hoares, Fleet-Street.			
6 Ditto of Sir Thomas Gresham; paid quarterly by the Chamberlain of London, 2l 10s. per quarter ·	10	0	0
7 Ditto of Mrs. Mary Simcott, paid by the Chamberlain of London, 65 penny loaves			
8 Ditto of Mr. Jacobs, left in 1609, paid quarterly, by the proprietors of the Grainge Inn, Carey Street, at Easter ·	2	0	0
9 Ditto of Mr. John Marks, 1l per annum, and the interest of 21l. 18s. 10d. S S. Stock, paid by the Company of Mercers · · · · · · · · ·	1	10	1
10 A quantity of bread and money sent by the company of leather-sellers, is at the rate of 6s 8d quarterly.			
11 Legacy of Mr Robert Ramston, paid at Christmas	1	0	0
12 Gift of William Roper, Esq paid by the Company of Parish Clerks, yearly · · · · · · · · · · · ·	1	0	0
13 Legacy of Mr. J Gaythorn, by the Company of Cutlers, at Christmas · · · · · · · · · · · · · ·	0	15	0
14 Ditto of Mr. T. Dawson, paid by the churchwardens of St. Ethelbergh, Bishopsgate · · · · · ·	0	9	0
15 Ditto of Mrs Lettice Smith and Mr. Arthur Moses, paid by the Company of Fishmongers ·	0	6	8
16 Company of Salters send annually · · · · · · ·	0	6	8
17 Gift of Thomas Caster, by the churchwardens of St. Dunstans in the East, at Lady-day yearly, is a quarter of beef and a peck of oatmeal yearly.			
18 Legacy of the late Mr. Baron Smyth is fifteen stone of beef yearly at Christmas.			
19 Company of Drapers yearly, sixty loaves.			

20 Legacy of Mr. Ralph Carter, a quantity of beef at Christmas; paid one year by the churchwardens of Allhallows, and next by those of St. Andrew Undershaft.

21 Company of Ironmongers send yearly, on the 15th November, a quantity of beef and bread.

The following voluntary Donations are generally paid yearly.

1 Archbishop of Canterbury · · · ···· ·	1	0	0
2 The Lord Steward of H M. Household ··· · ····	5	5	0
3 The Steward of the Court ··· ·· ···· ·	1	1	0
4 Henry Thornton, Esq. ···· · ·· ··· ·········	5	5	0

A LIST of the Lord Stewards of his Majesty's Household, Knight Marshals, Stewards of the Court, Deputy Stewards, Prothonotaries and Deputy Prothonotaries, from the year 1773 to the present time. Also the present Counsel and Attornies of the Palace Court.

Lord Stewards

Earl Talbot.
Duke of Dorset.
Earl of Dartmouth
Earl of Aylsford.
Marquis Cholmondley.
Marquis Conyngham (present Lord Steward).

Knight Marshals.

Sir Sidney Meadows, Knight
Hugh Boscawen, Esq
Sir James Bland Lamb, Bart.
Sir Charles Montihen Lamb, Bart.(present Knt. Marshal)

Stewards of the Court.

Levett Blackburn, Esq.
Thomas Kymer, Esq
James Stanley, Esq.
Burton Morice, Esq. (present Steward).

DEPUTY STEWARDS.

Danby Pickering, Esq
Mr. Serjt. Sayer.
Mr Serjt. Runnington.
Mr. Serjt Marshall
Sir John William Rose, Knt (late Recorder of London)
Henry Revell Reynolds, Esq.
Robert Pooley, Esq.
Robert Reader, Esq.
G. Long, Esq (present Deputy Steward).

PROTHONOTARIES.

Richard Bulstrode, Esq
Charles Pierrepont, Esq (late Earl of Manvers)
Sir H. F Campbell, K C.B (present Prothonotary)

DEPUTY PROTHONOTARIES

Robert Stainbank
Richard Bulstrode
Evan Jones.
William Cruchley
J. C Hewlett (present Deputy), Palace Court Office, 39, Chancery
    Lane

PRESENT COUNSEL

Lewis Flannagan, Esq 4, Garden Court, Temple
William Erle, Esq 14, Paper Buildings, Temple
H. J. Ross, Esq. 7, New Square, Lincoln's Inn
J V. Thompson, Esq. 21, Old Square, Lincoln's Inn

PRESENT ATTORNIES

William Railton, 4, Clifford's Inn
Dobson Willoughby, 13, Clifford's Inn
Edward Dolman, 14, Clifford's Inn
Joseph Arden, 15, Clifford's Inn
J H. Turner, 2, Clifford's Inn
Thomas Rimmer, 10, Clifford's Inn.

INDEX.

R

W M'DOWALL, PRINTER, PEMBERTON ROW, GOUGH SQUARE.

Ingram Content Group UK Ltd.
Milton Keynes UK
UKHW050752110423
419970UK00008B/192

9 781240 046881